Catherine Carolyn Jenkyns

Hard Life in the Colonies, and other Experiences by Sea and Land

Catherine Carolyn Jenkyns

Hard Life in the Colonies, and other Experiences by Sea and Land

ISBN/EAN: 9783337107239

Printed in Europe, USA, Canada, Australia, Japan

Cover: Foto ©ninafisch / pixelio.de

More available books at **www.hansebooks.com**

A HARD LIFE IN THE COLONIES, AND OTHER EXPERIENCES BY SEA AND LAND

NOW FIRST PRINTED. COMPILED FROM PRIVATE LETTERS

BY C. CARLYON JENKYNS

ILLUSTRATED

LONDON: T. FISHER UNWIN, PATERNOSTER SQUARE. MDCCCXCII.

To

MY FIVE NEPHEWS,

HALN, SYLVESTER, GILBERT JENKINS,

AND

LIONEL AND NELLO WENDLING,

I DEDICATE

THESE PAGES ADAPTED FROM THE DIARIES

OF THEIR

FATHER AND UNCLE AND THEIR FRIEND.

C. C. J.

PREFACE.

HE following pages are offered to the public in the belief that the Colonial experiences they record are of sufficient interest to justify their transcription from a series of private letters written twenty years ago. It is not claimed for the book that the adventures it contains are specially remarkable, or that many men now living are not more competent to speak of the ups and downs of a colonial life than the three writers of these letters: it is rather as presenting a picture of the life of young Englishmen who have knocked about a little before settling down— a picture the interest of which, perhaps, lies in its being fairly typical of many thousands of cases— that these sketches have been put into print.

In compiling the volume, the editor would add that she has kept as much as possible to the writers' own words. As, however, the latter have not had the opportunity of reconsidering their *impressions de voyage* by revising letters struck off in more or less haste, it is hoped that the reader will excuse any inaccuracies or errors he may meet with in the narratives.

CATHERINE CARLYON JENKYNS.

November, 1891.

CONTENTS.

		PAGE
(1)	SHANG-AIED, OR ROUND THE HORN. By A. C. JENKINS	1
(2)	A VOYAGE TO CHINA. By G. C. JENKINS	40
(3)	VOYAGES TO MELBOURNE AND CALCUTTA. By G. C. JENKINS	91
(4)	HARD LIFE IN THE COLONIES—	
	(1) AUSTRALIA ... ... ⎫	117
	(2) NEW ZEALAND ... ⎬ By G. C. JENKINS and H. K. DUNBAR	168
	(3) AUSTRALIA AND 'FRISCO ⎭	225

LIST OF ILLUSTRATIONS.

(1) San Francisco (*see page* 311) ... ... *Frontispiece*
(2) Arthur Cardew Jenkins ... ... *To face page* 40
(3) Shanghai ... ... ,, ,, 55
(4) Gilbert Chilcott Jenkins ... ... ,, ,, 117
(5) Taipari ... ... ,, ,, 150
(6) Haln Killegrew Dunbar ... ... ,, ,, 168
(7) River Scenery—New Zealand ... ,, ,, 195
(8) A Maori Belle ... ... ,, ,, 198
(9) Gum Trees ... ... ,, ,, 239
(10) Scenery—Gipps Land ... ... ,, ,, 286

ERRATA.

Page 53, line 19, *for* almost as many of them *read* almost as large a proportion of them.
Page 102, line 17, *for* £3000 *read* £1000.
Page 107, line 14, *for* one story *read* a story!
Page 127, line 15, *for* Dromanagh *read* Dromana.
Page 154, line 4, *for* their *read* there.
Page 172, lines 1 and 2, *for* Tristan Ditcunha *and* Curguelan's Island *read* Tristan D'Acunha *and* Kerguelen's Island.
Page 177, line 9, *for* clearly *read* almost.
Page 179, line 18, *for* Geelong *read* Queenscliff.
Page 181, line 1, *for* Landridge *read* Sandridge.
Page 189, &c., line 12, &c., *for* How-Hows *read* Hau-Haus.
Page 194, &c., line 22, &c., *for* Tanronga *read* Tauraga.
Page 196, &c., line 8, *for* Pahéhă *read* Pakèhă.
Page 212, line 20, *for* Farmium *read* Formium.
Page 217, line 24, *for* schiser *read* schicer.
Page 230, line 34, *for* Sidney *read* Sydney.
Page 232, line 11, *for* Daudenmy *read* Dandenong.
Page 238, line 9, *for* iriantilopes *read* triantilopes.
Page 240, line 5, &c., *for* carnivorous *read* herbivorous.
Page 250, line 13, *for* Dauderong *read* Dandenong.
Page 258, line 1, *for* Brinston Steevens *read* Brunton Stephens.
Page 258, line 22, *for* Arnothoryneus *read* Ornithoryncus.
Page 261, line 10, *for* Miomi *read* Miami.
Page 263, line 7, *for* Gipp's *read* Gipps.
Page 270, line 34, *for* New South Wales *read* Australia.
Page 338, line 5, *for* Sacramanto *read* Sacramento.
Page 346, line 16, *for* come *read* came.
Page 362, line 30, *for* nihil *read* nihilo.

SHANG'AIED; OR, ROUND THE HORN.

IN 1873 I happened to be in 'Frisco. How or why does not matter: there I was, and terribly hard up too. I was barely sixteen at the time, small and not over strong, therefore of no particular use to any one. This fact had been made so painfully apparent to me, that, desperate and wounded, I resolved to free myself and go to sea as a last resource.

Now sailors are, or were, procured for the merchant marine by a modified system of the press-gang. That is to say, fellows nicknamed " crimps " are kept for the purpose of following men who look like sailors, and offering them the hospitalities of the house to which they have the honour to belong. Once in their hands, he (the sailor) becomes simply a division sum. If he is a man who drinks, so much the better; he will be more easily divided, and only wake up to his fate to find himself on an outward-bound ship, where growl and swear as he might, he must *nolens volens* remain, and generally ends in becoming resigned. If, perchance, he does not drink, so much the worse for him; he will then be disintegrated in spite of his struggles, for the "crimps" are very powerful men, gigantic of build and liliputian of conscience. Should the unfortunate victim dare to show a desire to leave their entrancing society, he will be looked at with reproachful sorrow, and mild methods will first be tried to convince him of his folly; a romantic and preposterous bill of charges will be thrust at him: "Can he pay that? Does he imagine that they are going to keep him like a prince for nothing? Does he want to talk to a policeman about it?" &c., &c. The other methods do not involve so much arithmetic; a charge of a different kind is made, in a nice lonely room, with overpowering numbers on the wrong side, and the victim emerges, breathless, bruised and bleeding, but—convinced. The result is precisely the same in either case.

Now all these facts were perfectly well known to me; still I fancied I could work it a little better than an ordinary common sailor. So having fully made up my mind to go to sea, I commenced operations at once. Proceeding to the sailors' quarter, I soon detected a "crimp," standing in front of his house, apparently admiring the landscape. I sauntered slowly by on the opposite side of the street, perfectly aware that he was in reality watching me. Before I had gone quite fifty yards, I heard a step behind me, and the same womanish instinct that had told me he was watching me as

I passed, now told me he was following. I kept on my way slowly and without looking back.

"Sa-ay, I want to speak to you a minit," sounded in a would-be gentle voice behind me.

"With me?" I asked, turning and facing the man, with a look of guileless surprise on my face.

"Yes, come right away and have a drink. I have seen you before somewhere. Were you ever in Liverpool?"

"Yes," came unhesitatingly from my lips.

"Do you remember," continued my disinterested friend, "the Constellation Hall in Whitechapel?"

"Rather," I replied; "it must have been there you saw me."

Needless to say I had never been in either, but such a man must be fought with his own weapons. My shady companion scratched his head and stared at me, then led the way into a public-house and called for drinks. While waiting for them, he studied me with pleased yet puzzled scrutiny. He was a professional liar, and when there was no business reason for it, lied instinctively, and for the benefit of that practice which makes perfect. He knew that *he* had lied, but his statement had been so promptly endorsed, that he commenced to have doubts as to whether he had not committed an error, and inadvertently spoken the truth; in short, whether he had not really seen me before.

The drinks appeared, and we clinked glasses; he took out a short black pipe, carefully filled it, and began to smoke. I gazed with apparent unconsciousness at the wreaths of smoke, while my respectable friend continued to take my measure. When I considered he had had time enough for the survey, I looked at him and found his eyes riveted on me.

"Wouldn't you like to be in Liverpool again?" asked the crafty wolf.

"Shouldn't mind," answered the innocent lamb.

"I know a ship—you're a Britisher, ain't you?"

I nodded.

"Wall, this is a Britisher too. The skipper has got his wife aboard, and coming out a kid was born, and all hands were drunk for three weeks. Now that's the sort of d—— ship you want."

"Yes, she would do right enough," I assented.

"Ever been to sea before?"

"Only as a passenger."

"Wall, the skipper wants a boy to help the steward in the cabin, and I guess you'll do as well as another. You won't have to go aloft, and if you behave yourself you can have a d—— good time."

Had my distinguished friend made me this proposition one short year ago, I believe I should have called for the police; but raw wheat and tarpaulin beds had worked their demoralizing effect upon me, and I accepted this enchanting offer with alacrity.

"Let us go and see what the 'boss' says," suggested the "crimp," and he led the way out of the inn where we had been drinking, to another of the same calibre, where my future captain had taken up his abode.

"Captain Billings in?" asked my companion of a dirty-looking waiter who stood at the door "contemplating" the passers-by.

"Guess," was the concise reply, and I followed the "crimp" into the tap-room, where several men, all of seafaring appearance, were smoking and drinking. Picking out a burly and somewhat flashy-looking Yankee, Watts, as I afterwards found out the "crimp's" name to be, spoke to him in a low voice, evidently about me, as the man turned, and stared at me fixedly and keenly, as though to discover whether I was a *bonâ-fide* "tenderer" or not. The look of innocent and wide-eyed curiosity that met his glance apparently satisfied him. He asked me my name and age, and merely said, "Wall, I guess you had better stop here till I can get you a berth, and I'll take it out of your advance note."

This being settled, I was permitted to have the run of the "bar" and, what pleased me more, of the table. The meals were good, and both Jackson, the boarding-house keeper, and Watts, the crimp, were kind, if scoundrelly. I made the acquaintance of several sailors, and pumped them, not always with satisfactory results. As a general rule, they were grumpy. Some felt injured at being addressed by a mere boy and a gentleman; for my poverty and bad clothing could not hide that fact from voice and manners, and they resented it. According to their code, if a man is a gentleman let him keep with gentlemen, and not come amongst them taking the bread from their mouths, and treating them with calm condescension. I was quite unconscious of any such manner, which would have been very foolish and unsuitable on my part, and in my position, but they evidently considered me as not one of themselves, and took care to let me know it with a directness of statement that I confess somewhat staggered me. But more of this further on.

The days wore away, and I found some really pleasant kindly acquaintances in men, afterwards pointed out to me as some of the worst characters in the city. I can only say they never attempted to lead me wrong, and even their language was not so bad as I have often heard since from so-called "gentlemen."

"But everything comes to him who knows how to wait," as the French proverb says, and one morning Watts, the crimp, came to see me, and told me that my ship was going to be manned that day, and that I must go, in company with a select band of eminent mariners, and affix my name to the ship's articles. He furthermore informed me that I would have to sign myself as "ordinary seaman."

I ironically inquired if "extraordinary" seaman would not be more to the point, but he ignored my feeble attempt at a joke and said severely, "You'll hev to sign as O. S. 'cause that's the lowest thing there is, and as yer are to be in the cabin you kin say that yer've been to sea afore. The skipper will never know no better, 'cause yer wont 'ave to go aloft, and so yer've no call to go and make a show of yerself. Now go right along to the British Counsel (Consul), and do as I've told yer."

I went to the English Consulate, and found my future mates there before me, a seedy, motley group; my heart sank as I looked from one surly sodden face to another. The Consul, a commonplace rather rough-looking man, was evidently in great haste to get away, and read out the agreement with such frightful rapidity that the only distinguishable words were, "no grog allowed." This sentence was received with muttered imprecations. The reading ended, we all drew two months' advance money (we got the order, not the money), Her Majesty's Consul being good enough to say, "A lot of d——d fools you are to draw your money now, it will only go to the boarding-house keepers; why don't you ship on your own hooks?" No one replied; what was the good? When I went up for my paper the Consul eyed me sharply, and muttered, "Another gentleman; poor devil! he's going to the devil young. Got no parents or home, eh?"

"No," I answered, shortly, and hastily followed the others out of the room, where we were greeted by the lodging-house keepers waiting outside, with open arms. The advance notes were delivered up, and my future companions went to drown care in drink. Heart-sick and weary, I wandered up and down the quays wondering if it were not better to make a hole in the water and have done once for all with this wretched life. What was the good of toiling at unsuitable work among a lot of uncongenial men, simply to get bread to keep alive my useless and wretched self? In the mood I was in then, I think a very few minutes more of my own society would have solved the question, and this story would never have been written; but Watts had followed me, forced me back with him, made me eat and drink, and sent me to bed early. The following morning he fitted me out from his own stores, at liberal terms (to himself), gave me five dollars and his blessing, and sent me on board accompanied by another "crimp"—to help me carry my bundle was the pretence, to prevent my running away, was the reality.

On the quay I found all the crew mustered; they were more or less drunk, most of them too stupefied to know or care where they were going. I noticed one sailor, seated in the boat by my side; he was a sickly-looking fellow, less drunk than the others, and was coatless. As it was bitterly cold, I asked him why he didn't put his coat on. He answered me, with an oath, that the boarding-house keeper had taken his clothes to pay expenses; he had nothing but what was on him. The poor wretch was going round the Horn in winter time in his shirt-sleeves. But we were now drawing close to the ship, and all the sympathy I had in me was required for myself, for my spirits sank lower and lower. She was pointed out to me, an iron barque of outlandish build, very deep in the water (no Plimsoll's mark just then), very cheerless looking and dirty. As I gazed around me, and saw the gang of marine blackguards with whom I was to be shut up for the next six months at least, and reflected that I did not know how to do any work, and consequently they would have to do it and might not feel grateful towards me, I wished myself ashore with all the heart I had left in me.

Arrived at the ship, the whole disorderly crew scrambled up the side, and, saying farewell to the disinterested "crimps," staggered off to the forecastle; and I followed them, not knowing what else to do. The foc'sle, as the shell-backs pronounce it, was a house on deck about twelve feet square, and held twenty-four bunks, their owners and chests. When I entered the door, it was fairly reeking with the fumes of bad whiskey, cloudy with tobacco-smoke, and hell-like with blasphemy.

"Oh, here's the bloated swell!" was the greeting with which I was saluted. "'Ave a swig?" "Wet yer whistle?" "Ain't yer got a cigar, Bill? baccy ain't good enough for the gent!"

I turned to fly, but a burly half-drunken fellow barred the way with a rough "None of that, you white-livered cur. 'Ave yer ever been to sea before?"

"Yes," I answered, facing the lot of them, and looking braver than I felt.

"The gent has been to sea before," said Muggins, the man who had barred my way, looking at the others with a drunken leer.

"As skipper, of course," cried another, which sally was received with a roar of laughter.

"The darned boy is going in the cabin, though," remarked a surly old fellow who had not yet spoken.

This had some slight beneficial effect as far as it went.

"Wall, yer can just remember us poor devils when you are there," said a far-seeing seaman of pot-hunting proclivities.

I answered I would do what I could, but further conversation was cut short by an authoritative voice at the forecastle door, "Some of you men come out on deck."

Those who had not taken the precaution to get dead drunk were obliged to obey, and I was swept along with the rest. It was the second mate who had called, a tall black-bearded man, from Bristol, with nothing remarkably good or bad about him. Having disposed of the more important members under him, he turned his attention to me, looking down at me with open contempt.

"What's your name?"

"Brown," I answered, after a moment's hesitation, for I wasn't perfectly sure what name I had given at the Consulate—certain only of one thing, that I had not given my own.

"That's a lie," said the second mate sharply, "but it doesn't matter. Ever been to sea before?"

"Yes."

"Yes, what. Don't you know how to speak to a gentleman? Keep your d—— mouth still; I'll teach you to sneer at your superior officer."

How small a thing sometimes leads to great results; my foolish boyish action of curling my lip at the mate's calling himself a gentleman, and omitting the customary "sir" due to a superior, made that man my enemy; many an ill-turn he served me, all my after deference being powerless to take away the first impression my unlucky sneer had made upon him.

"Ever been to sea before?" he asked again, sharply.

"Yes, sir."

"Oh, you have, have you? Well, I'll see what a smart seaman you are," he answered, with a malicious grin. "Just take that grease-pot, and go and sign your name on that fore-top-gallant-mast."

Had I been told to go in a tiger's cage, and sand-paper the tiger's claws, I should not have been more scared. I looked around me helplessly, desperately, thinking whether I wouldn't jump overboard. My tyrant watched me calmly.

"You know how to do it, of course?"

"With a wad, or piece of canvas or something," I stammered almost unconsciously, with my eyes fixed on the slender swaying mast, that seemed to my fevered fancy to lose itself in the sky.

"Then you had better take a wad, or piece of canvas or something, and the grease-pot, and be off," said the mate, pointing to a heavy dirty tin filled with fat.

I went silently towards it, when the mate said amiably, "You'd better take off that good coat before you go up; our sailors usually do so, as the grease is apt to drop about when the mast sways."

As if it mattered to me, who expected to be dashed to pieces in ten minutes' time, whether I spoilt a coat over it or not!

However, I went obediently into the forecastle, took off my coat, and carefully folded it up. One of the men raised his head and asked sleepily what work I had been set to.

"To grease down the fore-top-gallant-mast," I said, adding, with bitter calmness. "It would be a pity to spoil a nice coat over it."

The man stared at me a moment; then his head dropped on his arms with a snore, he was asleep. No one else even looked up, and with a feeling of quiet desperation I went out alone to meet my fate.

The second mate was where I had left him. He glanced at me curiously as I silently took up the grease-pot and moved towards the mast.

"If you are afraid, young shaver, say so," he remarked.

I looked him steadily in the face as I answered, "You had better move from here, sir; I might splash you with my brains if I fell, and it would be a pity to spoil your nice coat."

"Go to the devil!" he cried, furiously, and in another minute I was on the rigging, with the heavy grease-pot dangling to my wrist.

"Don't come down until you have put some grease above the sheave hole in the royal-mast," shouted the mate.

The "coatless" seaman, who passed at that moment, whispered hastily: "Keep yer knees close to the mast, and yer eyes on the top. 'Taint as bad as it looks."

It certainly looked very bad, nay, to my unaccustomed eyes, an impossible feat that I should ever reach the top of that swaying mast, that stood a hundred and fifty feet from deck.

My head swam, my heart turned sick within me; for a horrible moment I felt as though I should faint. A sneering laugh from Mr. Mason brought the hot blood to my cheeks, and courage to my shaking nerves. Pulling myself together, I set my teeth firmly and commenced my perilous journey, sustained by the knowledge that the second mate was watching me, hoping to see me fall, and I felt a grim determination not to give him that pleasure if I could help it.

I got on very well until I reached the cat-harping, where I was delayed a little, some of the grease having slid down my sleeve. Getting out the cold slimy stuff as best I could, I screwed up my courage another peg and proceeded on my journey, passed the topmast rigging, and in due course arrived at the cross-trees.

Two-thirds of the journey was accomplished, but the other third! I looked up—there was no Jacob's ladder to step on, as there is in decent ships; the wind was howling and shrieking through the rigging, and seemed to rejoice at my danger and scream with joy at my peril; and far ahead the royal pole loomed up gaunt, naked, and apparently as unapproachable as the North Pole itself. Shuddering, I turned my eyes away and foolishly looked down: the ship appeared like a little boat, and the men mere specks, only the second mate seemed, to my disordered brain, to have grown in size until he reached half-way up to me, and the yelling wind seemed but the echo of his sneering laugh. I was completely demoralized, my knees knocked together. With a groan I folded my arms across my breast, when I heard the rustling of paper. I put my hand inside my shirt, pulled out the little packet that had never left me since my sister had put it there two years ago, and drew out of the oilskin bag a small engraving of the "Ecce Homo." I gazed at the pictured image of the "Man of Sorrows," and as I gazed my fears left me. Fastening it up carefully again, I turned resolutely to the rigging and commenced the last and worst part of my task. It was terrible work; my greasy hands had no power to hold the pole, and I slipped again and again. But to make a long story short, I finally reached the royal-yard and knelt on it. I had not much higher to go, but that short bit was without aid of any kind, and I was rocking to and fro with sickening jerks. Remembering the "coatless" man's advice, I pressed my knees tightly to the pole, and taking as firm a grip as my oily hands would allow, reached the top. Without staying a moment, I hastily dabbed on a handful of grease and slid down to the royal-yard again, and thence to the cross-trees; there I could breathe more freely. My fright was passing away, when the voice of the second mate came up to me : " Fore-royal, there "—they always hail the part of the vessel you are on, never by your name—" I don't want you to varnish the d—— mast; come down."

I joyfully prepared to obey, and with a lightened heart began my downward descent with a confident, even comfortable, feeling. About half-way down, a sailor called Fitzgerald passed me on his way up with a marling-spike and some spun yarn; he looked at me and said, with a surly nod, " Thought yer'd 'ave came down head first, so did Mr. Mason. Better luck next time."

I didn't answer this Christian-like wish, and in a few minutes more was safely standing on deck. The mate received me with a jeer, but I heard afterwards that he was in no small anxiety until

I was down, for had an accident happened, the blame would fall upon him, for sending a boy into such danger. He now gave me some odd jobs to do on deck, and went away to his own part of the ship.

At six o'clock we knocked off work, and the cry of "Tea-oh!" resounded from the galley. When I got there, I found it was my privilege to fetch the biscuit, beef, &c., from the galley as required by the men of my watch; I also had the advantage of washing their plates and pannikins, trimming the slush lamp, and sweeping the foc'sle floor after meals. This made me handy and smart, I was told. It was another portion of my duties, when my watch was on deck at night, to pass the word from the officer of the watch to the watch itself; to keep always awake, and to be ready and grateful to keep the men's look-outs for them, to prepare the sand-glass, to heave the log every two hours, and above all to be vigilant with the clock and strike eight bells with astronomical punctuality. This made me alert and watchful. Even when sound asleep on the deck, or in any hole I could find to rest in, I heard the mate's voice when he called, and awoke sufficiently to repeat his orders without blundering as soon as he had finished giving them. Incidentally, I learnt that a boy must never speak until spoken to, nor must he help himself to anything to eat or drink until everybody else has been served; he must also be tolerant when kicked or struck, and irresponsive when cursed or insulted. By strict attention to these precepts I became meek and submissive outwardly, but the iron entered into my soul.

To return to my first night on board. It was indeed a cheerless one. Some of the men were drunk, and were violent or affectionate according to their habit when in their cups, some half-drunk and very sulky, while all the old hands were nasty and exclusive because they had no chance of getting drunk. Outside, the night was cold, windy, and damp; inside, these uncongenial companions. Under these dispiriting circumstances, I thought that bed was the best place, so wrapping myself in the quilt—by no means too clean—that constituted the bed, I stretched myself out in a corner and prepared to pass the night as best I could. I had thought that at least I should be left in peace during the hours of darkness, but I was quickly undeceived. Voices were heard outside the forecastle, and some one indignantly demanded, "Where's that confounded boy?" This swelled instantly to a chorus, "Boy, get out of that and go on deck." I crawled forth from my corner, and was met outside by a deputation headed by the second mate, who landed me clear of the door by my coat collar, and holding me at arm's length, asked furiously, "Why the devil didn't you stop on deck? Who the devil gave you leave to turn in?"

Determined to keep my temper, I answered quietly, "I did not know I was to stay on deck, sir."

"Didn't know you had to stay on deck," cried Mr. Mason. "Why, the lad must be mad, or a fool," he cried, looking round on the grinning seamen, who were much enjoying this entertainment, to judge by their faces. Then turning to me again, he asked with a sneer, "And who do you suppose keeps the watch—Providence?"

As I made no answer, he pushed me before him to the forecastle-head, and ordering me to keep a sharp look-out for lights, and watch that the *Polly* didn't drag her anchors, left me.

It is a little strange that I had never given the watch business a thought, for having been at sea before, even though only as a passenger, I knew quite well that the ship was not delivered up to "Providence" every night; but I did not know, never having been in one before, that on board these small merchant vessels this duty often fell upon the cabin boy.

I stood shivering at the forecastle-head, for it was bitterly cold, and I was worn-out with fatigue and sorrow. But I never even closed my eyes for a moment, being far too scared to think of drowsing. In two hours, which had seemed to me like two nights, I was relieved and ordered to bed. Going into the forecastle, I found all quiet and every one asleep but one man, who swore at me fiercely for daring to come in, and ordered me to trim the lamp before I lay down. I did so, then looked around for my tattered quilt, but observing that my swearing friend had taken it, curled myself up in a corner and fell asleep, with the sound of the howling wind in my ears, and the lapping of the water against the sides of the vessel. But even in my sleep I was pursued by the insults and abuse that had been heaped upon me, and again and again seemed to be climbing up that swaying mast, ever striving, and never attaining, to reach a place of safety.

At dawn the next day I was awakened from my restless slumbers by a hideous uproar, and opening my eyes, beheld the last look-out man standing in the midst of the forecastle, shouting through his hollowed hands the following summons: "Watch ahoy! Oh ye sleepers, eight bells below there! all hands on deck!" the last words being delivered in a peculiarly strident yell that sent a cold shiver right through me. I staggered to my feet, and looked around for some basin in which I might wash at least my face and hands.

"What are yer turning yer eyes inside out for?" asked Fitzgerald.

"A basin to wash in," I replied.

A roar of laughter greeted my words, and a volley of witticisms, more or less filthy, were showered upon me. I moved to leave the cabin, where a grim, weather-beaten looking man said, not unkindly, "Don't notice their blarney, my son, but go ahead and see if there's a southerly wind in the bread barge."

I opened my eyes in astonishment at this mystic order. Seeing I did not understand a word, he translated it into plain English as follows : " Go and see if there's any biscuit in that box, and if not, go aft to the steward and get some."

There was none, so I departed on my errand, one man calling after me, " Don't stay to wash your 'ands on the way, we ain't partic'lar."

I found the steward in his cabin ; he gave me a basket of biscuits, with which I returned to the forecastle. There I found the whole crew dressed, seated on their chests, awaiting my arrival. My appearance created a general move to the centre, where each man grasped a biscuit, and retired with it to his lair; inquiries were made about beef and pork, but the locker having been searchingly investigated, yielded no results, so they had to content themselves with more biscuit and more growls.

Shortly after, a tin of hot coffee was served to each, and all hands were then summoned on deck.

There we were all set to work, some to heave up the anchor, some to loose the sails. I was sent up to the main-top-sail-yard, and helped to cast off the gaskets that held it ; this being accomplished without accident, we descended and were set to the (to me) far more agreeable duty of hauling on the braces. By this time a tug had us in tow, and we were fast nearing the heads; the sea was choppy, and we commenced to pitch and toss in fine style. Soon the tug came along and took the pilot off. How I wished I was a pilot, or a deck hand, or any one that would be taken ashore ; but it was useless giving way to any such desires, and my time was too fully occupied to spare many minutes in repining. Soon we were dashing along with every stitch set, and the wind in our favour. Towards evening the men were mustered to be picked into watches. There are two watches, the port and starboard. The port is generally the crack watch, and is commanded by the first mate; while the starboard is commanded by the captain and second mate, but as the captain usually sleeps in all night, his command is merely an *ex-officio* one.

The chief mate picked me out for his watch, much to my pleasure, though I fear to his disappointment, for when he found I could not steer, and was really of no particular use to him, he demanded indignantly of the sky "why such things were sent to sea to torment him." He grew more reconciled when it was discovered that the "ordinary seaman" in the other watch was a soldier, and hopelessly useless.

The other "fraud's" name was Rogers. He had deserted from the American army, and been taken in hand by the benevolent boarding-house keepers, with an eye to his advance. They had been exceedingly liberal to him, and had shipped him as full-fledged "able seaman." Before the dazzling lustre of this swindle, mine became a shadow into which I gratefully retired.

So the days wore on, and my scare wore off. I no longer turned dizzy when ordered aloft, and began to settle down as best I could into the uncongenial life. I found out that the captain's name was Alexander, a little sandy-haired Scotchman, a good seaman, though addicted to the consumption of whiskey rather more than was good either for him or for us. He had his wife and baby on board, and I had shipped on the understanding that I was to wait on them. But the captain soon told me I was not wanted, never had been, and I was ordered forward among the men, and expected to do a man's work.

The men were so tickled at the fact of my having been so cleverly fooled, that in their appreciation of the joke they were somewhat disposed to be kindly towards me. The chief mate, Davis, was a Welshman, and though harsh at times, was on the whole pleasant and forbearing with my ignorance. Being a thorough seaman, I learnt a great deal from him. He was a middle-aged man, with a shrewd but not unkindly face, and sharp black eyes. The second mate, Mr. Mason, I have already described, the one I had so unfortunately offended. He never lost an opportunity to show me that he had neither forgotten or forgiven my offence. The rest of the watch on my side numbered eight men. One, an Englishman by birth, called Smith, was a type of sailor fast disappearing, a man that believed in Dibdin and his songs, really loved the sea, was always contented and jolly, and was an old "man-o'-war's" man to boot. I do not know how I could have borne the life on board but for him; he not only helped me when I had work beyond my strength and knowledge, but his bright manner cheered me on, and helped me out of many a fit of depression into which I too often fell. The next man was a Welshman, called Jones of course, also a good-tempered fellow; he had been a navy man, and though only about twenty, had deserted from the ship *Repulse*. Of the others, three were Irish, one good, one indifferent, and one downright nasty in temper. By a strange coincidence they had all three come from the part of Ireland I had once lived in as a child, and the familiar names of places and people gave me a queer sensation. Needless to say that I did not say who I was, though I more than once heard them mention my father's name, and one spoke of his funeral. The rest of the eight were Germans, and simply outrageous in every way.

We were now getting into warm weather, and the trade winds blowing steadily there was little work aloft, and consequently, or so I thought, no danger; but an incident happened one fine morning that opened my eyes to the fact that danger might lurk on deck as well as aloft. It happened in this way. I had been sent to scrape the paint off the rim of the forecastle-head. There was no rail to it, so I seated myself on the edge with my feet on the jib-guys, and began gently scraping away the paint, whistling softly meanwhile. Suddenly the ship gave a fierce lurch, my feet slipped off the guys, and down I shot between them and the forecastle-head. My right hand happening to strike against the guy in my descent, I clung to it with the tenacity of death, and hung suspended over the water, while the surf of the bow-wave roared and buzzed in my ears, and the roll of the ship swung me outwards. Strange to say, I never felt calmer in my life; watching my chance, I drew myself up by one hand, and then with a sudden spring caught at another guy-rope, and in a moment had climbed on board, and calmly walked down to the main-deck to announce the loss of the scraper. Had I missed the rope, I must inevitably have been killed, as, falling so close to the side of the vessel, I should have been sucked in before help could reach me.

Truth to say, this danger appeared as nothing to me when compared with the sickening terror I had felt on climbing up the fore-top-gallant-mast, perhaps because this had come too suddenly to allow me to think about it.

I reported the loss of the scraper to the second mate, who said with a scowl, "Then why didn't you go in after it?"

"Well, I did, sir, but couldn't catch it."

He paused a moment, then said, "Be more careful another time; you have not only lost the scraper, but raised a cry of 'Man overboard' for no reason. Don't do it again."

I ventured to remark that I didn't cry "Man overboard," and knew nothing about it, but Mr. Mason made a step forward as though he meant to knock me down. I think he would have done so, had not Mr. Davis here come up and said kindly, "Glad you are safe, my boy. Were you frightened?"

"No, sir; I had no time," I answered.

Here a sailor remarked that he had been watching me, and it struck him that I was too lazy to put up two hands to save myself, preferring to do it with one.

"Be more careful another time," said Mr. Davis, in the same words as Mr. Mason, but such a different tone. "You can't expect to play such gymnastics with impunity on board ship."

So the incident ended, but it had the advantage of raising a feeling in my favour among the crew, and it became a common belief that I knew rather more than I cared to own to, in a nautical point of view, but, like the monkey, feared to show it lest I should have more work put upon me.

Mr. Mason, too, never let it be forgotten, and when, later on, the first mate doubted the advisability of sending me on a highly dangerous mission, such as casting off a preventer-sheet from the mizzen-top-mast-stay-sail, and mentioned his doubts to the second mate, would reply with a sneer, "Never fear, he won't fall, unless the stay-sail falls too."

Accordingly, I was sent up, and executed the task with that assumption of frozen calm that I had learnt so well how to assume, and which hid my sinking heart and trembling limbs,

The other "impostor" did not manage even as well as I did, and must have led a life of hell. He had shipped in a man's place, whereas I had shipped in a boy's; and the gulf that separates an able-bodied seaman from a boy on board a short-handed merchant vessel, is one too awful and far-reaching to be lightly regarded.

Time wore on, and we crept farther south; the days grew shorter, and the weather colder. The scantiness of my wardrobe now began to show painfully. The slop clothes that I had been so lovingly provided with by Mr. Watts commenced to "carry-away." The much-lauded imperishable oilskin had already bleached white, and the boots —those picturesque sea-boots that show so well in pictures—were giving signs of tender spots, which filled me with gloomy forebodings as to how they would act towards me when we encountered Cape Horn weather, or "Cape Stiff," as the sailors called it.

Shorter and darker grew the days, and one morning the first large snowflake descended into the black-looking water, like some lost spirit from heaven sinking into bottomless perdition. It was soon followed by more and more of its brethren, until nothing could be seen of sky or sea, and we worked with benumbed fingers and frozen feet, while the snow made its way down our necks and, melting, trickled down our backs. I began to understand the horror and terror of the poor for the "beautiful snow."

I understood more still before we got into warm weather again, and have never quite lost the feeling of hopeless misery and depression when I see the snow come whirling down, silent and pitiless, into the dark, gloomy waters.

One incident happened at this time that may be worth mentioning. The captain had brought a goat on board for the purpose of supplying the baby with milk; but whether it felt lonely and sighed after pastures green, or what, one thing was clear—poor old Nanny sank into a decline, and, to avoid any charge of wilful extravagance that his owners might possibly bring against him, Captain Alexander ordered her to be killed and served out to the men as mutton. This was done, and she was eaten with many a complaint against her leanness and toughness. Jones managed to secure the head, and worked up a little joke with it as follows. The snow lay deep on the deck wherever it had a chance, for the seas were tumbling heavily overboard every five minutes or so, and all above the main deck was shrouded in white. Mr. Jones waited until black night fell upon us, and the look-out man had taken his post, when having carefully prepared the goat's head he placed it on the fore-bits, and retired a short distance to await results. They came with all the force and rapidity any practical joker could desire. The "out-look" happening to turn round, saw an unearthly apparation, and expressed his feelings in a blood-freezing howl; after standing a brief moment paralyzed with terror, he jumped for dear life down on the main deck. Hearing the yell, we all went up on the forecastle to see what had happened.

The sight was certainly sufficiently alarming to excuse the poor " look-out's " terror. For standing boldly out in relief from its black snowy background, shone the head of " Nanny," its unearthly wide-open eyes glaring with sulphurous and steadfast malignity out into the inky night, with an expression that harmonized beautifully with its black face and long Satanic horns.

" No wonder that Mick yelled," chuckled Jones, as he prepared to take down the head; but before he could reach it his experienced ear caught a familiar sound. "Look out," he shouted, " and hang on anywhere you can."

The next moment I too heard the hoarse roar of the coming surf, as a white-capped mountain of water loomed suddenly out of the darkness, and came with awful speed and force straight for the vessel.

" Jump for the rigging," yelled Jones, setting the example. With a dexterity taught by desperation, I followed him as he flew to the side the wave was coming from (the other side would have meant certain death), and dashed up the rigging like a sunbeam, just as the great "comber" charged resistlessly over the deck, burying the vessel completely out of sight, leaving us clinging to the frail mast in the midst of the raging waters. Well it was for the "look-out" that he was absent from his post, for his part of the deck resembled Niagara in spring-time. After a short time, the water poured off, the ship righted herself, and we descended from our perilous positions. Poor Nanny's head had been washed away in the rush of water. Mick always vowed that the devil in person visited him that day.

This was only one of the many excitements we enjoyed in our passage round the Horn. In the midst of the dark cloud of our discomforts there were, however, two specks of brightness. One was that at midnight the cook served out a pannikin of hot coffee to each one on watch; it was black and horribly sweetened with molasses, a fearful compound, without doubt. When I think of it now it makes me feel sick, but then, when we had been out in the night air for four hours in a snowstorm—for it generally was snowing—we found the smoking hot mixture simply delicious. The other ray of comfort was, that whenever it blew a gale which necessitated the taking in of the main-sail, and splicing the main-brace, grog was given at the end of it. It did not matter to the men that the pulling in of that particular sail meant two or three hours' grasping and clawing at canvas that was frozen into the semblance of sheet-iron, while the snow drove persistently down one's throat and neck, and the sail itself made back-somersaults over us to the imminent danger of our lives—if only they got their grog at the end of it. The memory of those nights stands out hideous as a nightmare. I often thought that hell should be thus described, instead of the usual theory of fire.

About this time a curious phenomenon used to present itself. We had now got so far south that the day only lasted about six hours, and then we had to take the clock's word for it that it was daylight in other places; with us it was a sepulchral kind of twilight, wonderfully uncanny to look at. The sun would rise about six feet in the heavens, then retire in disgust, leaving us in the "gloaming." Shortly afterwards it would reappear something in the shape of a switch-tailed comet, and almost immediately after a full gale of wind would set in. The sailors consequently connected the two together, and appreciated them accordingly.

The next thing of any interest that happened was the total ruin of all the drinking water. Part of the cargo (wheat) was in bulk, and the water-tanks had been fitted with wooden man-hole covers to admit of the pump pipes being led into them. During some of the heavy weather we had encountered round Cape Horn, these covers had shifted, and quantities of the loose wheat had rolled in, also divers rats had found a last resting-place there; and so it came to pass that the water became unpleasantly diversified thereby, and our daily allowance was enriched by the presence of portions of black fur and swollen wheat, while a fascinating bluish oily scum dwelt ever on the top of the water, and an astonishing smell that could be tasted pervaded the whole forecastle.

This disaster soon took the spirit out of the ship's company; two of them got the scurvy and were very ill, others followed, and we who escaped that painful disease were obliged to do the work of those on the sick list.

It was fully two months before we got any fresh water, and then only by a lucky chance. Becoming becalmed, we saw not far off another vessel in the same plight, and from her the captain obtained one thousand gallons of water in return for a cask of whiskey. There were five ships besides ours becalmed for three weeks off the Western Islands (Azores), and quite a brisk trade was carried on between them, and visiting to some extent took place. One of the other captains had his wife on board, who came to see Mrs. Alexander. Our skipper's wife was a nice young thing, and without, of course, having the smallest pretensions to be a lady, had an innate tact that many a born lady might have envied. One morning, when it was snowing and blowing, and I had been four hours exposed to the stormy elements, she called me into her cabin and brought me some hot tea and a huge Cornish pasty. For a moment I hesitated, finding it easier to accept insults than kindnesses, but she pushed me gently into a seat and said, "Don't refuse me. I have a brother just your age, and just in your position; perhaps if I am kind to you, his skipper's wife may be kind to him."

Another time, seeing how miserably clad I was, she sent me some garments. On my venturing to remonstrate with her, she said, laughing, "You shall pay me back one day when you are in your right position—for I know you are not now—by giving my Will a help on in the world."

"Will" was at that time eight months old. The poor little chap never needed my or any one else's care, for before the voyage was ended, one bright sunny morning, we laid him to rest in the sparkling waters, with a ten-pounder at his little feet. The distracted mother was dragged away before we lowered him, for a shark had followed us closely all through the little one's five hours' struggle with croup, and we were not sure whether we could save the body from the great brute's jaws. I am happy to say we did so—a well-directed ball from the first mate killed the monster. We did not wait to take him, but hurried from the spot. Mrs. Alexander was even kinder to me after her loss than before, for Baby Will had always crowed with delight when I took him in my arms.

But to return to our becalmed days. They passed on wearily enough, though it must not be supposed that we had nothing to do but lean over the bulwarks and whistle for wind. Far from that, we used to "turn to" at 6 a.m., wash the decks, and tidy the ship for the day. We did not "spread the awnings," as in the ships one reads about, for a very good reason—there were none to spread. At 8. a.m. our watch went below, and the other one came on deck, and were set to work scraping paint or rust, splicing, putting on chafing-gear, &c., &c., until 12 a.m; then our watch rushed eagerly on deck and joyously took up whatever work was going, until our unappeasable industry was checked at 4 p.m. (eight bells), when we went below for the first dog-watch, 4 p.m. to 6 p.m., during which time we had our tea; then on deck again until 8 p.m., the second dog-watch; then below until 12 p.m., and so on. No speaking or singing was allowed during work time, and whistling was high treason. We painted that vessel seven times over during the voyage, Captain Alexander seemingly having a perfect passion for the smell of turpentine. But the culinary arrangements of the British merchant marine leave a good deal to be desired. Dinner consisted of salt horse or salt-junk, as the case might be, with pea-soup twice a week, into which we used to pour vinegar so as to congeal and keep it from jumping overboard. Three quarts of water was allowed each man daily, but as his soup, tea, and coffee were taken out of it, there was never enough for drinking purposes in hot weather. Of bread, of course, there was none, but ship biscuit was allowed *ad libitum*; personally I always detested it. We never washed in fresh water unless it rained, when each man caught all the water he could for himself, and washed first his clothes, then his body. On Sundays we did no work beyond scrubbing the decks and working the ship on her onward course. After three weeks' calm a strong breeze suddenly sprang up, and the five ships, signalling farewells, resumed each her way.

Shortly after, we caught a shark and had pieces of it fried in vinegar for dinner; but every one was ill from it except myself, chiefly because I hardly touched it. (N.B. I don't think shark can be as healthy food as some people, probably landsmen, like to make out.) A week after the voyage was resumed, we came up to a large dismasted ship, the *British Princess*. She looked very grand and romantic, stationary in the midst of the ocean, with her men swarming up aloft looking like flies, taking down the remains of her rigging and removing various spars which had been thrown across her deck. She was only twenty-two days out from England, and was bound for Calcutta. As she needed no assistance, we saluted and left her alone in her glory.

More days passed on, succeeding each other with wearying monotony, until the time came when we commenced to make preparations for coming into port. The last coatings of paint were, for the seventh time, daubed on; the masts scraped and varnished. The officers and men grew less surly; even Mr. Mason ceased to always greet me with a curse or an insult. The commissariat improved to a slight degree, and the weekly rations of fourteen ounces of sugar sometimes swelled to a full pound.

At last, in the fulness of time, came one morning the electrifying cry of "Land." Oh! my dear long-suffering readers—if I have any—did you ever know what it was to sight land after one hundred and fifty days cramped up in a 700-ton barque, with a crew of more or less blackguards for company? and that land England! Whether you have a home there, or loving friends longing to see you, or as I was, without father or mother, and with only relations utterly indifferent to my welfare, makes no difference to the feeling of joy that pervades one's heart and soul at that magic cry, "Land!"

There it was, merely a blue cloudy-looking line in the far distance, but the sight seemed to put us all out of our senses. The watch below came rushing on deck to view that blessed sight, and gazed and gazed at the glimpse of the promised land, until ordered to resume work; even then they did not murmur or grumble.

But we had not yet reached the much-desired haven where we would be, and the old adage, "There's many a slip 'twixt cup and lip," was again proved true. For the wind rose with sudden fury, blew a gale that increased to two gales with alarming swiftness. Sail after sail took itself away before it could be taken in, flying over the seething mass of stormy waters like some huge birds mad with joy at their freedom. Some of the head-sails were still remaining, and I being so expert a climber—heaven save the mark!—was ordered by my friend the second mate to go and haul them in. I went to the forecastle-head to do so, and the fury of the elements invested me with some of their wild excitement. The barque plunged up and down mountains of water, quivering from bow to stern, and I climbed up the swaying mast shouting wildly with a very frenzy of delight at this battle between man and Nature. I had got the sails in, and was descending, when a sudden gust of wind threw a coil of rope against me and knocked me clean overboard. Instead of falling into the sea and being no more seen, I fell astride the shank of one of the anchors. I should hesitate to speak of so astounding a fact, knowing how apt people are to believe that sailors and travellers generally draw the long bow when recounting their adventures, had there not been a witness to my marvellous though unconscious feat of gymnastics. Mr. Mason saw me blown off, and looked over the side; before, however he could raise the cry of "Man overboard," he observed me sitting astride the anchor.

"Well, the devil must be taking care of you for some purpose or other!" was his remark as he gave me a hand and hauled me on deck.

We were working slowly up to Caernarvon Bay, and the wind now shifted to the west. This was a very serious affair for us, as, with the exception of the lower-main-topsail, we had lost all our sails, and that one was no great good to a ship clawing off a lee coast with a strong current setting landwards. The result of the change in the wind was soon apparent; for every point of headway we made seven points to leeward, which was sufficiently alarming.

But bad as was our plight, our sympathy was soon called forth for a vessel in greater need. Away to leeward of us, perfectly within sight, a large Norwegian vessel was vainly striving to beat out to sea; but the current was too strong for her, and little by little, in spite of her desperate efforts, she was driven towards the deadly rocks that showed themselves now and again through the heaving surf, like wolves in ambush awaiting their prey. Nearer and nearer the merciless breakers hounded her on to her death. We watched with painful interest, but could do nothing; our man at the wheel had as much as he could do to keep us out of the fatal current. At last the end came: a billow seemingly stronger than the others lifted the vessel on her crest, and dashed it clean against the cliffs that towered three hundred feet above her. Above the roar and din of wind and waves we heard the crash of her timbers as they broke against the rocks; then the hungry waves, gathering force, rushed towards her in one huge pyramid of foam and overwhelmed her. She emerged from it for a minute, and we saw her in a sudden hush, upright with all her crew clinging to the masts, then she plunged bows forward and disappeared. And the waves dashed against the cliffs and the winds blew as before, and there was nothing to tell that over a hundred men had gone down with their gallant ship that had borne them so long. Another hour's fair sailing would have landed them safely. There would be many a desolate home and broken heart in the far Northland amongst those who watched vainly for husband, father, or friend. Sorrow on, brave hearts, but not for them; their last gale is weathered—they keep their solemn watch below "till the sea gives up its dead."

We learnt afterwards that the ship had been out three years. An occurrence like this could not fail to affect the most hardened and callous among us, the more so as there was some probability of our sharing the same fate. One or two of the men ceased swearing for a while, and Rogers (the soldier) with white lips asked me if I did not think that the people on the cliffs were wishing and praying we might get in in safety. On my suggesting that he would do well to pray himself, he answered he didn't know how, but he'd a sort of idea there was a God somewhere who could help us if He would. Poor ignorant Rogers, he knew nothing; but in the moment of danger, instinct drove him to the only real place of safety, "the everlasting arms."

But our own position was becoming perilous, and we were drifting nearer and nearer to land, which, as Captain Alexander had no knowledge of the coast, was fraught with considerable danger. We looked around in vain for a pilot, who had been signalled for long since. Hour after hour passed by, and our position got worse and worse; the crowds on the cliff increased in number, and they were doubtless expecting to see us sink like the great Norwegian vessel. At last a pilot put out, and before long we were hailed by the joyful words, " Ship ahoy! do you want a pilot ? "

" Want a pilot ? " Hadn't we been signalling for one the last three hours and more. He was warmly received, but the captain cooled down when £30 was demanded for the job, and seemed inclined to back out of the business. The pilot, a crafty old sea-dog, protested that he couldn't do it for a farthing less. " Keep your luff, you at the wheel ! " he yelled. " By George, you'll lose her yet. Come, hurry up, Captain. Yes, or no ? I don't want to make food for the fishes."

Captain Alexander surrendered, paid the money, and in a quarter of an hour we were in safe anchorage. In fact we had been so at the time the pilot boarded us, but the skipper did not know it. Of course he was furious when he discovered the trick, but it was too late then. We came to an anchorage at Holyhead, and the voyage was practically ended. Two days afterwards we were towed up to Liverpool, where the barque unloaded and was laid up for repairs. I bade good-bye to Mrs. Alexander, who on parting gave me a ringlet of Baby Will's hair as a keepsake, and begged me to write to her sometimes. That lock of soft golden hair I still have, though I never wrote to wee Will's mother, and our paths have never crossed again. But I shall not forget as long as my life lasts her kindness to a desolate boy; nor will she, I think, forget one on whom her dead baby used to smile.

A VOYAGE TO CHINA.

SOME twenty years or more ago, I sailed in the iron barque *Peep-o'-Day* then going to China. The weather was favourable, and until we reached the Bay of Biscay nothing occurred of interest, at least to me. There I nearly lost my life through one of those acts of ignorance and foolishness that sailors more than other peple are so apt to commit. One day, the breeze freshening somewhat suddenly, the second mate ordered in the flying-jib. As it is always considered the boy's place aboard ship to furl all the small sails, I hurried out on the boom to do so. It was my first voyage, and I knew little or nothing of seamanship. Making my way out, I kept to the lee side, whilst I tried to gather in the sail in order to get the gasket around it. After tugging vainly for some minutes, I had nearly succeeded, when a fierce gust of wind blew the sail against me, and in another moment I was knocked clean off the flying-jib-boom. Oh! the horror and length of that moment; the sickening sensation of utter powerlessness as I shot through space; the sudden plunge deep down into the ocean; the terrible feeling of despair and loneliness when, on reaching the surface, I saw the ship

ARTHUR CADEW JENKINS.
(*After a Photograph.*)

already far off! Luckily for me, the man at the wheel had seen me fall, and putting the wheel hard down to fetch the ship up in the wind, and so stop her progress, cried out, "Man overboard!" That thrilling cry always brings every one on deck; a boat was soon lowered, and I was picked up half a mile astern, well-nigh exhausted.

Fair weather accompanied us right on to the Western Tropics, where we witnessed a very curious spectacle. As far as the eye could reach, a distance of about some three miles, was a seething mass of fish, closely packed together by the million. They were the Bonita, a short, sturdy fish, reddish in colour outside, and very good eating. The first mate, who was very knowing in all piscatorial matters, said that they had probably been pursued by some finny monster, and were migrating. They were starving, and devoured each other ravenously with much apparent relish. All hands on board were called up to catch them, which was by no means difficult to do. It was an odd sight to see the various men at work. Some, with true instinctive love of angling, got out their lines and caught them in the approved fashion; others, on the contrary, disdaining such slow measures, lowered buckets, bringing up hundreds each time. The chief mate seated himself on the top-gallant-yard with a sack slung to him, which he rapidly filled with his hands as the ship ploughed her way slowly through the living waters. An Irishman on board, not to be outdone by the chief mate, sewed up the ends of an old pair of trousers, lowered it with a weight in each leg, and hauled it up "alive and kicking" amidst a roar of laughter.

Some of the hands got poisoned eating these fish; for, in spite of the first mate's warning, they would leave them out in the boats to dry after having cleaned them; and the moon, which is very powerful in the tropics, poisoned all the fish exposed to her light. One of the seamen got moon-blind from obstinately lying exposed to the rays of the moon at this place. He could see as well and clearly as any one else during the day, but at night, no matter how clear the sky might be, he was quite blind. I have never heard that there is any cure for moon-blindness.

A few weeks after, we witnessed a battle royal between a Sword-fish, a Whale, and a Thrasher. Their mode of warfare was peculiar and decidedly interesting to watch. On this occasion it was two against one, *i.e.*, the Sword-fish and the Thrasher against the Whale. The Thrasher would make a sudden rush, rise into the air, and come down on the top of the Whale, with a tremendous whack and crash that could be heard half a mile off. The poor Cetacea, to escape from this enemy, would dive, when the Sword-fish, being on the lookout, would dash at him like a flash of lightning, driving his sword into him up to its very snout—I had nearly said hilt. This defence and attack went on for some half-hour, when the

Whale began to spout blood and died. We left the victorious ones feasting upon him.

It was through a whale, of which there are quantities in these seas, that the monotony of the life on board was at this time considerably disturbed. An enormous bull, fully sixty feet in length, came alongside so quietly that the first intimation we had of his proximity was his spouting a few gallons of water over our taffrail, and uttering a deep, hollow roar that might be heard a mile off. The man at the wheel was nearly frightened into fits, and Ching, a Chinese dog on board, and a universal pet, became literally mad with terror. Ching soon had sole possession of the deck, for all hands took to the rigging, fearing a bite from the mad dog, who ran to and fro with tail lowered "half-mast," and all his hair down his back bristling. After some talk, the carpenter undertook to cure him, and as we had no gun at hand with which to shoot him, beside the desire we all had to save his life, the man was allowed to try his powers of curing a mad dog. We all looked on with great interest as he made a noose from some cord cut from the rigging, and, the next time Ching came his way, he cleverly threw it over his head and drew it tight enough to keep him still, though not tight enough to strangle him. Then jumping down from the rigging, he quickly fetched an axe and chopped off the tip of Ching's tail to let the blood flow. That done, he dipped him overboard twice, and brought him on deck restored and in his right mind. Never afterwards could Ching be induced to sleep on the taffrail; indeed, he always passed it with a rush.

Meanwhile the whale was keeping abreast of us, and some fears were entertained of his attacking the barque. He was as long as the ship, and it would have gone hard with us if he had taken it into his small head to do so; but apparently he decided that it was not worth while, for, with a final roar and dive, he went away to the right, and we saw no more of him. Not long after this we very nearly lost Ching's saviour, the carpenter. It was a dead calm. Orders had been given to rig stages out over the ship's side, and some of the men told off to scrape the barnacles off her bottom with long-handled spades. Some of these barnacles were a foot and a half long, and considerably impeded our progress. It was very hot, and during the change of watches some of the men and myself jumped off the stages and took a delightful bath. It gives one a curious sensation to be alongside of the vessel one minute, and the next wave would take her some twenty yards or so away, the next again bringing her up so close that you felt she was coming on top of you. Mason—that was the carpenter's name—seeing us enjoying ourselves and swimming about so easily, thought he could do the same; so, undeterred by the trifling fact that he could not swim a stroke, he hastily undressed, and, getting on the rail, jumped clean overboard, feet first. It seemed a long time before he came up nearly on the spot he went down, but, as he expanded his hands and opened his mouth, down he went again immediately like a shot. The first mate, with some others of us, happened to observe him, and the former sung out, "Man drowning!" Two sailors immediately jumped on the stage with ropes and a life-buoy, and the next time he appeared threw them to him. He had just strength to clutch one of the ropes, and was hauled on to the stage, where he fainted. It is really astonishing that so many men whose whole lives are on the ocean should not know, or even care to learn, how to swim. That very same day I came near losing my life in a horrible manner. There was another boy on board beside myself, who could not swim. The captain wished me to teach him, and ordered him to get down on the stage and strip; he also gave him a life-belt. But Jennings was too timid, and only stood shivering, unable to summon up courage enough to venture into the water, particularly after the carpenter's adventure. Therefore, after swimming about for a time on the life-buoy, to show him how easy it was and how safe, I threw it on the stage, and struck out for a long swim, boy-like, to show off. After going some little distance, I heard a fearful yell, and, looking back to the ship, saw the men gesticulating madly for me to come back. Frightened by their actions and their looks—for after the one shout they kept silence—I swam back to the vessel as fast as I could. As soon as I reached the stage, half a dozen hands grabbed hold of me and hauled me on deck, where the captain, collaring me, naked as I was, dragged me aft and told me to look over the side. I did so, and there was a tremendous tiger-shark over twenty feet long. His small eyes looked straight up at me, and he snapped his jaws with a yapping sound that made my blood run cold. In fact it gave me such a shock and made so deep an impression on me, that I vowed from that day forth nothing should ever induce me to take a swim in broad ocean. The sailors were not long in giving me a nearer and pleasanter sight of him. A large iron hook attached to a strong chain was thrown over, after being baited with a piece of salt pork. The greedy brute grabbed at it at once, and in his struggles to get away tore his jaw badly; nevertheless back he came for the meat, was caught, and after some hard work, hauled on deck. The first thing he did was to knock down the black cook who was standing by, and smash the binnacle-stand with a flap of his tail. With great difficulty he was got down to the main-deck, where the carpenter, who seemed to have a speciality for such operations, chopped off his tail with an axe; that quieted him. But sharks cling to life with horrible tenacity. This brute, after his head was cut off and he was opened, had muscular movements all over him; his backbone measured twelve feet; well cleaned and cut to a suitable size, they make handsome walking-sticks. We caught twenty-seven sharks altogether of different kinds and sizes on this voyage.

A few days after entering the Straits of Sunda we sighted Java, and soon after anchored off Anger Point. This was the first land we had been near since leaving England, a period of one hundred and eighty-six days.

A week before this we sighted a ship, the *Pembrokeshire* from London. On signalling us, and finding we had been out so unusually long, the captain concluded that we must be short-handed from scurvy, or loss of life, a gale or some other accident which had prevented the barque from being properly worked. Being a kind-hearted man, he came on board bringing two sacks of potatoes, some newspapers and tracts. Hearing that two of our men were down with scurvy, he sent his boat back for another load of potatoes, while he stayed on board the barque to lunch, for which state occasion the last fowl aboard was killed and roasted; it being little but skin and bone, Ching got the most of it. When the boat had brought the second load of potatoes, the captain of the *Pembrokeshire* returned to his own ship, and we soon parted company, as she was a fast sailer. We were all of us the better for the short visit—nothing is so refreshing as the sight of new faces after months of always seeing the same. That captain (I am sorry to say I forget his name) was a good and humane man. He would, I think, be sorry if he knew that all his kindness was thrown away, Captain J—— being one of the meanest and most cowardly men it was ever my misfortune to sail under. On this occasion, after giving us one meal of fresh potatoes and several times a few raw ones sliced in vinegar to the sick men, he kept all the rest for his own use in the cabin.

But we were now anchored off Anger Point, the captain's gig was ordered out, and I, being a good hand at the oars, was allowed to make one of the boat's crew. When we got ashore it was like entering into Paradise. The most magnificent tropical fruits and flowers were in the wildest profusion; crowds of natives running about almost in a state of nudity, the men well made, with shapely limbs, the women with soft eyes and small hands and feet; a great many shops, mostly kept by Chinamen dressed in their silken robes heavily embroidered with gold and silver; Dutch soldiers, still wearing their old-fashioned uniform of a hundred years ago; Europeans in their sombre modern dress mingling among the crowds of natives. The latter, men, women and children, were many of them bathing together in the clear sparkling water. All was so bright, so fresh and lovely, that it made up a scene never to be forgotten.

The Chinese shopkeepers were very polite, offering us such tea as they only can make, in tiny delicate cups about the size of egg-cups, and endeavouring to get us to teach them some English words in return for their kindness. They are remarkably quick, and picked up not only words but whole sentences with marvellous rapidity. When we returned to the ship, a great many natives followed us in their canoes, loaded down to the water's edge with the most delicious fruits; pine-apples, cocoa-nuts, bananas, sugar-canes, plantains, oranges, lemons, and the famous mungastine, to taste which epicures have been known to come all the way from Europe. It only grows in this place, and I believe all attempts at propagating it elsewhere have failed. I was as eager as the rest to taste this great delicacy, and must confess that it exceeded my expectations—it is a most delicious fruit. Its outward appearance somewhat resembles the poppy-head when gone to seed. On opening this outer skin, the fruit is seen lying inside, shaped something like a peeled orange. It melts away on being placed in the mouth, leaving a most exquisite flavour.

The natives trade their fruits for old clothes, soap, or any European articles. A good lot was bought by the hands on board, and the natives proceeded to return, when a stiff breeze sprung up suddenly, capsizing several of their canoes. They seemed quite unconcerned about it, getting straddle-legged on them, and paddling for shore through a heavy sea. It was here that the most awful thunder-storm took place that I ever witnessed in my life. Piles of black clouds had been slowly making their way from the west, and towards afternoon hovered over the ocean, ominous, grim and still. The silence was almost awful; we all felt depressed and fearful, while Ching whimpered sadly and tried to hide himself. Suddenly there came an appalling crash of thunder that shook the ship from bow to stern, and she quivered and shuddered at her moorings. All hands rushed on deck, thinking that the masts had been struck and gone overboard. It lasted about an hour, flash after flash of forked and sheet lightning, violet and purple, scarlet and opal in colour, followed immediately by crashing peals of thunder that literally deafened you. The sea rose and added its roar to the thunder, and the heavens opened, letting the waters pour down in torrents. In another hour the sun was shining and the sky was clear; only the ocean heaved and moaned, unable to calm itself so quickly after the angry storm.

The sailors laid in a stock of yams here, a kind of potato, as large as a man's head, and very good eating, besides being nutritious and wholesome; after which we set sail for Shanghai.

I have mentioned that our captain was a mean and cowardly man, much disliked by all his crew. Discontent was rife. The men commented in no measured terms at his stinginess in not getting in fresh provisions at Java, and things came to a climax when, scurvy again attacking some of the crew, the remainder of the men had double work, and were still kept on short rations on account of the long voyage. So they mutinied, and in the height of a fearful hurricane. Captain J——, who had never been in these latitudes before, having always sailed in the Mediterranean until he got this command, was ignorant of the danger of these tropical hurricanes. We had all sail set at the time, and although the squall was seen coming, he imagined it was of no importance and gave no orders to shorten sail. The men went about their work with sullen anger, whispering among themselves. The hurricane was not long in approaching, and struck the barque with fierce fury. Smash went the two royal and top-gallant masts, the flying-jibboom with all the yards and sails attached. The force of the wind, added to the wreck of the masts, threw the *Peep-o'-Day* on her beam end, where she was in imminent danger of filling and going down. At this moment it became of inky blackness, the wind howled and shrieked like wild fiends let loose, and the sea was lashed to fury; the waves poured over the vessel, which, encumbered by the fallen masts, could not right herself. It was in this time of awful peril the mutiny occurred. The captain came running forward with axes, and ordered the men to cut away the riggings and throw the masts overboard that the ship might have a chance. The men folded their arms and flatly refused to obey him, their spokesman saying that they would rather go down with the ship at once, than to go on starving and being overworked as they had been. Captain J—— was so frightened that he actually wept with terror. He promised the best the ship could give—"Only, for God's sake, clear the deck of the masts, or we shall all be lost in a few minutes!" At first he wept and prayed in vain. Finally four men did go to work, cleared the wrecked masts away, and the *Peep o' Day* righted herself. The sea was one sheet of white foam, and rose mountains high for a day and a night after the hurricane was over, that only lasted twenty minutes. Things went on somewhat better after this, as the captain was too much afraid of another mutiny not to keep his promise. Nothing of interest occurred until within about a week's sail of Shanghai, when we narrowly escaped being destroyed by a waterspout. These spouts contain thousands of tons of water, and if they should burst on a ship would sink it instantly. The one I mention was making straight for us, a stately but awful object. There was scarcely a breath of wind stirring, and the captain, after vainly trying to get out of its way, ordered one of the large guns to be loaded with a heavy charge of powder. When all was ready, a red-hot poker was obtained from the cook's galley and the gun was fired. Instantly the tremendous pillar of water tottered and fell headlong into the sea, about a quarter of a mile from us.

A week from this date we arrived at the mouth of Yang-tsze-kiang River, leading on to Shanghai. This river runs a great distance into the interior, and is one of the principal means of traffic.

The most striking feature that struck us on

entering the harbour was the large number of ships, most of them flying their ensigns half-mast, the token of death. Over eight hundred vessels were at anchor here, the largest number in a foreign port I ever saw, with one exception: that was at New York just after the war had ended.

We soon found out that there was no chance of getting a cargo, as most of these ships had been waiting here, some three, some four months for that purpose. The distress and misery occasioned by this forced delay was something truly frightful. Trade all over India and China was very dull at this time. The captains, obliged to pay heavy harbour dues as well as keeping the men at full wages, became despairing and desperate. It was useless to go elsewhere for freight, all trade being at a standstill. This state of things so worked upon the minds of the captains and mates, that almost as many of them died by their own hand as did the common seamen from dysentery and exposure. Some deliberately drank themselves to death; others blew their brains out; and many jumped overboard and let themselves drown, while their crew looked on with stolid indifference. It was one of the usual customs to go round to the different neighbouring ships every morning to find out who was alive, and how many had died a natural death or had killed themselves. In the afternoon of the day they died they would be buried, the body or bodies being placed in boats and taken down to Fu-chow (I think the name was) Reach, which opens into the river, and there, without a word of prayer or ceremony of any sort, were thrown over to sink or swim, and became food for the fishes. The town was so full of seamen who could get no ships that every boarding-house was filled to repletion, and fearful quarrels, often ending in murder, took place for the sake of a filthy corner in which to lie. The heat was stifling and the stench appalling. Many of the men would take their blankets at night and sleep on the beach for coolness. Most of them would be dead by the morning, which did not in the least prevent others attempting the same thing the following night. The heavy steamy malaria arising from the swampy ground after the great heat of the day made the night-air fatal to most. Sailors are very much like children, having no thought or care for themselves, without a child's obedience to protect them from danger, and therefore they do not give themselves a chance in these eastern countries. They will eat voraciously of vegetables and fruits, which, not being accustomed to, brings on violent diarrhœa. Unless this disease can be taken in time, it causes a sure and painful death. A man taken with it has no appearance of sickness, he keeps his colour, and his eyes are bright, but he gets rapidly thin, and so weak as to be unable to lift his hand to his mouth. I, amongst others, was taken down with it. Captain J—— declared I was shamming, and ordered me to work, threatening otherwise to send me to the

SHANGHAI.

French hospital, where, it was said, a knife was run into the heart of any one whose recovery was not rapid enough to satisfy the doctors. I attempted to crawl aft to the main-deck, but was so blinded by weakness that I could not see where I was going, and stumbling against one of the masts, fell heavily. A Nova Scotia seaman, who had often shown me some kindness, dragged me back to the forecastle, cursing the captain, the climate, the heavens and the earth in no measured language. For weeks after I lived on nothing but rice-water, if the state I was in could be called living, for I lay all day and night with no feeling but one of utter powerlessness and weakness. Tears of weariness would roll down my cheeks when forced to the exertion of swallowing a mouthful of rice-water. The doctor coming one day, pronounced me dead; but when in the afternoon I was placed in the boat with two men who really were dead, I was seen to breathe, so carried back to my berth again, where I finally recovered, chiefly from being left alone. We lost four men from diarrhœa, and two died in the hospital from scurvy. During the three months and a half that we stayed at this port, over seven hundred died or committed suicide.

The *Peep-o'-Day* lay out in the stream opposite the English Town. In these Chinese cities each nationality has its own separate town, known as English Town, French Town, American Town, and so on. The river Yang-tsze-kiang is 3,158 English miles in length, and has a current running eight or nine knots. It is of a dirty, muddy colour, and has but little beauty to recommend it. There is one curious thing about it, and that is that in these large Chinese cities more than a quarter of the population live on the water, having their streets and towns built on the river. Shops and markets, business of all sorts, is carried on by the people as though on land. But these floating towns are often scenes of terrible accidents, owing to the swiftness of the current and the carelessness of the people. Often the *sampans*, sort of boats, miss their hold of the ship they intend to reach, and are swept down the cable of the next ship, capsized, and not unfrequently dashed to pieces. A Norwegian captain and his wife got drowned in this way, trying to reach their ship. Poor girl! she had only been married about a month. When their bodies were found, they were so tightly locked in each other's arms that they were placed in the same hammock and buried down the river, with more ceremony and display of feeling than was given to events far more tragic and awful. I remember being struck with the great length and beauty of the young wife's hair, of that pale gold colour that Norse women often have. The water had washed it around her husband's neck and arms, and it glittered on him like rays of gold.

These *sampans*, although safe enough for those who understand them and know something of seamanship, are very dangerous to the inexperienced and careless. They are exceedingly light, and shaped something like a cockle-shell, capsize easily, and, although universally employed in China, are a frequent cause of accident and loss of life. It seemed to me that they might, without much cleverness or difficulty, be made safer, but no one troubled their heads about it. The small passenger *sampans* are propelled by a man at the stern, who sculls and steers at the same time. Where the current is very strong, some of the passengers will condescend to put out oars at the sides or bows to prevent being carried off or capsized.

The European Town appeared much as in Europe, the shops being built, stocked, and kept by Europeans, and so had nothing particularly interesting about them. But the China Town was exceedingly curious, and consisted chiefly of a great number of small huts, bazaars, and stalls. in which, huddled together in wild confusion, was a heterogeneous mass of Chinese toys, sweetmeats, jewellery, roast pig, vegetables, embroidered stuffs —in fact, everything that can be imagined. The ground was low, filthy with putrid matter left to rot, and the smell something too awful. We used to stuff some cotton-wool up our nostrils, but it was not much good, for it was a smell that could be tasted, and even a bit of camphor kept in our mouths —when we were lucky enough to procure a bit— was only a short relief. The dirt and smell were only exceeded by the frightful discordant noises that never ceased day or night: men quarelling in all languages, merchants bawling out their wares, dogs yelping, a din of pipes and a wild beating of gongs that certainly did not impress me favourably with the Celestial City. There was a wall around the town covered with spikes, on which were stuck the heads of Chinamen beheaded for murder or robbery. The effect of these grinning heads was ghastly in the extreme.

At the time I am writing of, any European was justified in killing any Chinaman he found outside China Town after eight o'clock at night without his pass, which was a Chinese lantern having the pass inside. Most of these Chinese ports belong to England, and disputes, fights, and murder were of everyday occurrence. Besides which, war was raging up the country, and it was a common thing for us to go over the ship's bows to clear her cable of dead Chinamen brought down by the river. They would float up and down with the tide, it seemingly being no one's duty to bury them. One is said to become accustomed to all things, but I must confess that it was never without a shudder I saw, as I often did on looking into the river, the hideous face of a dead Chinaman grinning up at me from the muddy water.

During this time of forced inaction, the morale among the European seamen became very bad. Those who at the commencement had been discharged and could get no ships and no work were in a bad way, and would induce sailors, who although on board a vessel, were almost as destitute as themselves, to join them in attempts to get food and money. All sense of right and wrong, of honesty and truth, seemed lost. English and Dutch, French and Spaniards, Germans and Italians, would band together to plunder. One party, rendered desperate by starvation and misery, boarded a two-masted lighter anchored at the mouth of the river, threw the Chinamen overboard to sink or swim—most sank—and then went up into the interior of the country, exchanged some things on board for raw silk, which they sold again in the cities, and having paid no duties on it managed to make some money. So callous had the authorities become that even this outrage passed unnoticed.

Another favourite mode of obtaining money was to watch where the rich Chinese were buried, and at night a party of men would dig them up and cut off their tails, which were more than half made of silk, and were worth from six to eight dollars apiece. These fellows also obtained a hearty meal at the same time, as after all the screaming and yelling, the beating of gongs, burning of incense, dropping coins and other death ceremonials have been gone through, the relations leave the dead, placing beside him a good roast pig and plenty of rice, in order that he may not starve on his journey to the next world. The rich Chinese are buried within a large inclosure of white masonry shaped like a horse-shoe. I never saw a Chinese woman buried, but as the Chinamen do not believe their women have souls, they probably do not think it necessary to provide them with food for the long journey. Parents will sell their children quite readily, and you can purchase a very nice girl for thirty dollars.

Frequently, during the weary months we lay by in the river, we were visited by ivory-men, fellows selling Chinese curiosities made of ivory, sandal-wood, and bamboo. Whilst we were looking over their collection of fans, jewellery, and knick-knacks of all sorts, they would stealthily take notes of how many men were on board, how many guns the vessel possessed, what sort of man the captain was and so on, for they were all spies paid by the pirates. After making the rounds of several ships, they would despatch their information to the pirates waiting out at sea, more particularly the information when certain ships would leave the harbour, and the number of her crew, guns, &c. Directly the unfortunate vessel left the river and entered the high seas, down would come the pirates, take the ship, and kill all hands with the utmost barbarity and torture. Woe betide any woman that fell between their hands—their fate was too awful to put into words. Whenever there was time, their husbands killed them with their own hands, or they drowned themselves rather than fall into the power of the pirates. Some of these pirate junks were quite as large as any European ship, having seven masts and carrying twenty guns, while they were manned by a crew of not less than two hundred men. They are splendid seamen, and can sail in the wind's eye with any European ship, and they weather the heaviest gales. Nearly every week the English gunboats would bring in one and sometimes two that they had captured. In most cases men of European nationality were found aboard, having entered into the service of the pirates to work their guns for them in exchange for high wages, it being a matter of perfect indifference to them from whom they got the money as long as they did get it. It was very hard at that time to find out who were pirates or who were not. The only way to be sure was to examine their papers, and if they had been out over a year they were pirates. They seldom sink the vessels they plunder, and only care to plunder those taking stuffs from the country. In order to be revenged for the loss of some of their junks, seven of them joined together and attacked one English gunboat; she resisted and defended herself gallantly, but what chance had she against so many? She was taken, and all hands not killed in the fight were murdered slowly in cold blood with the most revolting tortures. These pirates fight like devils; they seem to rejoice in it with a fierce insatiable joy. One morning we witnessed a fearful fight between two junks and a Spanish barque. The latter was attacked just on leaving the river. The barque put two shots into one of the junks at long range, and so smashed her at the water-line that she sank in less than twenty minutes with all hands on board. The other junk then came close to the barque and threw "stink-pots" aboard (a sort of Greek-fire with a most horrible and suffocating smell), but as fast as they were thrown aboard the Spaniards pitched them into the sea. The pirates then tried to use their boarding pikes, but the Spaniards kept them off for some time. Then many of them got on board the barque, but the Spaniards, who use the knife splendidly, picked them off one by one, while two or three of them standing in the bow shot down the Chinamen as fast as they could load. Finally, seeing that they were gaining no advantage, the pirates became panic-struck, and all that were left rushed back to their junk hoping to push off and escape; but the wily Spaniards had lashed the vessels together, and pursuing them into the junk stabbed all they could lay hands on. Many of the pirates jumped overboard and were drowned. In the chief cabin they found an English lady of rank half dead with terror; she had been barbarously outraged, and would doubtless have been murdered had the pirates had time to think of her. The Spaniards found plenty of treasure aboard, and having towed this prize into Shanghai, were handsomely rewarded not only by the lady, who was very rich, but also by the different Governments, for their gallantry. They all made enough by that capture to enrich themselves for life, but, like true sailors, they spent it all while in port in the most foolish and extravagant manner.

The week after this capture by the Spaniards, an English gunboat brought another pirate junk into Shanghai. It had been taken after a hard chase. Many of the pirates jumped overboard, knowing what fate awaited them, but most were picked up alive by the boats of the English vessel and brought into port—a hundred and fifty of them. Amongst them, dressed as Chinamen, were four Europeans—one Irishman, two English, and one French. They aimed their guns for them, and were paid over one hundred and sixty dollars a month. Being caught red-handed, there was very little time wasted over a trial; they were all executed, the four Europeans being hung from a church steeple, and the Chinamen beheaded by their executioner, who with a long sword cuts off three heads at once. It is the simplest arrangement in the world: the men laid their heads on a bamboo bench—on this occasion placed on the beach—and the executioner with one blow of his sword cut off the three heads at once, when another three men were placed on the same spot, reeking with blood, and so on until all were dead. Two of the chiefs were sliced to pieces with swords, the executioners cutting off ears, cheeks, shoulders, arms, sides, &c., with cool deliberation. It was a sickening spectacle. The pirates themselves never uttered a sound or even winced—nor had they been drugged, as is sometimes the case.

Their power of endurance and stoic indifference to pain is something I have never been able to understand.

In the charred remains of a barque found floating out at sea were discovered several bodies with their eyes and tongues torn out, the nails pulled from their fingers, and other atrocities too horrible to mention. After we had been at Shanghai for three months and a half, Captain J——, finding that there was no chance of getting a cargo here, resolved to go elsewhere and seek one; so we took in stone for ballast, and a pilot to take us safely out of the harbour. As we were slowly making our way down the river, the *Peep-o'-Day* suddenly struck on a sand-bank. The shock of the sudden stoppage sent us all flying, the masts cracked and creaked, but luckily stood firm. Orders were given for all sail to be taken in at once and the kedge anchors to be run out. This was done, but to no purpose. Then a tug-boat was sent for; even then we did not budge, although we had out our lower anchor, heaving on the windlass, to help the tug. All we succeeded in doing was to break the hawsers; next we tried with the cable, with the same result; then by the captain's orders we gave up trying, which order struck us all as being, to say the least of it, singular—for this bank was of quicksands. Before night the bow had sunk eight or ten feet, and the stern was raised up in the air at an angle of about forty-five degrees. We had to hold on to the rigging going from one end of the ship to the other, and had the pleasant anticipation of being sucked in. We remained in this state all night; the next morning the captain, taking the pilot with him, went to Shanghai to find lighters to lighten her, which of course should have been done fifteen hours before. On the second day of his absence, during which time we were gradually sinking, there happened a spring-tide, and a tug-boat passing by, the chief mate determined to make another effort to get her off. Putting a cable out to the tug-boat, and attaching a second to the lower anchor which we worked with the windlass, we succeeded after some hours' hard work in moving her into deep water; then getting our anchors and boats aboard, were towed up the river. On the way we met the captain, who, instead of being pleased at his ship's having been saved, got in a violent passion with the mate, used the most abusive language, and finally, losing all self-control, dashed him off the poop. He dismissed him at Shanghai, actually daring to say that the chief mate had attempted to run off with his ship. It was the firm opinion of the men that Captain J—— had intended to lose the vessel, having in fact been put aboard for that purpose. She had been built for a steamship, but would not answer in that capacity; finding which, her owners changed her into a barque and offered her for sale at the low price of £3,000, but failed to sell her; then they insured her heavily and sent her out under command of Captain J——, with the probable understanding that she would do them more service at the bottom of the sea than at the top. Twice afterwards we went ashore, once on rocks coming out of Hong-Kong, and the other time on a sand-bank away up north near Nui-Chwang. Taking a new mate on board—there being no lack of them ready and willing to leave Shanghai—we once more went down the river and into what is called the Inner Channel on our way to Nui-Chwang. It was tiresome work with a great deal of tacking to do, owing to there often being land on both sides. Several times we were obliged to anchor at night to avoid the danger of running ashore. One evening, after beating about all day, we had got our anchor ready to drop in some safe place, and had taken in most of the small sails, when we heard firing. Rounding a point of land, we saw in a little cove, where we had intended anchoring, more than a dozen seven-masted pirate junks, mostly riding at anchor. They were firing and fighting among themselves, probably over some plunder. At any rate, we were not anxious to stay and find out the cause of dispute, but 'bouted ship at once, put on all the canvas we could and fled for our lives; for although we had nothing worth their taking, they seemed just in the mood to find a pleasure in the amusement of murdering us and scuttling our ship. We did not venture to anchor all night, every man was kept under arms, with smothered lanterns, ready in case of attack. I do not think any of them followed us; it soon got dark, and the next morning we saw no more of them.

The pirates were so numerous and so powerful at this time, and so many ships had been taken by them and all hands murdered, that the merchant captains joined together and sent a memorial to the Home Government, stating that the English men-o'-war and gunboats, instead of being out cruising on the high seas in order to protect the mercantile service, thought of nothing but keeping in port and giving large balls and entertainments amongst each other. Also that the man-o'-war ships were so disgracefully neglected and dirty that it was impossible to go up their gangways without soiling one's hands. There was a great row, of course, but on investigation the facts were proved, and the upshot of it was that the admiral was recalled, and a law passed that merchant vessels going to China were to have double crews, and to be fully armed. Things went better after that, but as it was some time before the law could be enforced, the pirates worked doubly hard—I suppose on the principle of making hay while the sun shines. Among other affairs of note, they took one of the magnificent French Havre mail-boats by stratagem. As these boats were always so well armed and manned, no fears had been entertained of their ever being molested by pirates, but on this occasion one hundred and fifty of them, dressed as respectable Chinese merchants, took their passage on board ostensibly to go to some Chinese port—I forget which now. In such an immense ship as the *Havre* mail-boat, even so large a number as one hundred and fifty merchants would not excite notice. Directly they were in full ocean the pirates took possession of the ship, killing no one but the chief officer and one sailor, who offered resistance. The passengers were too paralyzed with terror and surprise to do anything, and the crew had all been bound. Some junks came alongside, and into them was transferred all the specie, opium, and silks, with which the mail-boat was heavily loaded. After taking everything of value, the hundred and fifty respectable Chinese merchants entered their junks and made off with their booty.

These Chinese seas are the most curious in the world. Within a radius of thirty miles one has all weathers. I have seen three different vessels, one having her square yards out; the second under top-sails with a stiff breeze and a heavy sea; while the third had all sail set in order to catch any little zephyr that might reach them—all three within sight of each other. It was dangerous work, at that time, navigating to these far northern Chinese seas, not only on account of the capriciousness of the weather, but also that they had not been surveyed, even by the Government ships; so the pirates had it all their own way. We, however, escaped; so poor a thing as the *Peep-o'-Day*, having no cargo on board, was evidently disdained by these lordly pirates. I assure you we bore them no ill-feeling for their contempt. After some two weeks' hard work we began to near our destination. A pilot was taken on board, and we crossed the dangerous bar at the entrance to Nui-Chwang safely; but on working our way up the river Leao, under the pilot's directions, he landed us high and dry on a green field! The land all around being very low and flat, the water at this time of year (winter) is on a level, and not unfrequently overflows, as had happened on this occasion, making it very hard to distinguish the channel. The captain got into one of his furious rages again, and was only restrained from pitching the pilot overboard by the recollection that without him we should be in an even worse plight. So he contented himself with abusing him in the most violent manner, storming and raving with passion till he foamed at the mouth. The poor pilot, a quiet Norwegian, bore all the abuse with lamb-like meekness, which only seemed to exasperate Captain J—— the more, who continued abusing him until his voice became a shrill shriek, when, giving him a kick as he passed, he retired to his cabin to drink. We lay all night on the green field, not without anxiety, first from pirates, who might take it into their heads to murder us for fun, and secondly from the position of the barque, as she lay well over one side. The next morning we started early to lighten her of some of the ballast, and with the incoming tide managed to get her off and work her up under easy sail into Nui-Chwang, where we anchored opposite

the town—if such a word could be applied to the
cluster of poor huts, which with a few larger and
better, built for the Europeans, comprised the
whole of it. On turning out the next morning we
were disagreeably surprised by finding two feet of
snow on the deck. After sweeping it away and
putting everything in order, I, amongst some
others, was allowed to go on shore with the
captain, who wanted to see his agent in order to
obtain some money and see about getting in a
cargo of small beans. There was literally nothing
to see but dirty huts and dirtier streets, still it is
one of the few Chinese ports where apples, pears,
and carrots can be obtained as well as sheep, and
is an important port; at this time there were
thirteen other vessels lying there besides our own,
mostly English and Germans. The natives, who
are of the Tartar tribe, are fine well-made men,
most of them six feet in height, and many six feet
three and four. The women are equally tall, and
beautifully formed. They dress very warmly in a
sort of linen, padded with cotton. As we wandered about they brought us different kinds of furs
to look at; some were really very magnificent,
made into cloaks and caps and mats. After some
hours' wandering about we returned to the beach
to await the captain. Soon we beheld him in the
distance flying towards us, hatless and breathless,
with a mob of natives at his heels. As soon as he
reached us he gasped out, "Jump in, and pull for
your lives!" We required no second bidding, sprang

in and plied our oars with such vigour that the water was dashed on all sides; showers of mud and stones and sticks were pelted at us, without, however, doing us any harm. It transpired that some of the natives had an inkling that Captain J——— was going for money, so waited outside the agent's office to meet him. Suspecting something unpleasant from their looks, and measuring the distance to the beach with his eye, he took to his heels—the wisest thing he could do, for they were half savages, and always in a state of rebellion against the Imperial Chinese Government. At this time they were commanded by a prince, some relation to the Emperor, and their cause of revolt was the intense dislike they had to the admittance of foreigners to their country. Most of the time we were there they were fighting not far from Nui-Chwang, and we were lucky in leaving when we did, as after-events proved to us. Having got in our cargo, we and seven other vessels were piloted down the river, and all fortunately crossed the bar, with the exception of a Hamburg barque, which stuck fast and had to be abandoned. That night the five vessels left in port were taken by the rebels, and all hands murdered with unparalleled atrocity. It made a great effect on us, for we knew all the men personally; the thought of the tortures those poor fellows had undergone threw a gloom over us for some time. But at sea, more perhaps than anywhere else, there is little time for retrospection; three days after the horrible tragedy, a terrible monsoon came on, every recurring day getting more frightful. On the fourth day a tremendous gust smashed the top-gallant-masts as well as the top-mast-boom, bringing the whole wreckage on deck with such force that the broken boom went clean through the deck. For six days we saw neither sun, moon, or stars, and were without any knowledge of our whereabouts. We could get no soundings, as it was certain destruction to try and bring her to, running as we were under bare poles, at the mercy of the monsoon. The sea was of a thick muddy colour, and the sky grey and lowering; every minute we expected to go on the rocks. A spare mast that was lashed with chains broke loose, and was blown across the deck, breaking the leg of a man, who was endeavouring, with a second seaman, to go aft, in order to relieve the man at the wheel. The captain had brought on board, as a private speculation, a good many pigs; these were kept in a strong wooden house, and were being carefully fattened up for sale. Alas for the captain, a fiercer gust than usual tore the pig-house from its fastenings and pitched them overboard, where we heard the poor piggies' dismal squealings mingling with the roar of the wind for a brief moment. Any attempt to rescue them was of course out of the question; we lost the cook's galley at the same time. On the seventh day it cleared a little, sufficiently to take note as to where we had been driven. The captain found that we were within one day's sail of Hong-Kong, having run most of the distance under bare poles. It was considered one of the quickest trips ever known. One of the seven that had left when we did, an English barque, went on the rocks during the monsoon, was smashed to pieces and all hands lost. She was seen by another vessel to hang out signs of distress, but no help could be given.

It was sad to think that out of the thirteen vessels lying in the port of Nui-Chwang, six only reached Hong-Kong, the other seven all being destroyed in less than a fortnight. For ourselves, we arrived at Hong-Kong without further incident. It was Christmas Eve, I remember, and the men, true sailor fashion, forgot the past hardships and sorrows and spent Christmas Day in eating and drinking. Hong-Kong is an island, a pleasant, fertile, gay little place, as it is frequented by vessels of all nationalities. There is a very high mountain or peak, called Victoria Hill, over which came twice a number of pirates and rebels from the other side of the sea, entering Hong-Kong at night, securing all the treasure, murdering the inhabitants, and, sacking the town, left it in flames; getting away back over the mountain and into their junks before the Government troops and gunboats could pursue them.

A few days after our arrival, we, with thousands of people on both sides of the bay, witnessed the taking of a pirate junk right in the middle of the harbour. A short time previously, the watchmen on two separate ships had been found murdered, the captains and mates bound in their cabins, and the thieves had succeeded in escaping with the cargoes and everything of value. They were discovered through the pluck and coolness of a boy not yet fifteen years old, in the following manner. This lad, Hartmann, belonged to a Hamburg barque then anchored in the bay. There were some hundred or more vessels from all parts of the world, and amongst them a great number of six and seven masted junks. On the night in question, it was so hot, that the boy got out of his bunk about eleven o'clock, and going on deck looked about for some cool place to lie down. Observing that the sailor on watch was asleep, he crept forward to the forecastle and coiled himself up under an old sail. He had not been there long before he heard sampans moving about, but as this was a common occurrence he paid no heed to it. Suddenly four Chinamen appeared over the bow and came up to the sleeping watchman. Poor fellow, he never woke again in this world, for a pirate split open his skull with great dexterity, and he died before he had time to utter a sound; they then all four descended into the cabin. Hartmann having witnessed this scene, waited until the pirates had left the deck, when he noiselessly crawled aft, passed the poor murdered watchman, and having let himself overboard into the water, dropped quietly into the next vessel. He lost no time in rousing the men to whom he told his story. Ten minutes after a boat was manned, and they were rowing as hard as they could to give information first to the gunboats and then to the towns. Some of the gunboats were always under steam in case of an emergency; two of them were soon hurrying up to the scene of the murder. As soon as the pirates waiting in the sampan saw the gunboats coming, they immediately knew that somehow or other they were discovered. The alarm was hastily given to their comrades on board the barque, who, springing into the sampan, made for their junks, hoping to escape. But the gunboats were too quick for them, and opened fire upon them as they were attempting to get away. The noise of the guns had awakened all the inhabitants of the various towns, who came trooping out in the wildest excitement. It was brilliant moonlight, and I remember being struck by the contrast between the calm, lovely night, the moon flooding land and ocean with almost painful glory, and the scene of carnage going on below. The booming of the guns, the shrieks of the wounded and dying, the yells of the lookers-on, all made up a spectacle not easily to be forgotten. The two gunboats blazed away at the junk in grand style. Many of the pirates attempted to escape by their boats, but over a hundred of them were drowned by their sampans capsizing. Five boats did succeed in getting away from the junk, and were pulling for their lives to try and gain the opposite shore, but by this time the beach was crowded with spectators who fired upon them, and compelled them to turn back. The two gunboats had now manned their boats, and an exciting chase ensued. The firing on both sides was hot and deadly. The pirates were pursued for hours up and down and across the bay. Finally all that had not been shot or drowned were captured and soon after executed. The gunboats lost only three men, although a great many were wounded. Hartmann, as you may imagine was made quite a hero of, and his future well looked after.

The Chinese merchants are some of them extremely wealthy men and have no small power. One of them, by name Jardine, owned a whole fleet of European vessels, all his own. His riches were fabulous. One of the islands in the bay was almost entirely composed of his storehouses, watched over by his soldiers, in a special and private uniform. Captains always liked to trade with him, as his teas, opium, silks, &c., were all of the best, and they could therefore get higher prices for them.

We only stayed at Hong-Kong long enough to take in our cargo of tea and fire-crackers, after which we set sail for New York. Our captain was certainly one of the worst sailors I ever met with, for the pilot had not left us half an hour before we went ashore on the rocks. We could not suppose that he had done it purposely this time, as we had a tolerably valuable cargo on board. After immense trouble we managed to get her off, and having passed a thrumbed sail under her bottom, got the services of a tug, who towed us up to Whampoa, where we had to go into dry-dock for repairs. It was found that she had broken a plate on her starboard quarter exactly where she had once been repaired before.

Whampoa is a dull little country town, built on the river, and looks not unlike a government dockyard on a very small scale. The only thing worthy of note seemed to be the extreme cleverness and ingenuity with which the natives carried out their thefts. So expert are they, that they have been known to strip two or three sheets of copper off a ship's bottom, although there was a boat containing an armed watchman both ahead and astern. When the *Peep-o'-Day* was once more in sailing order, we quickly replaced the cargo and sailed down the river. One evening when we had entered the China Sea, and were preparing to anchor for the night, not without carefully reconnoitring as these were dangerous parts, Captain J—— called us all up, and in a nervous and somewhat lachrymose manner informed us of what we already knew, viz., that we were in waters not only difficult to navigate, but beset with pirates, and that it was very doubtful if we should ever reach our destination. After this pleasing and inspiring speech, he provided us with old tower-muskets and cutlasses, informed us that England expected every man to do his duty, and proceeded to do his by going to his cabin, where, having placed two loaded revolvers on the table, he locked himself in, and proceeded to get drunk, doubtless in order to keep up his spirits. We were fully alive to the dangers we ran from pirates; every chain and rope had been carefully taken in so that they could catch hold of nothing; we went about armed and with smothered lanterns. About eleven o'clock on the night of the captain's characteristic speech, I was on watch with another man. It was a clear moonlight night, very still and beautiful; a slight breeze played around the masts. We had anchored some time before, and Scott and I were lazily talking on indifferent subjects, when suddenly, without changing his voice, he nudged me, and stealthily pointed to leeward. There were six pirate boats dropping down on us. We gave the alarm, and as soon as the boats were abreast of us we fired into them, both Scott and I killed our man. The rest of the crew now joined us, and helped to make it hot for the enemy, who, finding they were getting the worst of it, tried to regain their ship. Unfortunately for them, they got into a strong current which swept them down in an opposite direction. Suddenly, to our great surprise, they abandoned all attempt to reach their ship or to disable us, and pulled off in the direction of land with all their might. Looking ahead of us we saw two Chinese Government Mandarin boats coming down in grand style, each having fifty men at the oars. They commenced firing at the pirate boats without delay, killing many, and pursuing them towards land. On nearing it, many of the pirates jumped overboard and swam for shore, but most were killed before reaching it. Those who did succeed in landing ran for shelter to the paddy (rice) fields, but the Mandarin boats sent men out to set fire to the rice. The scene was awful and grand in the extreme, the flames ran along the ground with fearful rapidity, burning many of the poor wretches before they could escape. Horrible as the death was, it was doubtless merciful compared to what the few who were captured underwent afterwards. Daylight began before the scene of carnage was over, nor did we wait to see the end of it, but, weighing anchor, proceeded on our way. Some days passed on, and we were well out at sea when one day two pirate junks were seen waiting to interview us, one at each bow. To our astonishment and relief, Captain J—— showed no little pluck and cleverness. Having crowded on all sail, he hoisted the English ensign, and loaded the two guns, and a breeze springing up in our favour, he ordered us to stretch up as if we were going to tackle one of the enemy. The *Peep-o'-Day*, having been so lately repaired, sailed fairly well; half-way towards the first junk we squared away as if to attack the second, by which manœuvre we got a good start of them, and managed to keep it, as the wind was with us, but against them as they tried to close on us. We gave the last fellow one of our big guns, damaging him pretty badly to judge by the crash of timbers, and the fact that they neither returned the compliment or attempted to continue the pursuit. These were the last pirates we saw. We were now in the Malay Archipelago, and pirates seldom if ever venture so far, so the captain took in his flag and breathed freely once more. He was in such high good-humour at the result of his stratagem that he ordered a grog for all the crew, and himself got gloriously drunk. It was here that I saw a very fine lunar rainbow of a pale yellow colour; it lasted some time, and had a singular and most beautiful effect.

Nothing of importance or interest happened until we were nearing St. Helena. Although we were on the look-out for the island, we had no idea that we were so close to it: the first intimation we had was the look-out man shouting "Land a-head," and then we could plainly hear the roar of the surf, and see right in front of us, looming up through the mist, a very high peak of land. Most vessels land there, and we fully expected to do so, the more so as both the captain and second mate were suffering from fever and ague. But orders were given to ease away at once, and we continued our voyage for three days more, when we sighted Ascension Island, and after a few hours anchored outside some of the most beautiful coral reefs I ever saw. Having got out a boat, we took the captain and second mate ashore to try the effect of change of air. Whether from that, or any other cause, they both rapidly recovered. It is not often vessels stop here; they mostly call at St. Helena. But this is a beautiful island, where the people seemed to lead a peaceful, not to say lazy, life. On the long, low, level beach many turtles came to lay their eggs; we were lucky to arrive just in the season and had a real feast of turtle eggs and some turtles too; but they are sent to all parts of the world. The Government men appeared to have nothing to do but turn over the turtles when they had caught them. We succeeded in catching some very fine specimens of the flying-fish; one or two measured over two feet long, and had four pairs of wings. It was a pretty sight to see them skimming above the water, seemingly rejoicing in their double power of flying and swimming.

We stayed only a very short time here, as the captain was in a hurry to get to New York. So one fine morning we set sail and went on; the weather was very favourable, the men all well, and Captain J—— satisfied, as he had got a clean bill of health from Ascension Island. I do not remember anything especially worthy of note; I am sorry I was not a better observer in those days. Sailors see so many wonderful and extraordinary sights, that they are astonished at nothing. But to return to my narrative. As soon as we neared New York we signalled for a pilot, who, coming on board, sailed us up the East River in fine style. The scenery was beautiful and the buildings gigantic in size and magnificent in form. We anchored in the stream off East River, and before we could get on shore experienced a sand-storm. Cloud after cloud of sand came swooping down from the land in immense columns, driving everything before them. The decks were soon deserted, for the sand cuts like a knife. It lasted an hour or more, blowing with terrible violence; when it was ended there were some inches of fine gritty sand on everything. After the storm was over we went to our pier, No. 46, in the North River, and on the way, short though the distance was, were nearly all killed, which shows that as much danger lies near the shore as in mid-ocean. It was full tide, and a steamer full of passengers came steaming right down upon us. Before we could get out of her way, or she out of ours, she struck us with great violence in the bow. She did us very little damage considering the force with which she came upon us. Had she struck us amidship, as she was pointed, she would have cut us in two without the smallest doubt; as it was, the man at the wheel had time to sheer her off a little, with the above result. She carried away our flying-jib-boom and fore-top-gallant-mast, which was nothing compared to the damage she did herself, for the collision made a clean sweep of her. All the starboard rigging, davits, boats, masts, and funnel were torn off with a fearful crash. The passengers all crowded to see what was the matter, and a waiter coming out of the saloon was so terrified that he jumped overboard, and no one having time to look after him, he was drowned. The man at the wheel was killed by a blow from one of the falling masts, but beyond those two deaths there were no fatal accidents, which, considering the gravity of the disaster, was really marvellous. The steamer did not stop or even turn back, but continued her way, and we soon lost sight of her. Captain J—— got a new foremast and jib-boom out of the steamer's company, though he had no earthly right to demand it, there being no injury to life that had happened to any one on board the *Peep-o'-Day*. But he asked for it, they gave it to him, and he was immensely elated at what he called a good stroke of business.

There was no little excitement in the harbour at the departure of the *Red, White and Blue*, a small boat of only three tons burden which sailed from New York to cross the Atlantic. She was a lovely thing, but like a toy, being fully rigged like a large vessel, and sailed down the river with her three top-sails set amidst such cheers and thunders of applause as had rarely been heard. Every one knows how the gallant little craft made the voyage in safety and was afterwards exhibited at the Paris Exhibition. The life and traffic on North River were something tremendous; everything was on such an enormous scale. The warehouses covered immense pieces of ground, and so close to the water's edge that many of the jib-booms of ships anchored there, touched the windows and roofs. The river itself teemed with vessels of every sort, size, description and nationality. Floating mills carry on their work as though on shore, and the beautiful Mississippi passenger boats come steaming grandly along looking like some huge mass of white buildings floating on the water. But New York is too well known nowadays to need any description. At the time I am writing of, the American war had just ended, and the whole country was in a most unsettled state. There was literally no law at all, except the law that Right is Might, by which the weakest of course went to the wall. It was not safe to go out with a decent coat on—any man doing so ran a good chance of being assaulted and robbed of it, and might think himself lucky if he escaped with his life. I have seen German policemen shot down in the open streets in broad daylight by the free negroes and Irish roughs, and no notice taken of it, the dead bodies simply carried away and a double number of men put in their place. I have seen a whole cargo of splendid wines from France broken into by a gang of these roughs, who would tap various barrels, and if they were not to their taste would let the wine run away while they tapped another cask. And the policemen dared not interfere—indeed they took good care to be out of the way, for a policeman's life was not worth a breath. I have seen a carpenter, for refusing to lend some of his tools to some negroes for the purpose of opening a brandy cask, seized by four of these fiends, who tied a rope under his armpits, threw him overboard, and dragged him up and down in the water until he was dead. No one interfered, the negroes had it all their own way in those days.

I have seen a dozen or so of these tall, lanky blacks come down to the wharves where the cotton bales were discharging, and sitting on them pick a hole and begin stuffing the cotton into their big, long calico coats and loose trousers until they swelled out like giants, when they would walk away unmolested by the public. Why should they interfere? it was not their business. They have even been known to bring down a large dray with two horses, pile it up with cotton, and coolly drive off with the load into the city, where they sold it, nobody venturing to ask how they came by it. But their favourite mode of proceeding was to take a boat alongside the wharf just underneath where the bales were placed, and to fill their boat with cotton, which they would land a little further down the same wharf, some returning for more, while others carried what was landed into the city. Every vessel had a well-armed watchman, but they were frequently overpowered and murdered, and it was an every evening's occurrence to hear an interchange of pistol and rifle shots going on in the harbour and on the wharf. In the city things were not much better; every gentleman's residence was guarded by ten or twelve watchmen, and no one ventured out unarmed. Murders were as common as paving-stones, and although in many cases the criminals were caught red-handed, the magistrates dared not hang them, or their own lives would not have been worth an hour's purchase. It was a terrible state of things, so much misery and crime in the midst of so much magnificence and grandeur. I was walking about the wharf one day and went up to a fruit-stall to buy some fruit. The old lady hearing I had been to China, had in fact just come from there, anxiously asked me if I had not met her son, who was somewhere there. When I informed her that I had not had that pleasure she expressed much astonishment and surprise, and evidently suspected that for some dark reason of my own I was not telling her the truth. She kept looking at me askance and repeating, "Bin to Chinny and not seen my Tom! Wall, I guess I never heard anything like that;" and all my explanations failed to convince her that it was anything but most unheard-of on my part not to have met him, to say nothing of my bad taste. I could never get her to accept any of the friendly advances I made her, and I should not be surprised if at the bottom of her heart she did not suspect me of doing away somehow or other with her Tom. Poor old soul, it was very probable that her son had fallen a victim either to dysentery or the pirates.

Having discharged our cargo, we prepared to go over to New Jersey to take in petroleum for England; but the night before we anchored there, a most frightful conflagration took place. Hundreds and hundreds of barrels of oil were consumed, the whole wharf destroyed, and half the lower part of the town. Many ships were burnt at their moorings, and the water-police having cut away some of these burning vessels, they floated down the stream, getting entangled with others and setting them also on fire. Quantities of river boats or lighters, full of raw crude oil, took fire, they had families of women and children on board whom it was impossible to rescue. It was an appalling and heartrending sight to see the poor creatures running from side to side imploring help, with little babes in their arms and young children at their skirts. It was impossible to get anywhere near them, for the stream was one sheet of devouring flame. The shrieks of the dying and screams of the women rose above the roar of the fire. God grant I may never witness anything so fearful in my life again. Several people went mad with the sight, and strong men sickened and fainted. The oil burnt on the water almost as well as on land, and in both places burnt with such fury and power that the people almost gave up trying to save any one or anything, it seemed so hopeless. This oil is almost as dangerous as gunpowder, yet these families fetch it down from up-country in open boats, along canals, drawn by horses doing all their cooking with careless indifference to, or ignorance of, the awful danger they run. This fire delayed us some weeks in procuring our cargo. The crew were so terrified at the disaster that they felt inclined to cut and run when they knew that the captain intended to ship petroleum, but having been out over two years on this voyage, they had a good deal of money due to them, and thought better of it, all but two who gave us the slip the day before we sailed.

There was a brig called the *Telegraph* that had sailed with us from England, had followed us all over China and now to New York, getting the same cargoes and passing through the same dangers. We had become quite friendly, and always hailed each other like old acquaintances. She now loaded with petroleum the same as we did. The strictest orders were given about smoking, it being absolutely prohibited; and the cook did all his business ashore, for if a spark had touched the escaping gas, it would have blown us all into eternity in less than a minute. The casks of oil were most carefully stowed, trestles being placed under each one to keep them in place, and to prevent the upper casks from pressing on the lower ones, which might open the seams, and the oil escaping, the vessel would become top-heavy and she would run a good chance of capsizing. The captain of the *Telegraph* laughed at our extra care; he had not stowed his oil away with such precautions, and was thus enabled to set out on the homeward journey a day before we did, but he must bitterly have repented of his carelessness before many days were over. He dined with Captain J—— the day he left, a fine, big, good-natured Cornishman. "Good-bye; we shall be home before you," he cried from his boat as his men pulled him to his brig. They were, but not the home he meant,

The day after the *Telegraph* left, we were towed down the river, and set sail for England. That cargo was the bane of our lives; it was like working over a powder magazine the whole way. Once we sighted the *Telegraph* and signalled greetings. Soon after an easterly gale came on, and the *Peep-o'-Day* plunged and tossed, and we were all in a panic about the oil, but, thanks to the trestles, the casks stood firm; on examination when the gale was over, we found all safe and in order. We were sailing along smoothly and comfortably, when the "look-out" sighted an object; we steered towards it, and saw to our sorrow that it was our old friend the *Telegraph* floating bottom upwards. She had evidently become top-heavy during the gale, from the bad stowage of her cargo, capsized and all hands lost. We continued our way, saddened and depressed for a time, but recovered as we neared England. We made the voyage in thirty-six days, but it took us twenty-one to beat up Channel in the teeth of an easterly wind, but finally we had the felicity of anchoring off Gravesend, and soon after were towed into the St. Catherine's Docks. Pay day came in due course, where our estimable friend Captain J——'s last meanness was exposed. Most of the crew being unable to write, I had done so for them and they had then been delivered to the captain for postage, for which he charged when paying them off. But several of them soon found out from their wives and sweethearts that he had never stamped them, and they had been obliged to pay double postage. I don't know how it ended, I left them disputing about it, but I think never did a captain and his crew part with less cordiality than did Captain J—— and his men. For my part I saw no more of Captain J——, nor have I ever heard what became of him.

VOYAGES TO MELBOURNE AND CALCUTTA.

WHEN I was quite a youngster, I started with two other middies on board one of Money Wigram's ships, the *Yorkshire*. She was a fine vessel, half clipper, half frigate, but so beautifully built and proportioned that it was a real pleasure to see her on the water. We left from Plymouth, where we took in passengers, and then sailed on for Melbourne. Money Wigram's ships go nowhere but from London to Melbourne and back. The wind being in our favour we got on splendidly for several days, and the first exciting thing that happened was the madness of one of the crew, who became suddenly and violently insane. He was half-Italian, half-Irish, a bad mixture at any time, and aggravated in this case by the fact that the man suffered from chronic neuralgia. When the pain was on, he would sit, with his two hands pressed to his head, glaring before him. If any one came near to offer consolation or suggest remedies, he would answer, without moving or even turning his eyes, "Don't pity me; if you value your life, don't pity me." The surgeon took him in hand, and seemed at first to have succeeded in alleviating the pain, but one day when no one thought anything more about him, he suddenly jumped on to the poop with a dagger in one hand and a Bible in the other. Seeing what had happened, the captain and surgeon tried to coax him down, as many lady passengers were about. But in vain; the unfortunate man began to preach a really powerful sermon on the sin and sorrow in the world, and offered to stab to the heart every one on board, that they might be freed from the torment of living. Some of the ladies were nearly frightened into fits, particularly when, discarding his Bible, he began to dance a jig, waving his dagger about wildly. The mate crept up the rigging behind him—while the surgeon drew the madman's attention to himself—and threw a bow-line over him, by which he was secured and confined. The poor fellow never recovered; he was placed in a lunatic asylum at Melbourne, and, I believe, died soon after his entrance.

Neptune came on board at the Line, but it is needless to describe so well known a ceremony. When we were a month out, the "Dead Horse Night" was celebrated, a singular and curious scene of great interest. An animal in the shape of a horse is rigged up by sewing sacks together and stuffing them with straw. The whole is covered with brown blankets, tail and ears not being forgotten. One of the seamen personates an old farmer, and is dressed in character. Two farm labourers attend him, to assist in reining-in the fiery steed. Everything being ready, the horse is drawn three times around the main-deck by the two farm boys with innumerable "whoas" and sundry blows over the head with thick sticks. The old farmer is on his back, and it requires no small skill to keep his equilibrium, so prodigious are the bounds of the fierce animal. . The sailors follow, singing dolefully:

> "Oh, poor old man!
> Your horse will die,
> And I say so, and I hope so!
> Oh, poor old man,
> Your horse will die!"

After the third round he is brought to a standstill on the quarter-deck, where all the passengers and crew are collected, and put up to auction. After some spirited bargaining it is knocked down to the highest bidder. A dark night is generally chosen for this performance as it heightens the effect of the "death of the horse." The chief officer gets into one of the quarter-boats and sets fire to a quantity of blue lights, which burn with ghastly effect in the blackness of the night. A tackle is then fastened to the horse, and he is slowly hoisted over the ship's side, away out to the yard-arm, with a sailor on his back. All the other sailors follow, singing their mournful ditty. As soon as the yard-arm is reached, the mounted sailor cuts away the "dead horse" from under him. It looks a frightfully perilous position—by the glare of the blue lights, the man is seen suspended in mid-air, over the black waters, with no apparent support, not even a rope to cling to. As soon as the sea receives the "dead horse," the sailor, with cat-like ease, comes on deck, when the passengers generally make up a purse for the crew, which is presented to the old farmer by the highest bidder at the time of knocking down. The meaning of this ceremony is as follows : Sailors, as a rule, obtain a month's pay in advance before joining their ships, therefore they are working the whole of the first month for nothing. Drowning the "dead horse" is in token that they have done with that moneyless month, and are now beginning to work for pay.

Soon after the "dead horse" ceremony we had a birth on board, a woman among the steerage passengers. Every one made a great deal of her and the baby, who was really a jolly little chap by the time we reached Melbourne. A young married couple had come aboard at Gravesend; they were the most loving pair I ever saw—one always came across them cuddled close together in some little sheltered nook. The young man looked delicate, but every one was surprised and shocked at hearing one morning that he was sinking fast, and could not live out the day. He died the same evening, and the next day was buried. I never saw anything so heart-breaking as the expression on the face of the poor little wife during the reading of the burial service. She looked from one face to the other with utter bewilderment, but when the sailors lifted up the body to put overboard, she gave a cry like a wild animal and had to be dragged away by force. Every one was very kind to her, but she seemed to care for nothing, and it was pitiable to see her sitting alone day after day in the little nooks that they used to be in together. We brought her back with us on our return trip, the captain giving her a free passage. Another sad death occurred after we had arrived in Hobson's Bay. A lady going out to join her husband had been sea-sick the whole voyage, and was reduced to such a state of weakness that she was carried on deck to meet her husband, who had come in a boat to take her to his own large steamship, to which he had just been promoted. We saw a little commotion and confusion, and were horrified to hear that she had died in her husband's arms before they had spoken a word to each other.

We went on to the Canary Isles. When we were some distance off, long before we could see land, we witnessed a splendid mirage of the country. It was the best optical atmospheric illusion I ever saw, the shore, the trees, and the city with the houses clearly defined. It was difficult to believe but that up there in the sky this wondrous country was not really fixed. We landed at the Isles to take in bullocks, as we had run short of beef. Funny little fellows they were, not larger than a good-sized English sheep, some even not bigger than a dog. They were most delicious eating, being tender and juicy, and much appreciated by the passengers. A large quantity of ducks were obtained here, and the captain, a good-hearted man, thinking to give the sailors a treat, ordered ducks for them all; but his well-meant kindness was a failure, for they only growled, wanting to know " Who ever heard of ducks without green peas?" and this hundreds of miles from any land. I only know we middies rejoiced in them, and soon put ourselves outside a duck apiece, with infinite satisfaction. Sailors are proverbial grumblers about trifles, though it must be allowed that they will put up with terrible hardships when necessary, without a murmur.

One morning whilst I was assisting the sail-maker, who was doing some repairs to the mizzen-royal-sail, I was watching the passengers on the deck instead of attending to the instructions being given to me, when a sudden lurch of the ship shot me clean off my airy seat, and I fell, striking the shrouds, rebounding from that straight into the sea. The man at the wheel, who saw this involuntary gymnastic performance, had the wit and *sang-froid* to throw over to me the main-brace, which, directly I came up from my plunge, I grabbed hold of and hung on to for grim life. It was a horrible experience. I was nearly dragged to pieces before he could haul me up, as he was obliged first to stop the vessel. One moment I felt I must give way, the strain was so great, and my hands were all torn and bleeding, but the cry " Man overboard!" had brought many willing hands, and I was finally deposited on deck, where I fainted like a woman, much to my after disgust, as it served as an endless source of amusement to the other middies, who were never tired of teazing me about it; the more so as some of the lady passengers took me up and made a good deal of me, one attending to my torn paws like a true sister of mercy. The hanging on to the main-brace was, however, no easy thing to do. I saw a man drowned in that way on one of my after voyages to India. He held on bravely for a while, but before we could rescue him he shouted out, " Good-bye, mates," let go, and was sucked under the vessel. We were going, as in my case, at a speed of fifteen miles an hour. This happened a short time before entering Port Phillip, where it was put out of my head by a catch of very fine horse mackerel. They were a great treat to every one. On board a vessel, particularly when on a long voyage, every trifle assumes immense proportions. Having entered Port Phillip Heads, we signalled for a pilot, and soon a tug-boat with the pilot on board of her came alongside and towed us into Sandridge Pier, a very fine piece of work, some seven or eight miles from the city of Melbourne. No ships can go nearer, although the river Yarra-Yarra runs into the midst of the town, as the water is so shallow that only barges and small boats can ply up and down. The city of Melbourne is too well known to need description. Its Houses of Parliament, Post Offices, Town Hall, and Parks are not to be surpassed in any of the great European cities. We stayed here three weeks when taking in our stores, freight, and passengers, were towed out to the Heads, and set sail for England. The poor little widow continued to seek out the nooks where she and her husband used to be together, and did not seem at all able to get over her grief. We had favourable weather, and no accidents of any sort, nor any encounters of interest until we neared Cape Horn. Here we came to immense fields of ice and tremendous icebergs. These vast mountains of floating ice are wonderfully beautiful, and of every fantastic shape; cathedrals, palaces, old ruins, giants and forests. Picturesque, indeed, but terribly dangerous, and requiring most careful navigation to avoid striking against them, particularly during the night. Nevertheless our captain kept his ship going ahead under double-reefed top-sails, although we passed several vessels who were anchored, fearing to be run down, or otherwise damaged by these icebergs. The cold was most intense, the hail coming down sometimes with such force as to cut the flesh like a knife. Often at night all hands would be called up to shorten sail. It was really horrible to leave the warm bunk and go up on deck. Every man was given a "tot" of raw Jamaica rum, 11° above proof, and having tossed that down went out to the rigging. It being wire rigging, and covered with a thick coating of ice, acted almost like an electric machine when you touched it. On you go up aloft, tumbling one over the other in the dense darkness, and having got over the tops reach the yards and lay out to gather up the sail, tearing off your finger nails in the endeavour to haul in the frozen sails bellying out every minute in the furious gale of wind and hail. I have seen great, bearded men sit in the tops so benumbed with the cold that other sailors, not being able to see them, would trample on them in the dark without their having either the energy or strength to resist or move out of the way. The *Yorkshire* was so strained going round the Horn on this voyage, that we were at the pumps the whole way to England.

A very sad occurrence took place a week or so before we sailed into England. One of the lady passengers in the second cabin had a handsome little boy about four or five years. He was a great pet with all on board with all classes, he was taken ill and, after a two days' illness, died. Every one felt for the parents; it was an only child, and they were taking him home to show their people, who were farmers in Cumberland, I believe. The carpenter made a little wooden box, full of holes, so that the water might rush in and sink it. The captain read the burial service, which seems so impressive at sea, and I am sure there was not a dry eye on board. The service ended, the body was tilted over the side of the vessel on a plank, when, instead of sinking immediately, it floated. A large shark that had been following us ever since little Frank's illness—indeed they always do when any one is going to die—suddenly attacked the box, smashed it open, tore the child out, and ate it before the eyes of the mother and father. Her maddened, agonized shrieks were heart-rending, and it was impossible to tear her from the spot. Her husband, white and shaking from agitation, tried to calm her, but in vain; she tried to jump overboard, and was for the time quite insane, although she ultimately recovered her senses. It was a most painful scene, and threw a gloom over the whole of us, which lasted until we reached England again.

After two more voyages to Melbourne in the *Yorkshire*, I joined the *Enterprise* as third officer, then going to Calcutta. Most of our saloon passengers were officers going to join their respective regiments in different parts of India; many of them had their wives with them. They were a gay lot, up to every fun and mischief, dressing up like a lot of school-boys, and playing tricks that would not have disgraced a monkey colony. But some theatricals they got up were very successful and entertaining, and they certainly kept us all alive. We were racing another East Indiaman, the *Punjab*, all the voyage, and many were the bets made as to which vessel would run in to Calcutta first. Every man, woman, and child on board took a keen interest in the race, and discussed it with a gravity and sometimes warmth worthy of a better cause. I may mention here that we had the felicity of beating the *Punjab* by six hours, and the joy was as great as though we had won a mighty victory.

A curious incident occurred after we had been out a couple of weeks. One night as we were running under full sail with a favourable wind, the fore-mast, suddenly and without the smallest warning, sank fully four inches, and was consequently in considerable danger of going overboard, as it loosened all the rigging with it. Every seaman was called up at once to take in sail and set up the rigging, which was not accomplished until midday. The delay caused by this accident enabled the *Punjab* to pass us, but we soon got up to her again, and used to sight her at intervals of two or three weeks. It was discovered that the famous mast had never been properly "sent home" into the keelstone by the riggers, and the heavy rolling had displaced it. However, as it happened, no great damage was done, though it might have proved a most serious business. This voyage was almost without incident or accident of any sort. A shark or two caught, a small storm now and then, or a calm, was all that marked our days, and but for the officers and the constant look-out for the *Punjab*, would have been almost unbearably monotonous. In due course we arrived off Garden Reach, which is the entrance to the river Ganges going up to Calcutta. There is a most dangerous sand-bar here, the terror of every seaman whose ship has to pass it, for should a vessel touch it, no matter how large she may be, she rolls over and over helplessly and disappears, generally with all her crew. The pilot who came to bring us over this danger was the only man saved from a large ship that had touched this spot, all his companions and the ship being drawn in by the fatal bar and lost.

Pilots in India are the most stuck-up fellows in the world. No one and nothing is grand enough for them. They come on board dressed in the finest of white linen, or broad-cloth, with three servants, two leadsmen, two helmsmen, and a couple of huge trunks of clothes. They receive splendid pay, sometimes more than £3,000 a year. They serve a seven years' apprenticeship as leadsmen, and work gradually on to mates, and lastly masters. When they get old or disabled they retire on a pension. On this occasion, having received our imperial and imperious master on board—for the captain becomes a nonentity as soon as the pilot takes command—we set off to work our way up the Ganges to Calcutta—a very ticklish piece of work, as the river is so tortuous. Although not so long as the Yan-tsze-kiang in China, the Ganges is a decent length, being 1,570 English miles, and is far more beautiful than the Chinese river. But it is exceedingly dangerous not only on account of its frequent twistings and turnings, but because of its great narrowness in some parts, and the force of its current in various places. Most of the way up the carpenter, by the pilot's order, stood ready with his axe to cut the hawser if a current should take us and drive us down on the tug-boat. We went along very cautiously, under sail, the tug-boat keeping well ahead, and we were all employed trimming sails the whole way up. The scenery was most beautiful and varied, gorgeous as only an Eastern country can be. Now and then we passed a palace belonging to some king or native prince, magnificent in structure and immense in size. Each end of the piazza was guarded, one by a Bengal tiger, the other by a lion, in sign of the kingly rank. They were enclosed in large stone cages with iron bars, and we passed one so closely that we threw in a biscuit to the royal beast, which he was too grand to touch, at least while we were looking at him, but lay with his great paws crossed and his grand head raised, looking down the river with proud, mournful eyes. The tiger was running up and down his cage, for reasons of digestion probably, as the mangled remains of some four-footed animals showed that he had just finished his dinner.

We were two days before we sighted the city of Calcutta. It is situated on the right-hand side as you go up the river, and looks wonderfully imposing and grand. The manner of mooring ships here is very strange. They lay six in a row, right in front of the city; each vessel drops her anchor into the stream, and then pays out cable until she is hauled into her place by the side of a vessel, to which they then proceed to fasten her by hawsers. One after another is so fastened until the six are complete, and then another six are arranged in the same way, and so on with all vessels that come into port. This is done for two reasons: firstly, to enable a vessel to haul out easily when she has her cargo on board; and secondly, that she might free herself quickly should a "bore" (large wave) happen suddenly to come along. We had that pleasure two days after our arrival, and an awful and wonderful sight it was, and fearful destruction and loss of life and property it occasioned.

Great excitement prevailed directly the "bore" was seen far in the distance, coming up the river. It consists of a tremendous huge wave from twenty to thirty feet in height, which comes rolling up over the top of the other waves and water, and sweeps everything before it with resistless force. All the ships looked well to their fastenings, that they might ease out without danger; boats and sampans made for the middle of the stream, their occupants yelling and shouting in the wildest terror. It is much safer for small boats to meet the bore out in the middle than near land, where they run a good chance of being dashed to pieces, or sent flying along at lightning speed for a distance of sometimes a thousand yards. It made one feel the powerlessness of man when placed in opposition to any freak of nature. Take what care you may, protect yourself as you will with all knowledge science has put at your disposal, build your houses and enlarge your stores, work for years, spending all your strength, arrive at the summit of your highest hopes, and feel safe for the future, but you have forgotten Dame Nature, and one little playful trick of hers upsets all your calculations, ruins your property, and reduces you to despair. Watching this gigantic wave coming swiftly onward, sweeping all before it, cruel as the grave, resistless as death, I had a curious sensation that I stood alone watching the destruction of some world. I was at the time ashore in the officers' quarters of the Sailors' Home, and looked on from the verandah of that building. Away to the right was a long neck of land jutting out into the river, covered with houses, huts, gardens and fields, inhabited by both Europeans and natives. On came the wave, silently, swiftly, deadly, swept over it, and went on, carrying with it land, houses, huts, and people. A large steamboat, not having time to move far enough from shore, was lifted up and dashed high and dry on land; many of the crew were killed from the shock, and the whole of one side of the vessel was stove in. This "bore" was not considered one of the worst. I confess I thought it quite bad enough, and was thankful I was on shore.

I was young and foolish at that time, and because some misunderstanding had arisen between the captain and myself I resolved to remain behind. Captain K—— was a good man and a brave officer, but too strict to suit my ideas at that time, therefore when the *Enterprise* was hauled out to start on her return voyage to England, I, like a hot-headed young fool, slipped overboard with a small bundle of my belongings, and swam some distance to where I had a friend waiting for me in a sampan. Of course I forfeited all my money, not to speak of my position; but youngsters never seem to learn the lesson of life without bitter experience. Could I have looked on a few months and have seen to what depths of misery and starvation my ill-advised act would bring me, I think I should not have had the courage to do aught but let the waters close over my luckless head. My friend kept me hidden for three days until the *Enterprise* was gone, when I again joined the officers' mess at the Sailors' Home. If you want good living, go there; it was something wonderful. Young sucking-pigs boiled in champagne, roast duck, truffled pigeons, curried dishes of every description; while the wines, ices, and fruit were above praise, and the cost not at all exorbitant.

Some astrologer from England predicted the coming of a cyclone about this time, that was to pass over Calcutta, and to be of terrific force. For anything less serious, it would have been amusing to see the panic this prophecy caused. The palaces, the houses, in fact the whole town was soon emptied of their tenants, who, after securing their property the best way they could, went miles away, fearful that their houses would be blown down about them. In this case it turned out to be a false alarm, when, instead of being thankful that it was so, the unfortunate astrologer was overwhelmed with abuse and execration. Ravages made by the last cyclone were still visible on all sides. I saw parts of vessels that had been blown out of the river and carried a mile and a half into land, mixed up with *débris* of houses, wharves, trees, in fact anything that had stood any height from the ground. I heard one story that is worth repeating. A very fine ship, a three-master, had been taken up by the cyclone, whirled through the air like a dead leaf, and thrown on shore with such nice aim that the jib-boom and bowsprit were driven clean through one of the native huts. The next day, after all the turmoil and excitement was somewhat appeased, the owner of the hut came to the captain and requested him to take away his ship, as it obstructed the entrance, filled up the rooms, and prevented him and his family from living in the house. The poor captain, who desired nothing better than to see his magnificent vessel back again in her own element, instead of looking as if she had been caught red-handed in a bad housebreaking case, could not help smiling at the *naïveté* of the demand. That smile cost him dear. The infuriated native was so angry at what he chose to consider mocking at his misfortunes, quite ignoring that the captain was in a worse plight than himself, that he got numbers of his friends and literally broke the vessel up in pieces. I never heard that the captain could get any redress, nor could he probably have succeeded himself in moving so heavy a ship more than a mile to the water.

The hotels and houses are on a grand scale, with every comfort that art or money can devise; so that although the heat is, of course, very great, I doubt whether the Europeans suffer as much from it as from a hot summer in England, where no alleviations, such as are common here, can be got at. The delicious coolness of the air caused by the incessant moving of punkahs is beyond words delightful. They are kept going by coolies, who squat in corners or corridors for that purpose. Sometimes they drop off to sleep—the air instantly becomes stifling; then the man with the most energy among us would wake the coolie with a gentle kick, and lazily come back to his lounging chair, cigar, and iced claret. A very luxurious life this Indian one, but it takes all the energy out of a man, and one quickly sinks into a lotus-eating state of mind that makes work a terror, and even the trouble of eating almost too great to be borne. Yet nowhere is there more social intercourse, a greater number of balls, theatricals, and other amusements. The Europeans seem to live for that alone, and outvie each other in the grandeur of their entertainments, the richness of their wives' dresses, and the cost of their wines. The quantity of wine drank a year in Calcutta would, I should think, float a three-decker. Ladies are not at all backward, wine being said to be good for their complexions, and whether for that reason or any other, they certainly imbibe considerable quantities.

The Ganges is believed to be a sacred river; natives from the interior come long distances to bathe, and carry away some of the holy water to cure their sick. If they died after taking it, well—it was to be; if they recovered, it was the holy water that cured them: a simple childlike faith that many a Christian would be the better for possessing. Sometimes large parties of men, women, and children would come down to bathe, after which they would change their clothes in the water, go on shore, eat, and having made a day of it, fill their large bronze jars and return to their homes. They drive their teams with bullocks—a very small, handsome animal, and very powerful. That horrible disease, elephantiasis, is rather common. I saw a man sitting near the roadside, with a leg the size of his whole body. I entered into conversation with him, and he told me that he had been ill for many months, and the doctors had told him he could not be cured. It is a horrible disease, the whole skin being covered with incrustations like the skin of an elephant. We were talking about it at dinner that night, and I was horrified to hear that it is not by any means unfrequent in this country, is without cure, and besides being a dreadful chronic disease, is regarded as contagious. A surgeon who was present began describing several cases that had come under his notice, with such revolting details that we vowed to turn him out of the room unless he talked of something else. He refrained from any direct stories, although he still favoured us with many allusions.

There are an immense number of different religious sects here, and each as strict as possible in the carrying out of the various tenets and ceremonies belonging to their own particular belief. I have seen a whole side-walk cleared of some one sect, because a European happened to come down on the same side, they absolutely walking in the middle of the street, with the blazing sun beating down upon them, rather than risk the contamination that would come to them, by the contact with "a dog of a Christian." However, they are not always discourteous. I remember, when out strolling about one day, I saw some Hindoos drinking from a fountain that was placed at a corner of the street. Being thirsty, I asked one of them to allow me to have some water from his cup, as I had nothing with me from which I could drink. He hesitated slightly, then with a profound salaam handed me a beautiful little vessel, half saucer, half cup in shape, of fine china with curious emblematic figures around it. I took a drink, and returned it to him, when he immediately broke it in little pieces. I understood his hesitation then, poor fellow, and wished I had known before that anything touched by a Christian was defiled for them, so that he might have kept his beautiful cup.

About this time my funds were getting low, and I thought it quite time to rouse myself from the lazy, luxurious life I was leading and look around for something to do. I met an old schoolfellow, from Nelson House School, Plymouth, who was acting as railway engineer on the other side of the river. He introduced me to a first mate, belonging to the East India Pilots. He was a very pleasant man, who had seen many ups and downs in his life, and rather liked giving a helping hand to young fellows who through misfortune or their own folly found themselves in a difficulty. He intended to get me a post as leadsman, in which capacity I should have to serve seven years; but the post ultimately attained was well worth the seven years' work, and it would have been a fine thing for me. Alas, before things were at all arranged, the scheme was knocked on the head by his taking the command of one of the P. and O. boats to China. Disappointed and somewhat mortified, I left the office where I had heard the news, and walked with more speed than discretion back to the Sailors' Home. Suddenly I felt sick and dizzy, but staggered and stumbled on almost blind. Instinct must have led me right, for I had no notion where I was. I managed to get not only into the Home, but to my own room, where I seated myself on the edge of the bed, and went through the most miserable maddening sensations that can hardly be imagined, and certainly not described; then I collapsed utterly, and knew nothing more until I came to myself in the bed, with some of the officers bathing my head. The doctor, when he came, made me drink quantities of water, and in a few days I was all right again, with every one congratulating me on my escaping with so little harm from that dread illness sunstroke. Mine was a very slight stroke, it is true, but I found it bad enough; Heaven help those who have it worse, for even if they escape with their lives, it nearly always more or less injures their reason.

Just as I was fully recovered, a great disturbance occurred, caused by the ladies; whose excessive fastidiousness caused a regular revolt. There was a very large park about a mile from the city, part of which was beautifully laid out as pleasure grounds and was called Eden Garden. It was a favourite resort for every one, and military bands played there every evening. Owing to the great heat during the day, the ladies only took their drives and walks there after sunset, when they ventured forth in great numbers, elegantly dressed and generally well escorted. At this time the Sailors' Home happened to be full of sailors, who, having nothing better to do, also went to Eden Garden to hear the music and see anything that was going on. In order to make themselves more comfortable, as the weather was very hot, they left off their shoes and stockings, rolled their pants up to their knees, went without hats, and bared their (very often hairy) breasts to the evening breezes. Now all this was very disgusting to the ladies, who complained to the officers, and the result was, that a notice was posted up informing the sailors that they must put on shoes and cover themselves up generally, or they would not be allowed to enter Eden. This mandate considerably ruffled the "tars," who determined to see whether they could or could not force their way in. So some half-dozen in a greater state of undress than before went up to the gates. They were immediately collared and put outside, not without stout resistance. Another midshipman and myself were walking in the garden at the time, and although we were in uniform, our sticks were taken from us, and we were told that we could only claim them on leaving the grounds. This foolish little act of tyranny had the effect of placing all the midshipmen on the side of the sailors, who had called a meeting and had determined to enter Eden by force. One glorious evening they collected some six hundred strong, armed themselves with sticks, and were headed by a band, the instruments consisting of battered tin kettles, penny whistles and such-like, which, struck by vigorous arms, produced the most hideous noise you can conceive. Arriving at the gates, they broke down all opposition, marched to where the fine military band was performing the usual evening concert, coolly turned them out, and installed their own elegant musicians, who endeavoured to bray forth "Britons never shall be slaves."

The alarm having been given, the troops were called out to quell the disturbance, the officers hoping that the mere sight of a company of soldiers would be sufficient to induce the sailors to disperse. But the "tars" only continued their music! adding vocal to the instrumental, and jeering at the military. The order was then given to charge and clear the garden. The ladies had all been hustled out of the way before the fight began. Twice the military were beaten back, and a second company was sent for, when a serious battle ensued. After some hard fighting the sailors were scattered, but not before seven or eight had been killed, while the soldiers, although they only actually lost three men, almost all were wounded. Several midshipmen with myself joined in the fray, and I received a severe scalp wound from a sword-bayonet which laid me up for some time, and left a mark that I shall carry to my grave. This affair made a great talk at the time, and many of the sailors that were taken got three months in prison. When I recovered from my wound the Abyssinian war was going on, and I conceived a great desire to join in it. A transport ship was leaving, laden with provisions *en route* for the scene of action, and I found no difficulty in getting a berth. It was the old *Trafalgar*, one of Green's ships. We were under Government rules and law, and flew the blue ensign. Nothing of interest occurred on the voyage, which after all proved a useless one, for when we arrived the fighting was all over. King Theodore had shot himself, and the prince, a little naked savage, was running about the beach in charge of some English officers. We spent a short time there, chiefly employing the hours in boat-racing, and then returned to Calcutta, where I put up in my old quarters.

HARD LIFE IN THE COLONIES.

I.—AUSTRALIA.

SOME twenty years ago I happened to find myself in Calcutta penniless and friendless. How I, late midshipman in Her Majesty's Service, had come to such a mournful state of destitution I need not relate here. Suffice it to say that it was entirely owing to my own folly and waywardness, facts which did not tend to solace me in my trouble. Finding it a difficult matter to procure my daily bread, and discovering the fact that I might die of starvation without any one trying to prevent it, I went down to the wharf, where, not without considerable repugnance, I shipped before the mast in the vessel *Airdale*, bound for London. Any ship after the ones I had been accustomed to would have seemed poor; but this one was the worst I ever trod on. She was a long snaky iron vessel nearly 400 feet long, and would ride two seas at once. She was never dry the whole voyage through; always looked dirty, and was uncomfortable in every way.

Luckily for me, although the ship was detestable, the captain was a good-hearted man, and did what he could to make my position more bearable, for although nothing was said on the subject when I

GILBERT CHILCOTT JENKINS.
(*After a Photograph.*)

joined, he told me on parting that I was not the first gentleman he had had as "ordinary seaman," and whether owing to their own fault or to some misfortune, he always felt a deep sympathy for them. The crew, too, although rough and often coarse, were not unkind, and would sometimes teach me some part of my duty at which I was particularly awkward with a delicacy of feeling that a lady need not have despised. The men took their tone from the captain, proving once more the old saying that a good master makes a good servant.

One day, when we were some two weeks out, I was at the wheel, feeling somewhat glad that I should soon be relieved, for I found it rather anxious work. The sea was choppy, the wind cross, and every now and then the rain fell in spiteful gusts. Everything looked grey, dreary, and uninteresting. When the next man came whose turn it was to steer, I gave the wheel a somewhat vicious jerk, when to my amazement it walked clean out of the wheel-house and down the deck, as if it too were glad of a little change from its monotonous life. It was a very annoying accident, as it took two days' hard work before it could be replaced, and those two days were really terrible. Not only was the weather wet and boisterous, but steering was almost impossible. It took four men to tack, luff upon luff, and guy upon guy. I fully expected to be blamed, but Captain B—— was a just man, and on examining the wheel-house the pivot on which the wheel hung was found to have been bent. Christmas was upon us as we neared the Western Islands, but the weather had not improved. The forecastle was flooded, all our chests floated about, and it was a real difficulty to get any clothes out of them. I used to wade in knee-deep and push my chest against the side of the vessel, steadying it as well as I could while I opened it. The rats were very lively, and would dart over the lid and inside without a "with your leave" or "by your leave," burrowing under the garments, whisking their long tails, and squeaking defiance. One lady rat was pleased to honour my trunk by making it the birthplace of her six children, and fiercely resented my attempt to dislodge her and them. Being always weak where the female sex is concerned, I gave in to her evident wish and determination to remain, and left the lid open that she might receive her husband's visits. I took care, however, to remove my wearing apparel, with the exception of a flannel vest which madame had chosen for her bed. I may add that she and the six lived there for several weeks, and all departed one day, taking care to carry off the vest, which had been torn in pieces for that purpose. Though she was ungrateful, I confess to feeling a pang when madame's bright eyes no longer looked up at me from my sea-chest. On Christmas Day the captain presented us with a pig for dinner. We were grateful for the present, though we hardly knew what to do with it, for the weather was so bad the cook could not boil the water necessary to scald him. There was piggy very much alive, grunting in blissful ignorance of the fact that his fate was being even then decided upon; but how to manage to eat him without being scalded was the difficult question. Hot and loud grew the discussion, many and impossible were the suggestions. I remember one coming from the carpenter to the effect that as piggy couldn't be scalded, because boiling water could not be procured, he might be *planed*. Finally it was settled that he should be skinned, and soon after he grunted his last grunt, was skinned, and an attempt made to roast him. But the ghost of piggy seemed to hover over his remains, for he got smoked, he burnt in places, he fell asunder, he curled up, he stretched out; but cook like an ordinary respectable porker he would not. It was a Christmas dinner under great difficulties. The cook had peeled some onions, and finding it impossible to chop them up with sage as he had intended (for the ship was rolling like a drunken man), had pitched them in whole, with some potatoes, where they gaily ran up and down piggy's stomach, cannoning against each other like iron balls. The plum-pudding I think I won't mention; it is best buried in oblivion. I will only say that it very nearly buried three seamen, who were only saved by repeated doses of raw Jamaica rum.

This terrible weather lasted three weeks, during

the whole of which time the captain had not taken his clothes off or slept more than two hours at a time. Some of the men—and I among them—suffered very much from the state of our hands, the lines in them being open, raw to the bone, owing to the rain-water mixing with the salt whilst working on the ropes. Several were obliged to go to the hospital on arriving in England, and three, I heard, never fully recovered the use of their hands. I was more fortunate, for although I suffered very much at the time, the wounds healed quickly when once they could be attended to, and I felt no after bad effect.

We arrived safely in London, rather to every one's surprise, for the *Airdale* was not a vessel calculated to inspire her captain and crew with any confidence. Like a true woman, many were her moods and capricious her temper; but in times of trouble she came nobly to the rescue.

I bade good-bye to Captain B—— with real regret, and some weeks after shipped in the *Macduff*, bound for Melbourne, as third officer.

A third mate's position is far from being an enviable one; like a corporal in the army, he is at the beck and call of every one, and satisfies none.

I was unfortunate enough to offend the captain at the very outset. He was a Scotchman, very proud, conceited, and overbearing, with a painful sensitiveness of his exceeding ugliness. Women did not like him; he, on the contrary, was very fond of the fair sex, and would force his attentions upon them, with a disregard to their evident aversion that made one long to kick him. I had been able to offer some small attentions to one of the lady passengers on her arrival, for which she was far more grateful than there was any need. The captain offering his help, she turned away from him and called me. This trifling act was the beginning of his treating me with systematic hardness, and even tyranny.

The pilot we took on board on leaving London was an elderly man with great experience. He was pleased with my seamanship, and allowed me to steer nearly the whole way down Channel. On leaving he recommended me particularly to the captain, which had the effect of making that worthy more bitter against me than before. From that day my life was made a burden to me; everything I did was wrong, and everything I did not do, was equally wrong. I gave up trying to please him in despair, and only struggled to keep my temper, for I saw clearly that he was doing all he could to goad me into being insolent to him. Several weeks passed without any open dispute, but a row was inevitable, and one day it came with a vengeance.

The *Macduff* was a passenger vessel, and on this voyage had her full number in each class. Among the third class passengers were many very poor and miserable. As all the stores passed through my hands, I had taken a few comforts to the women and children. This was not perhaps strictly right, but any other captain would have passed it unnoticed; so indeed would Captain M—— had any man but my unfortunate self been the culprit.

He had me called up before the officers and men, abused me roundly for wasteful expenditure of the ship's stores, vowing he would make an example of me, and disrating me, sent me forward among the men. Such a piece of injustice completely dumbfounded me, and before I could find my tongue I was dismissed.

All the crew were very indignant at the way I had been treated; there was a good deal of talk about it, and the passengers hearing of it, took up my cause warmly. A petition was drawn up and signed by every one on board, begging the captain to restore me to my position as third officer. Angry at this show of favour towards me, Captain M—— tore up the petition, refusing the request in such insulting terms that I lost all control over my temper, and poured forth a torrent of passionate words at his injustice. I was furious with myself afterwards for giving him the very opportunity he needed for completing my disgrace. He now disrated me to an "ordinary seaman." But I had come to the end of my patience, and doggedly refused to work in this capacity. Captain M—— then ordered me to be put in irons and confined to the forecastle. After a week of this imprisonment I was brought on the poop before him, who asked me if I was prepared to obey him and act as ordinary seaman.

I answered, "No, I signed the ship's articles as third officer, and I will work in no other capacity. Let me take my duty again, and I will do all in my power to give you satisfaction, but work as ordinary seaman I will not."

So back I was marched again for another week, when the same thing happened with the same result. This went on for three weeks. Finding me determined not to give in, and fearing the bad impression he had made on the passengers by this act of palpable injustice, he commanded the irons to be taken off, and in a voice quivering with rage told me he dismissed me from the service of the *Macduff*, and for the rest of the voyage I was not to come aft of the fore-mast.

So the remainder of the voyage I spent in idleness, as far as seamen's duties went, but found plenty of work among the poor passengers, in helping and cheering them up. Many were going to Melbourne without the faintest idea of what to do when there. One of these emigrants, an Irishwoman, became very much attached to me; I had been able to do her some slight kindness the day she came on board, and from that moment she was my warmest partisan, and would make up little dainty dishes and bring them to me when I was supposed to be on the exciting diet of bread and water. Her husband was a carpenter in Newcastle, New South Wales, and she was going to join him after a five years' absence.

Among the second class passengers was a French

girl, with the most wonderful voice I have ever heard,—a pure soprano, clear as a bell and sweet as a nightingale. Often of an evening she would come on deck and sing song after song in the most good-natured way. There was also among the passengers a fine handsome young Englishman, who was going to join his friends who were mining in South Australia. These two were supposed to be engaged, they were always together, and all on board took a great interest in watching them; he was such a manly young fellow, and she had all the charm and grace of a Frenchwoman, without the capriciousness and inconstancy that so often mar the women of La belle France.

One morning we were just off the Cape, where the sea runs very high at any time, but now the billows were like mountains, and the *Macduff* flew before the wind with square sails set. So rough was it, that orders had been given that no passenger was to be allowed on the top-gallant-forecastle. Mademoiselle Vinot, however, pleaded so hard to be allowed to see the storm of waters, that her lover gave in, and with my assistance we got her up the ladder. I left them, advising them not to stay long, and above all to hold firm. I had barely reached the forecastle, when the ship gave a fearful roll, and I heard a shriek of agony, followed immediately by the cry, "A man overboard!" Rushing back, I was just in time to catch Mademoiselle Vinot, who, wild with terror and grief, was throwing herself after her lover,

The poor young fellow had lost his footing when the ship gave that heavy lurch, and falling had struck the chain-rail in the middle of his body, the rebound from the blow throwing him into the sea.

As soon as the man at the wheel heard the cry, "Man overboard!" he put the wheel hard down, and brought the vessel to a standstill, quivering from the sudden shock, from bow to stern.

The captain and mates, who were dining at the time, and several of the passengers, were on deck in a moment, and every assistance possible was promptly given, but alas in vain. I caught a glimpse of the poor fellow as he was passing astern, and never as long as I live shall I forget his beseeching, horror-struck look. Mademoiselle Vinot fainted, mercifully for her. In the excitement of the moment I forgot the order that prohibited me from coming aft of the fore-mast, and jumping into one of the quarter-boats with the second mate and one of the sailors, began to lower. Unfortunately one of the tackles broke, and we were nearly thrown out. The captain seeing our perilous position ordered us on deck at once, saying no boat in the world could live in such a sea. A man was sent to the royal-mast-head to see in what direction the drowning man would rise. He rose only twice, and the albatross and molly-hawks were tearing and pecking at him for about ten minutes; then he disappeared. The sight was sickening, and one of the men passengers fainted, while another ran madly up and down raving,

"For God's sake save him!" The poor young fellow could not swim a stroke, and besides was heavily capped by having a great overcoat and heavy top-boots on at the time he was thrown into the sea. He had also on his person a lot of jewellery and a large sum of money belonging to Mademoiselle Vinot.

A strange and sad incident about this drowning case is worthy of mention. Only the evening before, in conversation with several of the passengers, he had mentioned the fact that both of his brothers had met with their death by drowning, and laughingly said, " I don't think I need fear now, for I have not far to go, and we are told those who are born to be hanged will never be drowned."

I don't know what became of Mademoiselle Vinot for certain, though I was told some years after that she married a horsedealer, a man of great wealth, who had made his fortune by buying up horses in the Colonies and taking them to India.

When Mary Daly, the Irishwoman I have mentioned before, heard the cry of "Man overboard!" and the commotion that followed, she came on deck shrieking that they had killed me; she knew they'd been wanting to do it for some time! The more the men tried to explain, the wilder she got, and nothing would pacify her until I was brought into her presence, when she threw herself on the ground at my feet, embracing my knees and sobbing and laughing. I am afraid I was more irritated than pleased at this loud affection. Poor Mary, I never came across her again after she had reached her destination, but I have often thought of her, and hoped she is happy with her husband, of whom she seemed very fond.

After this, things went on their usual course for some little time. The captain ignored my presence altogether, and if by accident we met face to face, would not even return my salute, which I considered not gentlemanly. The lady passengers, however, amply made up to me for any unpleasantness I suffered at the hands of Captain M——.

At Port Phillip Heads, we took on board a pilot and were sailing between Dromanagh and Geelong, when we saw the wreck of a fine clipper ship. Her top-sail-yards were out of water, all her sails on, and masts unharmed, but her decks were blown up and she was a total wreck. There is no sadder sight to a sailor than to see a vessel wrecked, lying like some beautiful wounded bird, useless, helpless and desolate. This was the *Hurricane*, that had sailed from Liverpool, and was wrecked almost after reaching her destination. On board of her was a gentleman, whom it was my good fortune to meet a few months afterwards, and from whom I have never since parted. Many and varied have been the adventures we have passed through together in these long years, adventures that I will leave him to describe, for I have not the gift of writing as he has. Through sorrow and joy, poverty and ill-health, we have passed together, our hearts knit to each other with a deep and lasting affection that nothing can destroy in life, nor, I trust, in death, whose grey shadow hovers near my dear old friend. God help me when the blow falls.

Forgive me this digression and let me return to the *Macduff*. We reached Melbourne without anything more worthy of note happening. Captain M—— paid me what was due to me, and we parted mutually delighted to be rid of each other.

I now found myself again adrift on the world, without much idea what to do with myself. The lady who had been the innocent cause of Captain M——'s taking a dislike to me, had asked me if her husband (he was a large shipbuilder), could be of any service to me, but foolish pride had made me refuse her offer, and I preferred to wander alone and friendless, like a wounded animal who crawls to some solitary spot to die in lonely misery. I had only a few pounds, which, with an indifference to the future that astonishes me now, I spent in living quietly in a small lodging where I remained until, having paid up, I was left literally with one penny in my pocket, which I turned mechanically between my fingers as I paced the streets. A tiny flower-girl begged me to buy a bunch of violets—"only a penny," and my only penny passed into her wee hands in exchange for the sweet-smelling flowers that were not sweeter than the kiss the little maiden gave me *pardessus le marché*.

Now that I was literally penniless, I felt relieved, and looked about for some work to do. On turning a corner I ran against one of the crew of the *Macduff*. Our quickly uttered expletives turned into something more polite. Jackson informed me that he had " run " from the *Macduff;* why, he did not explain, nor did I ask—it was none of my business. After a little talk, he asked me if I could help him—" For I've only fourpence in my pocket." " Then you have fourpence more than I have, my man." I answered; "We must find work."

We set out together, with that hope that springs eternal in the human breast, and it was only after hours of fruitless search that we saw fate was against us, and for that day at least we should find nothing to do. Telling Jackson that I would meet him the next morning at the same place, I bade him good-night. Fourpence would get one man a meal and a night's lodging, but it was not enough for two. I satisfied the good-hearted sailor, by telling him I knew where to go to be comfortable; which was quite true—that I could not afford to go there, was another thing.

I walked off briskly in an opposite direction from Jackson until he was out of sight; then slackening my speed, I began to wonder what to do next. I had eaten nothing since I had left my lodging that morning, and wandering about all day in search of work had made me weary and footsore.

It was a lovely night, the stars twinkled and glittered in the deep blue of the heavens, and a young moon threw her pure, cold glamour over all. It disgusted me to find that all this beauty affected me but little, simply because I had been a few hours without eating. Poor humanity, what stumbling-blocks in the way of rising to higher things are the material needs of every day!

On I went, through street after street aimlessly, taking a faint interest in the crowds of busy people that were hurrying to their homes or to some amusement; but after a while they became fewer as I left the fine streets, and, as night advanced, only a policeman, a drunken man, or some homeless waif like myself, occupied the pavements. On I went, now walking mechanically, seeing nothing and feeling nothing, until from some near church clock chimed the hour of midnight. Shaking myself from the sort of lethargy into which I had fallen, I looked around me. The place was deserted, all was still and solemn. The church from which the clock had just struck twelve loomed before me, and towards it I directed my footsteps. To my surprise I found the door opened to my touch. On entering, I saw I was in a Roman Catholic church. Kneeling before one o the altars, which was lighted by two or three candles, was a priest. Hearing some one enter, he got up and turned towards me, and I thought I had never seen so venerable and good a face. He said something that I was too faint to understand or reply to, for a rushing sound came into my ears; I made a wild effort to save myself from falling into what seemed an ocean of darkness, then came oblivion. When I came to myself, the kind old man insisted on my going to his house, which was quite close, where he made me eat and drink, and afterwards gave me a bed—his own, I found out the next morning, when I rose early to thank him for his hospitality. He would not let me go until I had had a substantial breakfast, then bidding me Godspeed, he shook hands, and I left.

He had not asked one question about me, who I was, how I came there, or whether I was a Roman Catholic; but seeing my need, had simply helped me, in the spirit of true Christianity.

Strengthened and cheered, I walked briskly back to the place I had appointed to meet Jackson, and found him there before me, looking radiant, although we had not a cent between us, and yesterday's experience might have thrown a gloom over his brightest hopes. We went to the docks, but at first could find nothing to do; the place was crowded with loafers and men out of work. At last a man offered us a shilling an hour to load waggons with large stones. I couldn't help laughing to myself at the idea, but was too wise to refuse, so Jackson and I set to work.

Never shall I forget it! I suppose I had not entirely recovered a bayonet wound I had received some months before in Calcutta, and which had thrown me into a fever; at any rate, my back felt as if it would break, and my head throbbed wildly. I glanced again and again at Jackson, who was vigorously pitching the stones into his truck to the accompaniment of the song sailors sing when pulling up an anchor. He shouted out words of encouragement now and then, which helped me on, because they amused me by their singular inappropriateness.

I managed to put in two hours, at the end of which time I came to the conclusion that a man must be brought up to the business of loading trucks with stones, quite as much as to the higher walks in life. Jackson, although he had worked so bravely, was not sorry of the excuse to give up, for he vowed he would not leave me; so having received our two shillings each, we started again on our travels. I called for a small bundle of my things that I had left at the lodgings, the principal item being a fine Anglo-German concertina I had bought in London, and from which I could not bear to part. Jackson's luggage was even less bulky than mine, consisting of a shirt and a pair of socks tied up in a coloured handkerchief.

We walked twenty miles without stopping but once for a few minutes' rest, and late in the evening we put up at a small inn that we found near some clay works, and which looked suitable to our slender purses. After we had supped and rested a bit, I took out my concertina and began playing. In a few minutes the room was filled with men who had come in from the taproom. A rough lot they looked, unshaven and covered with yellow clay, yet I saw one of them, a big bearded fellow, sob like a child when I played "Home, Sweet Home," and none of the others either laughed at him or made the smallest joke on the subject.

The landlord was so delighted with my playing, or perhaps it would be more correct to say with the effect it had on his customers, that he offered to put both Jackson and myself on the clay works, that belonged to him. He would give us good wages, and I would get something more if I would play of an evening. All being fish that came to our net, we closed with the offer, neither of us having the very smallest notion as to what our work would consist of. The next morning, behold me trudging off with a small body of men to the clay pit.

The day before, I had thought the labour of filling trucks with stones a very arduous one, but it was as child's play compared to this. I was taken to a pit of wet clay, a huge shovel was put into my hands, and I was told to fill a rough, clumsily-made barrow that stood near. It was most frightfully hard work, the wet clay was as heavy as lead, and when I had succeeded in half filling my shovel, the weight was so great as nearly to drag me over. After frantic efforts I succeeded in piling up my barrow with the unsightly and evil-smelling mass, and then stood wondering what I was expected to do next. I was not long left in doubt. The man who had shown me my work came up, eyed me for a moment in silence, and then said, laconically, "Git on."

I stared around me to see what I was to "git on." Seeing nothing, I politely asked for information, and was rewarded with a snort of contempt, and the question, addressed to the landscape, "What do these sickly creeturs mean by coming and pretending to work when they aint strength enough in 'em to kill a flea?"

Nature not answering him, nor I either, he pointed with his thumb over his shoulder, and said, "Git yer clay up there; yer ought to have wheeled three barrers ere now."

I looked in the direction to which he had pointed, and my heart sank. A very short but almost precipitous incline led up to a single plank that was thrown across a ravine some seventy feet from the ground. On the opposite side of this primitive bridge was a brick kiln and all the necessary buildings for carrying on a small brick manufactory.

"Do you mean to say that this clay must be carried up there?"

"'Ivery shovel full, git on." And my companion turned away, leaving me filled with despair at the task before me.

However, I got my barrow up to the plank, and my seafaring life had made dizzy heights familiar to me; still, if I must confess the truth, I shrank back from crossing that wavering plank with both my hands rendered useless by the necessity of wheeling the barrow. In the very middle I was seized with a momentary feeling of intense and sickening terror. It passed away almost as soon as it came, but I reached the other side trembling like a leaf, and bathed in perspiration. Each time afterwards that I crossed over I felt the same sensation at the same spot, and dreaded it so much that I feel quite sure had I persisted in the work I should have gone over, barrow and all, into the clay pit that yawned some seventy feet below. How often afterwards in dreams have I traversed that dreadful piece of wood, waking only from the nightmare by the agony of falling down, down, down.

Well, I stood this work exactly three days, and they might have been three ages. On the evening of the third day, as I was playing in the taproom, I made a sudden resolution to go away at daybreak and get back to the Sailors' Home at Melbourne. I would not say anything to Jackson, for he would have insisted on following me, and that would have been a pity, for he was quite happy as a bricklayer and would make good wages; besides, having deserted, he might get into trouble if seen in Melbourne. I explained to my landlord, who, although sorry to lose my music, was evidently rather glad to get rid of so poor a workman. He paid me honestly what was due, and undertook to give Jackson a letter, in which I told him my reasons for leaving him, and said that I intended going back to sea.

Having settled my small affairs, I lay down for a few hours' sleep. At daybreak I rose, and with my beloved concertina in its case set out on my road back to Melbourne. I have not a very distinct recollection of that walk, for I seemed to be in a dream; at midday I stopped for food at a roadside inn, and must have appeared strange to the people, accustomed as they were to all sorts and conditions of men, for the landlord sent his son, a lad of fifteen or so, to walk with me for a time. Finding I went on all right the boy left me after a mile or two, asking for a shilling for the care he had taken of me. I was too confused and ill to protest, or even understand, gave him the money, and went on. How I got safely to the Sailors' Home has ever been a puzzle to me; however, reach it I did late in the evening, exhausted and almost delirious. I was carried to bed, where I remained three weeks in a sort of fever brought on by over-exertion.

These Sailors' Homes are a grand institution, and although, like with most institutions, there are many points that might be altered with advantage, nevertheless they are an immense boon, and have saved many a man from sin and despair.

As soon as I had sufficiently recovered I joined the brig *Greyhound*—the last voyage as sailor that I was destined ever to make. The *Greyhound* was the most perfect little model of a brig that ever was built to delight a sailor's heart. She was a Portuguese, and had been first used in that country as a gun-boat. She floated as easily and gracefully as a swan upon the water, and sailed better than any vessel I had ever put foot in. All her fittings were of the best, and from bow to stern there was not one clumsy or ill-done piece of work. I was as delighted with her as the captain, whose love for her amounted to a passion. He was never so happy as when he could get hold of some stranger to whom he could point out all the beauties and perfections of his darling. I firmly believe that I owed my berth as third mate, to my unbounded and really true admiration of the *Greyhound* as she lay daintily swaying to and fro, riding at anchor in the bay. Captain S—— was a short, round man, with a face that reminded one irresistibly of a rosy-cheeked apple. A good-hearted, good-tempered man, whose passion was never roused unless some real or fancied slur was cast on his beloved brig. Then his rage would pass all bounds. It was a curious sight to see him, dancing up and down the deck, his little fat legs thrown out in the funniest way; now abusing the man who could invent such lies, now addressing the *Greyhound* in terms of affection a mother might use to her babe. I am afraid the officers and men, too, sometimes made up stories of some supposed slight, in order to see "the skipper dance."

We were bound for Auckland, New Zealand. I went on board two or three days before we started, for I was not very strong yet, and I hoped the sea-air would do more to recover me than pints of doctor's stuff. The night before we had intended starting, as we lay at anchor out in the bay, a tremendous "sou'-wester" came on quite suddenly. In a few minutes the bay was lashed into a mass of seething white foam, and the wind and waves seemed to vie with each other as to which could howl and shriek the loudest. Several ships were torn away from their moorings and dashed into each other, doing endless damage, and causing great confusion and loss of life. We were anchored rather far out, and hoped to escape; but it was not to be. A large two-master, the *Homesdale* from London, if I remember rightly, broke from her moorings, drifted down, and a huge wave dashed her into us. It was a horrible moment. By the light of the moon, as she sailed across the sky, now obscured by black clouds, now shining forth with a strong light, we saw this huge dark monster bearing down upon us, and we powerless to do anything, for there was no time. Captain S—— gave the order to cut our anchor, a useless order, as he well knew, but right nevertheless; then stood with wide-open horrified eyes waiting for the destruction of his beloved ship. There was a moment's sickening suspense, as the immense black object hovered over us, then a thundering blow as the *Homesdale* struck against us; a crashing and smashing of timbers, mingled with the roar of the waves and the howling of the wind. The *Greyhound* bounded from the shock;

her boats were smashed to pieces, the masts broken, the sails torn to shreds, and one side bulged in: but to our utter amazement no lives were lost, nor did the *Greyhound* sink, as we fully expected. We got into the dry docks, where we remained over two weeks for repairs. Captain S—— fairly wept with joy when he saw his ship again sailing proudly on the waters.

We weighed anchor, and got off without further mishap. I found, somewhat to my distress, that my health did not much improve, and any sudden call upon me taxed my strength to its utmost. Among the crew of the *Greyhound* was a young fellow with whom I made friends. He was a gentleman by birth, and had been educated for entering the law. This, however, did not at all suit the young ideas of Master Curly, so called by a fond mother on account of his wavy hair, that was of the brightest gold that I think I ever saw in a grown-up person. As a boy he was expelled from one school after another, more for mischief and defiance of rules than for graver sins, and having exhausted the patience of his guardians (his father had died when he was a baby), and driven his eldest brother, a grave lawyer, almost into a frenzy by the tricks he performed in the office, he one day, after a worse escapade than usual, ran away from home, joined a ship going to Melbourne, with some vague idea of setting up sheep farming or "something," as he put it. Arriving at Melbourne, he wrote to his mother (whose darling he was) saying he could not bear the life in England any longer, and hoped she would send him money to enable him to set up as a horsedealer. He had changed his mind about the sheep farm. While awaiting her reply he led a gay life, thoroughly enjoying his freedom, and having no fears for the future.

Poor fellow, the letter from England was a sad blow to him. It was from his brother, saying that Curly's wicked conduct and cruel desertion, coming upon their mother's delicate constitution, had killed her. She had died calling for her youngest son. He added that it was useless his returning to England; he had better follow the life he had chosen. He enclosed a cheque on a Melbourne bank for £100, and told him he need expect no more until he came of age, when he would get £1,000 from his mother's will. Curly was heart-broken for a while, for he loved his mother dearly; but soon his gay bright nature came to the fore, and he quickly made an end of the £100. An appeal to his brother resulted in his letter being returned unopened, and Master Curly had to look about for means of earning his daily bread.

There was a great stir at this time about the supposed discovery of gold in the town Thames, in Auckland, and he, like hundreds of others, was bitten with the gold-fever. He got himself taken on board the *Greyhound* as "ordinary seaman," on the strength of having learnt a few things on his way out from England, and was now looking forward to the fortune he felt sure of making in the gold-fields of the Thames. From the first day, he began to try and persuade me to join him, and as time went on he would coax and scold, until I was fairly won over by his sunny character and wild enthusiasm; the more so as there was some sense in what he said as to a seafaring life being evidently unsuited to me, at all events in my present state of health. When I suggested that gold-digging was not likely to be child's play—for I had a shuddering recollection of the clay-pit—and also that we might find no gold at all, he eagerly protested against any such impossible thing happening, drawing vivid pictures of fortunes made almost from one hour to another, that I promised to go with him and share his fortunes, more, I think, because I could not bear to separate from him, than from any belief in the mountains of gold that were to be ours. The voyage passed without any incident worth mentioning. A sudden storm, during which the *Greyhound* bore herself "like an angel," as Captain S—— said with more enthusiasm than sense; the illness of one of the men, who swallowed some drug in mistake for rum, and thought he would throw up his immortal soul in consequence—" And serve 'im right, too," as the indignant owner of the drug observed; a catch of fish off Cape Regina: these and similar small events were all that happened to disturb the even monotony of our lives.

In due time we entered Kaipara Harbour, where

I bade good-bye to Captain S——, who, I fear, lost much of his regard for me when he found that I could dream of deserting the *Greyhound*, and preferred digging "in the dirty earth for dirty gold" to a joyous life on the ocean wave. But I had given my word to Curly, and we started off together with light hearts, lighter purses, and a photograph each of the *Greyhound*, a parting gift from the captain.

And thus ended the last voyage I was ever destined to take as a sailor.

Curly was in such a hurry to get to the gold-fields, that he would not allow me even to look around the town we were in. A queer little train took us some miles on our journey, then we were told that a four hours' walk would bring us to our destination.

"Did you observe how that fellow grinned when we said we were going to the gold-fields?" I remarked to Curly.

"Yes, he was rejoicing in our good luck," answered my light-hearted companion.

"Hum," I said dubiously, "such men are more likely to rejoice over our bad fortune. It looks fishy to me."

"Now don't croak like a bird of ill-omen, there's a good fellow," pleaded Curly. "Things are sure to turn out right, they always do, so shut up."

Having no answer to such an astounding assertion, I did "shut up," and we set out on our walk. It was impossible to give way to gloomy thoughts with Hope in person chatting gaily by my side; now relating to some boyish prank, now some tender reminiscence of the loved and loving mother, over whose death he would still have passionate outbursts of grief and remorse. But with Curly smiles soon chased tears away, and he would rattle on about some nonsense or fun, with his eyes still wet with tears.

Night came on before we had reached the town where we had hoped to sleep. We found ourselves on a hill, with nothing in sight but more hills that seemed to stretch away in an endless range. At Auckland we had provided ourselves with blankets and the other necessaries for a miner's life, the purchase of which articles had left us with two shillings between us. "Heaps enough," Curly had gravely observed, "for what's the good of taking coals to Newcastle!"

So we now decided to camp out on the hills. We quickly made a fire of bush-wood, quantities of which were strewn all around, ate some bread and beef we had been wise enough to put in our knapsacks, drank a modicum of rum to keep out the cold, saw that our guns were primed, then rolling ourselves up in our blankets, soon went fast asleep. I was aroused by feeling something cold touching my cheek, and opening my eyes found two dogs sniffing at me in an exhaustive but not unkindly manner. I uncoiled myself from my blanket and sat up, looking around me. The first faint flush of early dawn was tinging the sky with a rosy light that, as it advanced, seemed to put out the stars one by one. The summits of several of the hills were enveloped in a pink cloudy mist, very beautiful to see. Bringing my eyes back from the hills, I saw a man, the owner of the dogs, standing motionless, leaning on his gun, intently watching us. He was very tall and thin, with a face bronzed by exposure to all weathers, and scarred by frequent fights with man and beast. A pair of small sharp dark eyes gleamed from underneath the thickest eyebrows I ever saw on a human face. On his head was a soft felt hat that originally had been red in colour, but was now toned down to what I believe artists call "a neutral tint." A grey blouse, much the worse for wear, corduroy trousers, and high boots was the costume of our early visitor.

We eyed each other a moment in silence.

"Going to the gold-fields?" he asked, without changing his attitude in the least.

I nodded.

Then he raised himself with a jerk, and staring first at me and then at Curly, who had just woke up, put himself into the most extraordinary contortions, induced thereunto by a paroxysm of silent laughter. After a few moments of this exercise, various smothered "Hee, hee, hee; ho, ho, ho; haw, haw, haw's" broke from him, as he continued to double himself up in an agony of mirth.

"Here, I say," cried Curly, starting to his feet,

with his hair standing out all around his head like a halo, "when you have finished hee-hawing like a jackass, perhaps you wouldn't mind telling us why you stand with an annuity of a grin that reaches from y'ear to y'ear.

"Hee, hee, hee; ho, ho, ho; haw, haw, haw!" was all the answer he got. I began quietly rolling up my blanket and preparing generally for a start. Curly did the same. When we were ready, I turned to our mirthful friend and asked him if he could direct us the nearest way to Shortland, as we were going to the gold diggings. The last two words convulsed the man more than ever. He writhed and twisted about like an eel, and finally burst forth into a loud and long guffaw that was echoed by the hills around.

Irritated by this behaviour, I shouldered my knapsack, and with Curly, began to march down the hill, when we were called back.

"Don't be angry," he gasped out, "but I really couldn't help it when you mentioned the gold." The mere word nearly upset him again, but struggling against it, he asked if we would breakfast with him, and he would then give us any information in his power.

I didn't half like accepting the man's offer, but Curly closed with it at once, and in another minute we were walking along by the stranger's side, whose fit of mirth had left him as suddenly as it had begun, and who strode on in dead silence. Curly touched his forehead significantly as we followed our host into a roughly built hut, under the shelter of a hill.

The room we entered was of fair size, hung around with guns, knives, sacks of feathers, and skins of beasts. Nailed against the wall, without any frame, was an oil painting of John the Baptist in the wilderness. It looked strangely out of place in this hovel, and was evidently a relic of better days. There were two or three other things that showed plainly our host had not always been a bushranger in the wilds of New Zealand—one was a mug that he handed to me full of coffee; it was battered out of all shape and discoloured by time and want of cleaning, but it was of silver, and, what is more, was crested. Seeing my eyes fixed on it, he hastily filled a larger mug and passed it to me, taking the silver one from me with the muttered excuse that it was too small.

A large square table occupied the centre of the room, and there were four or five stools, beyond that no furniture. He went to a cupboard and brought out three mugs, the silver one aforementioned among them, some plates, a cold fowl, bread, cheese, and butter. A wood fire was burning brightly in the grate, over which hung a kettle. He soon made some splendid coffee, and placing it on the table, boiled milk in an old tin pan, and in less than a quarter of an hour after our entry we were seated at one of the best meals I ever remembered to have eaten. Our host told us his name was Richards—a polite fiction that we of course passed unnoticed; that he had lived here for many years, "Driven from the Old World," as he said with bitterness, "by the falseness and treachery of *friends*." He lived by hunting, and lately had kept a large poultry farm and many pigs, which he had sold to the crowd of miners that had flocked to the gold-fields. Again a spasmodic grin convulsed his face, so I asked him to explain himself. "If you know anything against it, please tell us at once. I have never been so sanguine about it as my friend here, and am quite prepared to find that the gold is not so plentiful as has been reported, and that there is an over-glut of miners."

Mr. Richards laughed outright, and forthwith informed us, in a few quiet sentences, that the gold-field was a fraud and a swindle got up by some storekeepers for their own individual profit. "But so great is the love of gold, so eager the rush after it, that without even waiting to find out what truth there was in the report, hundreds of men flocked to the spot from different parts of the colonies, and even from America and Europe. There are now," continued our host, "over seven hundred fine strong young miners, who can get nothing to do; let alone the crowd of other men who, ignorant of and unable to do miners' work, loaf about the place, half starving until the Government gives them a free passage back to their colonies."

Even Curly's bright hopes were clouded by this grim picture, and Mr. Richards, who was evidently much taken by the boy's face and manner, added kindly—

"Don't be downhearted. Seeking for gold is not the only object of a man's life. Take my advice, go back to England; this hell is no place for honest men, and it is easy to see that neither of you are fitted for a miner's life. It gave me a sort of fierce joy to see how men would leave home, and wife and children, all that makes life bearable, on the chance of picking up a few nuggets of gold, which, even if found, could never give them back their lost health and honour. I am a bit of a misanthrope, and it soothes me to see men act worse than the wild beasts; but to-day I would fain dissuade you from entering such a life—not for your sake," he added, with brutal frankness, "but he," pointing to Curly, "reminds me of some one I knew years ago, and I would spare him if I could. If you want money I will give you what is necessary, but take him back, take him away from here," and the strange man began pacing wildly up and down the room.

I hardly knew what to do, and certainly not what to say. Perplexed and embarrassed, I remained silent. Curly, however, settled the matter in his own bright way. Going up to our host, he said with his boyish impulsive manner: "It's awfully good of you, Mr. Richards, to trouble about me, but I'm all right; if there's no gold to be got here, well I'll turn hunter like you. It's no good returning to England—I've no home now, and no means to get there, and *gentlemen* who are strangers, do not accept money from each other. There, shake hands, and thanks for that prime breakfast. Now we'll go and look around a bit, something good is sure to turn up, it always does."

Mr. Richards, who had drawn back when Curly made the remark about gentlemen, now seized the boy's hands in his, wrung them with considerable force, as I could see by Curly's grimace, then shaking hands more calmly with me accompanied us to the door.

"Good-bye," cried Curly; "we will come and look you up in your diggings again before long."

Mr. Richards did not answer, but turned into his hut and we heard him bar the door.

"Decidedly a tile loose," said Curly, as we turned our steps towards the town.

"The man is a gentleman. Some sad history must be buried away in his heart. Poor fellow, what a miserable world it is," I remarked dolefully.

"Now there you go croaking again, and in the face of such a scene as this. I say, we will look over the towns and gold-fields, and if we find old Richards was right, why we'll turn hunters, that would suit your health far better."

So chatting now about one thing, now about another, we soon got over some ten or twelve miles and reached the Thames.

We found the Thames consists of two towns,

Graham Town and Shortland, connected together by a long straggling road of the roughest description. At intervals a few houses relieved the monotony of the scene; most of these were empty, and already falling into ruins. In Shortland, the most prominent feature was a construction known as " Smale's Building." It consisted of two long rows of rooms, reaching from the main street back to the beach, a distance of not less than a mile. It was a speculation on the part of an enterprising Methodist minister, at the time the gold fever first broke out.

Now that it was ended (for we soon found out that all Mr. Richards had said was true), the Rev. Smale increased his already large fortune by letting out the lower rooms to stockbrokers, while the upper ones were hired by any one who could afford to pay five shillings a week for the luxury of four walls with a roof over them.

The next building of importance belonged to a native chief, whose name was Taipari. He had a really fine residence, built according to European notions on many points, which looked odd, contrasted with several relics of barbarism, that I suppose the noble savage could not or would not dispense with. This house stood in its own grounds, the gardens being kept in order by Europeans, who were liberally paid by their dusky master.

Taipari was a tall handsome man, with well-shaped limbs, and a graceful carriage. His face

TAIPARI.
(*After a Photograph.*)

was very much tatooed, of which fact he was inordinately proud. When I saw him, he dressed like a European, and it was his delight to fill his palace with any European ladies and gentlemen who would go there. The whole town of Shortland belongs to him, for which the white residents pay him rent. He was named Colonel of the Hauraki Rifles (a company of which I subsequently became a member), and was by no means to be despised as a soldier. He gave balls and fêtes, of magnificent if barbaric splendour, to the white colony, and looked imposing in his colonel's uniform.

Before the gold rush broke out, Taipari's usual place of repose was an old cask, nor had he the traditional rag to his back. His followers were few and miserable, and he himself ignorant to the last degree. Now he possesses the whole of Shortland, with an income of over £8,000 a year. English ladies do not shun his society, indeed it is said that more than one would not have refused to become Mrs. Taipari, if the noble savage could be made to understand and acquiesce in the law that allows a man only one wife at a time.

But to return to the town of Shortland. We found it contained the usual grocery, fruit, vegetable, baker, butcher, drug, dry goods and liquor stores, demanded by any town however small. There was also an armoury of the Hauraki Rifles, which was sometimes cleared out and used for a concert-room. Shortland possessed also a theatre. Never having entered it, I cannot give any account of the performances enacted there, but to judge by the crude and horrible pictures on the signboard, lovers of the terrible and sentimental would be abundantly satisfied.

Where Shortland ends, a tiny pier juts out into the sea. Two small steamers plying between this settlement and Auckland, land stores and vegetables two or three times a week. The whole town is built on a level with the sea, so when there is a high tide the place is under water.

Graham Town belonged to the man from whom it received its name, an Englishman, who in a fit of inspiration and speculation built first one house and then another for settlers, and when the gold cry was raised, quickly made his fortune by building a town. In England one is not accustomed to hear of a town being built by one man, but in Australia there is nothing impossible in either the idea or the fact. Like Shortland, Graham Town is built on low land, and is generally under water. If you want to know what real mud is like, go there and you will see it in its perfection.

Nevertheless it is a far larger and more important town than Shortland, possessing a good wharf, three fine hotels, two banks, a large theatre, and some very fair houses. The rage for building was still very strong when we were there, for although that one particular gold-field was proved a swindle, other mines that had been long worked were in the vicinity, and Mr. Graham rapidly became a millionaire.

At the back of both these towns rose the mountains, from one of which the Karraka Creek ran straight into Shortland. On the hills around Graham Town are some of the most important mines, the principal ones being " The Golden Crown," " The Long Drive," and " Crown Point." Most of the others were what is called in mining phraseology " shysters, or wild cat," and were of little value.

Curly and I wandered about all day taking notes. We saw that the gold craze had already died out, but we also saw the effect of the cruel deception in the hundreds of able-bodied men that, homeless and penniless, were besieging the houses of the few rich people clamouring for work, or a piece of bread to keep them from starvation.

I sickened at the sight, and perhaps with a presentiment of our future; but Curly never lost heart, and even when things were at their worst had ever a bright word or a sunny smile.

I have put off speaking of this awful time as long as possible. After all these years, my heart shrinks back from the memory of that dire misery and black despair. Let me hurry over it. These are true bare facts that I am relating, and I cannot put them into well-rounded sentences, or enlarge upon the incidents that well nigh overwhelmed me at the time. That life is stranger than fiction is a trite saying, but only those who have passed a roving and adventurous life know how true it is.

Our first day at Shortland exhausted our money

—we had only two shillings—and we spent the next morning searching for work, without any success. So we sold our blankets for a few pence, their being a glut of them at the pawnbroker's. After our blankets went our guns, neckties, the one change of linen, and an extra pair of boots of Curly's. Then we found ourselves with what we stood up in, without a cent in the world, and little chance of getting any work. I remembered my beloved concertina, which I had placed in a corner of a half-finished house in which we had taken up our abode, rent free. Taking Curly with me, we went to the drinking-house, and I commenced playing. The effect was electric; pennies rained down, and on counting up we found I had netted four shillings and threepence. What castles in the air Curly built that night as we sat in our mansion, as he called it, discussing some bread and meat and beer that we had allowed ourselves on the strength of our fortune!

We were awakened by a feeling of wet. Starting to my feet, I found the place flooded. Hastily rousing Curly, we made our escape, not without difficulty, for the tide was coming in swiftly, increased by a sea wind. After some twenty minutes' unpleasant floundering about we reached dry land, wet to the bone and shivering with the cold. The night being very dark added to our discomfort, Curly's teeth chattered like castanets, and I made him keep moving about. We groped our way into the town, and I roused up an old fellow we knew who let out seats around a fire at a penny an hour. He grumbled a good deal at being disturbed, but I paid him threepence at once, pushed him aside, threw some logs on the nearly dead fire, and made Curly dry himself, and then lie down near the warmth. Suddenly he called out, "I say, Gilbert, your concertina, have you got it?"

I started to my feet. I had quite forgotten it; if that was gone, our chance of living was gone too. "It will be all right," I said, though my heart sank. "I know where I left it. I will go and fetch it the first thing in the morning."

Curly was soon asleep, but anxiety for the future kept me awake, and with the first rays of sunrise I was up, and, telling old Simon that I would return shortly, and Curly was not to be disturbed, went back to the scene of last night's disaster.

The tide had gone back, but the scene was desolate and miserable in the extreme. Wading through the liquid mud, I reached the half-built house that had sheltered us, and saw that the outer wall had been washed down. My concertina was buried beneath the *débris*. For two hours I worked at removing the stones, and finally succeeded in uncovering the instrument. It was smashed to pieces. I stood staring at it for a while, wondering what could be done now; then remembering Curly, I turned my steps sadly townwards, with my mutilated and dead concertina in my hands. At the door Simon met me with the words, "You must take that 'ere boy out of this, he's going to be ill, and I can't have no fevers here."

In a moment I was by Curly's side. He lay on the floor; his fair hair tossed about, and his beautiful face flushed. His hands were burning, and he muttered incoherently.

"Tek him away, I say; I won't have him here," cried Simon, who had followed me.

"I will not take him away. Move him into a room where there is a bed. I have money," I said, showing him one or two of the precious three shillings that were left to me.

The old sinner consented. Between us we lifted Curly into a cupboard—it was barely more, but there was a low iron bed there. I sat by him for some hours, but, finding he did not change, went out to the drug store and asked what was necessary in such a case as his. The man, who seemed intelligent, gave me a bottle of medicine, for which I paid a shilling.

The next ten days were a hideous nightmare. Having given Simon the last two shillings, I was forced to go out and seek for work. One day I walked to the coast of Tararu, thinking I might get some work at shovelling sand, but found at least a hundred men who had gone for the same purpose. Only ten were needed. I next tried to get work on a tramway up in the hills near the Karraka Creek, with the same result. I should most assuredly have starved had I not somehow made a friend of a waiter in one of the hotels, who sometimes of an evening would give me some food at the back door, and several times he gave me a bottle of soup for Curly, who lay still unconscious most of the time. Old Simon was always asking for more money and threatening to turn us out. I made a shilling one day carrying some of the luggage for one of the passengers who had come from Auckland, and that kept the old man quiet for two more days. My food was two biscuits a day, excepting when my friend the waiter gave me anything, that was not often, for all the houses were besieged with starving men. I would not go until, having passed two whole days without a bite or sup passing my lips, I was driven to it, fearing I should fall ill. One morning I heard of a Maori chief who wanted some white men to pick potatoes. Leaving Curly as comfortable as I could, I set out for the Maori settlement, some five or six miles beyond Shortland. I had to swim a creek to get to it, and when I arrived, wet and starving, found it was a false rumour. Doggedly I dragged myself back to Shortland. At the wharf I got a job of unloading a vessel of potatoes, but was so weak and wasted from want of food and misery that I was unable to carry the sacks. Seeing me stagger, four or five men, on the look out for work, rushed forward fighting and struggling, and so I lost that. The captain gave me a pocketful of potatoes. I lighted a fire on the beach and roasted them; then, somewhat strengthened, hurried back to Curly. Going to his room, I found it occupied by a stranger, who could not or would not answer my frantic inquiries as to where my friend was. Old Simon was nowhere to be seen, but on my swearing that I would set fire to the house if he didn't show, he emerged from the cellar.

"Where is Curly?" I asked, seizing him by the throat and shaking him until all his bones rattled. Some men separated us, or I think I should have killed him. I was desperate.

"Old Simon has ousted his mate," said one of the men. Turning to me, he added, "Don't yer take on. The boy's gone to a chum in the hills."

"But he couldn't move," I said. "I left him this morning unconscious. Do, for God's sake, some one, tell me where he is."

Simon then muttered that, a cart happening to be going to the hills, he had put Curly into it, as the boy had said that he had a friend there; that he couldn't keep him any longer—the room was wanted, and I might go too as soon as I liked.

In a moment I saw what had happened. Curly and I had spoken of Mr. Richards before old Simon, and I had said we would go to him as soon as he could walk. When we were starving, I went alone, only to find the house closed up and no trace of Richards. I had said nothing of my failure to Simon, fearing he might turn us out. Having a chance of letting his room, he had seized the excuse of sending Curly "to a friend," and had turned the sick lad out without a moment's pity.

Maddened with rage and grief, I sprang at Simon, and, before any one could interfere, dashed him with all my force to the ground, and, without waiting to see if I had killed him or not, went quickly out towards the hills.

Evening was coming on as I reached the bottom of the hill that led to Richards' hut. I seemed endowed with miraculous strength, and hurried on, tormented by fears as to how and where I should find Curly. No cart was to be seen returning, but then it might not come back; I had not thought of asking where the man was going. Perhaps he would take Curly on when he found Richards' house shut up, or perhaps Richards might have returned. At last I reached the little hut. It was still closed, and looked deserted. Sick at heart, I turned away, when I observed the trace of cart-wheels that had evidently stopped here, and then gone on. Somewhat cheered by this proof of Curly's near presence, and the fact that the man in whose care he had been placed had not left him outside the empty house—for life is held very cheap in these places—I followed the tracks of the cart.

Reaching the summit of the hill, I saw the cart at the foot of it. The horse had been taken out and was grazing. Giving a loud cou-ēē, I ran down at full speed. A rough-looking man came towards

me with his gun ready cocked, but lowered it on
my hasty explanation. I went to the cart, and
there, lying on a lot of straw, and covered with
some sacks, lay Curly. He opened his eyes as I
bent over him, knew me, and said, with his sunny
smile, "Don't croak, old fellow, but I must sleep,"
and immediately fell into a doze.

The carter told me that Simon had called him
in that morning, asked him to take the lad up to
the hut on the hill, that the man there would pay
him well. Curly had been lifted in, Simon vowing
that there was nothing the matter with him but
what food and rest would set right. Curly had
slept the whole way, and it was only when Richards'
hut had been reached that the man saw not only
that the boy was really ill, but that the house had
been deserted some time, and he had been tricked
by the old sinner. Too good-hearted to leave the
boy, he brought him on, meaning to put him in
the hospital at Auckland when he got there.

He made a fire, for the night was cold, and the
carter shared his meal of bread and meat with me.
He lived at Auckland, he told me, and was in the
employ of a corn factor, who sent him now and
then to Shortland with a cart of sacks of flour,
which he sold to the wayside houses. What was
sold in the two towns was sent by steamer.

The night passed on. The carter, stretching
himself on some empty sacks, fell asleep. I got
into the cart by the side of Curly, but I could not
close my eyes. Sitting there in the stillness and

solemnity of night, all seemed unreal to me, my life was, as it were, suspended. I seemed waiting for something, I knew not what. Curly lay sleeping peacefully, looking better than he had done since that cold had seized him, and I felt content about him, although I knew not what would become of us, or where I should take him on the morrow. The first rays of the rising sun shot across the sky as Curly opened his eyes and looked at me. My heart gave a throb of joy as I saw he was conscious. Raising him in my arms, I propped him up against the side of the cart. He looked towards the rising sun, his eyes shining with a wonderful brilliancy, then turning to me said, "There's a good time coming, Gilbert, a good—time—coming."

How can I describe what happened then? it is all blurred in my memory—for it was so sudden, so unexpected. I recollect only a short struggle for breath, a convulsive movement, a sunny smile, a peaceful sigh—and Curly was dead.

We buried him that same evening, pulling up a young tree by tying a horse to it, and enlarging the hole with spokes taken from one of the wheels. He looked so beautiful and peaceful with the smile still on his lips, that I could only thank God that for him the "good time" had come.

I think grief and misery must rather have affected my head for a time, because I utterly refused to go with the carter to Auckland; the sight of the man and the horse and the cart seemed to drive me into a frenzy. He gave me some food, and I set off in the direction of Shortland; but night found me on Curly's grave, though I have no recollection of how I got there.

With the morning came a change of mood. Reckless and bitter, I turned from the grave and, without looking back, mounted the hill, passed Richards' house, and on into Shortland.

The next six or seven weeks of my life I will pass over with but few words. It was a desperate fight among desperate men for bread to keep one from starving. Over and over again death stared me in the face, now through accident, now through a quarrel, now from hunger; but I always escaped. Once swimming across a creek I got cramp, and being perfectly indifferent, let myself sink, but found myself on the opposite shore some hours after, having been hauled in by a passing boat. The humanity of my rescuers, however, not being strong enough to do anything but toss me out on the sand. An old man who had witnessed the scene told me of it when he saw I was alive. It had not entered his head to help me until he saw me move. You see, dead men are useless, but a penny might be got out of a live one.

You may wonder, perhaps, why I, a sailor, could not get away to Auckland, and ship from there. It was impossible. Once in Shortland or Graham Town, a man was like a rat in a trap, if he had no money, for the two steamboats that called twice a week were so small that there was no chance of becoming a "stowaway." Many had tried it, but as the boats were strictly examined before starting no one had succeeded, and the passage money demanded was very high. To attempt to reach Auckland by land was hopeless now in November, with no shoes to my feet and no money to buy food to carry with me.

One cold wet night I was wandering about outside the town, when a man passed me and entered a half shed, half tent that stood near. I leant against a tree and lazily watched him as he lit a lamp, stirred up a wood fire and put something into a saucepan. I had eaten nothing for the day, but felt neither hunger nor thirst. I was simply numbed, morally and physically. We can only suffer up to a certain point, after that mercifully comes indifference.

The man came out for water, looked at me keenly for a moment, flashing his lantern into my face for the purpose of investigation, and said, "Down on your luck, mate? Come in if you like, there's plenty of room for two." I followed him in, and soon felt it was more agreeable to be near a fire than out in the pouring rain. He went on with his preparations for supper without noticing me, but when it was cooked he poured it out into two large plates, and shoving a knife and fork across the table, said briefly, "Eat."

It was a sort of Irish stew, I remember, and as I ate, the feeling of stolid indifference left me, and I again recognized that the world looks vastly different when viewed by a man warm and well-fed, than it does to that same man wet, cold, and starving. A tankard of beer unloosed our tongues, and Jack Ward, for such was my host's name, told me that I might sleep there, and if I cared to do so, take up my abode altogether. I was to provide my own grub, and when in luck to pay a dinner. He told me that he was working at an iron foundry a long way off, which prevented his being back until very late at nights. I thought his explanation unnecessary, but closed with his offer, and for many weeks had the shelter at night, and when more than usually unlucky in getting a stray piece of work, and consequently without food, Ward, who was always well supplied, would force me to share with him.

I had been with him for several weeks before I began to suspect that the story of the iron foundry was untrue. In the first place he was most unpunctual; I always left him rolled up in his blanket, and if by chance I came back during the day, very generally found him still asleep, or lazily doing nothing. The only thing he was regular about was returning late at nights; and he frequently had money that he rattled ostentatiously before me.

At last, one night he came in, in the wildest of spirits, and threw a handful of gold and silver on the table. "Why don't you ask where I get it from?" he said; "I might be able to put you up to a wrinkle."

"How do you get it?" I asked, quietly; "in the iron foundry?"

"Not such a fool. No, I make it by 'rolling drunks.'"

My readers will probably not know what the two words uttered by my respectable friend mean. Simply this, to "roll drunks" was to frequent drinking saloons, to follow any man who left drunk, roll him into the gutter and rob him of his watch or money, or whatever he had of value on him.

"Look here, I'll make you a handsome offer. You join me—two can do ever so much better than one, and I bet that before the winter's over our fortunes will be made. Here's my hand on it," and the scoundrel absolutely held out his hand to clench the bargain.

Choking with rage and shame, I told him in a few incoherent passionate words what I thought of him, and raising the flap of the tent rushed out into the dark night, once more homeless and friendless. I wandered about all night; for it was too cold to seek shelter in any half-built house, and could not help regretting the warm bed and good food that had been mine for so many weeks now. It maddened me to think that I owed it to such a rascal as Jack Ward; even the coat I had on me he had given, a heavy blue thing miles too big for me, but warm and without holes; my boots too were his gift, stolen from some poor drunken sot, no doubt. I wondered what I should do now, and my heart sank at the prospect of passing again through that time of black misery from which Jack Ward had rescued me. Had I only been taught a trade, little or none of the hardships need have happened; but like all other gentlemen's sons, I was taught only what was utterly useless, and soon forgotten. Latin and Greek will not keep a man from starving.

I had walked into Shortland by the time day broke, and was hesitating what piece of work to try for, when I was accosted by a soldier, who asked if I would join a company of volunteers who were going to the front against Te' Kooti.

I said "yes." When he further stated that we must depart the first thing to-morrow morning, I replied that I was ready to start on the instant if necessary.

"Well, cut off about two feet from that long coat of yours, and come with me to the armoury, where I will present you to the Captain of the First Hauraki Rifles."

I lost no time in doing what I was told, and proceeded to the armoury, where, having passed muster, I was accommodated with a rifle and a uniform, and ordered to return to the same place at daybreak.

It was a great grief to me that I had no time to go to Curly's grave, I should have liked to see it once more. For him, I had never sorrowed that his young life had been cut off; such a temperament as his would have suffered terribly as life brought him, as it must have done, one disillusion after another: but for myself it was long long before I could think of him without a bitter pang of grief at the knowledge that never again should I hear his joyous voice or see his sunny smile. I may state here that I wrote to his brother an account of his death, but never got any reply.

At daybreak the next morning I presented myself at the armoury, where I was a good deal astonished to see Jack Ward dressed in uniform, waiting with many others the order to march. He came up to me, and in rather a sheepish way said he had decided to give up the nefarious trade he had been carrying on, as it was unfitted to "a gentleman."

I congratulated him on his good resolutions, whereupon he asked me to shake hands with him, and begged me not to mention his past occupation to any one. I complied with both requests. Whenever we met afterwards we were always perfectly polite to each other, but we did not seek out each other's society. He being very flush of money—got, as I and the reader know, in that trade which he found "unbefitting a gentleman"— he was much looked up to and admired by the men, the more so as he was a good-natured fellow, and generous enough with his money.

So I left Shortland, that town which I had entered with such bright hopes a short three months before. Those hopes were buried with Curly, and I went forth to my new life feeling only that I might as well end my life in a battlefield by the hand of a savage, as die by inches, of starvation among my own people.

My adventures as " private of the First Hauraki Rifles" must be told elsewhere by my friend, for I observe that this narrative has stretched out to an unconscionable length. I herewith put the pen into his hand with profit to my readers and pleasure to myself.

II.—NEW ZEALAND.

My life has not been one that the most egotistic of men would be very proud of. I entered Trinity College, Dublin, where I did what most young fellows do—nothing of note. It was during my collegiate life, however, that I studied hard, became somewhat proficient in Hindustanee, Arabic, and Hebrew; was a fair mathematician; loved the Arab Antar more than Homer, and devoured all the English poets from Chaucer upwards.

My great wish at this time was to become an artist, painter, or sculptor, for either of which I had a great taste and was naturally endowed. I do not speak through vanity or in self-laudation, but truthfully and sadly too, the reason for which regret I will show further on.

Not being able to follow the profession I wished, I entered the Church, and was ordained July 12, 1846, and appointed as curate in the same parish as my father. Father and son brother curates, in the same parish, on the magnificent stipend of £69 4s. 7½d. per annum! You will wonder, perhaps, at the 4s. 7½d. So did I, but never knew the reason. The halfpenny was always strictly paid.

HALN KILLIGREW DUNBAR.
(*After a Photograph.*)

The great Irish famine began the same year owing to the failure of the potato crops. The scenes I witnessed were heartrending. Thousands died for want of food, of actual starvation. Then came malignant fever, whose breath, passing across a town or village, withered up its victims. Those who could, fled; those who could not fly, laid down and died.

Christian charity, if it could not save, could and did alleviate the torturing miseries of the poor stricken wretches. But all this has long since become matter of history, nor can any good be obtained by recalling it.

My life passed on monotonously, without much to mark the months as they slipped by. One amusing event happened in a neighbouring church, which I may as well relate. The church at Garrison, a small town on the south-east of Loch Melvin, had just been built, and the Bishop of Clogher appointed a day for its consecration. My rector, father and myself, were present, among other clergy. When the service was about to commence, the clerk endeavoured to sing the opening psalm, but having a very bad cold, could not produce a note, so turning to the bishop he said, " My lord, I cannot get out a note, but will whistle it." And whistle it he did, to the unspeakable amusement of all present, not excepting the bishop, whose episcopal gravity was very sadly upset.

In justice to the clerk—a man I knew very well, for he worked for my grandfather, whose residence was just outside the town—I must say his whistling excelled very much the usual excruciating vocal sounds with which he was wont to favour the congregation.

One more anecdote before I close this brief narrative of my clerical career. There had been a drought of some weeks' duration, and the prayer for rain was naturally used. One Sunday the clerk came into the vestry after service, and looking from the cloudless blue sky to me, said in a tone of contemptuous remonstrance: "Eh, sorr, whativer be the good of going on praying for rain, for sorra a drap will fall till the wind do change."

I remained twenty years in the same curacy, a lotus-eating but not wholly unpleasant life, during which I had time to study, and to increase my knowledge of painting and sculpture.

My rector dying, a successor was of course appointed, who brought his own curates. I had often thought of leaving "the Church," and not long after, having lost my dear father, and the home being broken up, I left Ireland in company with one of my sisters, who required my escort to Australia. We embarked on board the *Hurricane*, an iron clipper ship, commanded by Captain Johnson (he was captain in the Naval Reserve), a good seaman, and a kind, considerate commander. His wife was with him—she told me she always accompanied him; they were a most devoted couple, and seemed thoroughly to deserve all the happiness that was theirs. Mrs. Johnson was not only a beautiful woman, but was singularly attractive in manner, and had withal a fund of common sense as rare as it is delightful to come across.

My sister and myself were the only first-class passengers. In the second there were about thirty, a curious lot from all parts of the world, one and all fixing their hopes of wealth and prosperity on Australia, with a faith worthy of a better cause.

I used to like to get Mrs. Johnson to relate some of her adventures in previous voyages, or some particularly striking incident. I remember one in which the tragic and comic were strangely mixed. Among the numerous passengers on their way to Australia was an Irishman, his wife, and child. One morning the mother, being busily engaged, the man took charge of his baby, carrying it backwards and forwards on the deck. The little one crowed and jumped with delight, and in its extreme hilarity sprang overboard out of its father's arms and was drowned. Paddy at once rushed to the companion ladder, shouting down to his wife, "Och, Biddy, come up quick, the chile has bounched clane over the fince!"

We had our usual amount of storms and calms, neither being terrible or very inconvenient, and I began in my mind to accuse many travellers, who tell woeful tales of fierce tempests and weeks of a weary calm, of at least exaggerating. I forgot that we had not yet reached our journey's end.

The first land we sighted was Tristan Ditcunha, and next, Curguelan's Island. The captain was anxious to land on the former in order to renew his various stores, but the weather was so stormy, and the coast so rocky and dangerous, that he was obliged to give up the idea altogether; so all I saw of it was a dark mass looming in the distance, surrounded by wild white billows. When in the equator, I often stayed on deck the greater part of the night watching the brilliant phosphoric lights in the water. Millions of these tiny insects, more dazzling in their little spheres than the mightiest of men, lit up the waves with a golden luminous glory. One night the chief officer called me on deck to witness a most extraordinary sight. It was raining as it only can rain in the tropics, huge drops of water falling into the calmest of seas, and the whole sparkling like—I am at a loss for a suitable simile—not like diamonds, but like a white, clear, brilliant light, covering all the ocean, intensely beautiful, surpassingly magnificent in its glistening purity.

One day I happened to say to Mr. Farleigh, as we leant over the grating watching the bright waves sparkling in the sun, "I can quite imagine how a sailor loves this free life. You, I suppose, are perfectly happy in your career, and only desire to be a captain?"

"You are mistaken," he answered quietly, but with a concentration of feeling that startled me, "I hate it."

"Then why—" I asked, then stopped; it was none of my business to pry into the life of another, and although the first officer and I were very good friends, he had never mentioned his family or his private affairs, but he finished the sentence for me:

"Why did I enter the navy? Because, like many a boy, I thought it a very grand thing to go to sea; and because there happened to be a berth for me. I imagined all would be delightful; above all, looked forward to the freedom of a sailor's life—Freedom," he repeated, with a short laugh, as he knocked the ashes out of his pipe and rapidly refilled it.

"You have not found it a life of freedom?" I ventured to ask, for I was interested in hearing his opinion.

He laughed again. "Well, not exactly. Think a moment. What freedom can there be when one is confined to the narrow limits of a ship, where rules and discipline must be strictly enforced. One is actually in a sort of prison, with the additional comfort of not knowing what may happen from one hour to another. No, what with the storms, disasters, and shipwrecks, a sailor's life is not one to be envied, it is but one constant succession of hardship, toil, and misery."

"Could you not leave a profession so little to your taste?" I asked, still feeling somewhat puzzled at this unexpected view of a seafaring life from the lips of a seafaring man, who had always, as far as I could judge, been content with his lot, and what is more, skilful and proficient as a naval man.

"If I left, what could I do? What is a man who has spent years on the ocean to turn his hand to on land? Not one of all the branches of knowledge necessary on board a ship would help a man to get his living on *terra firma*, and my fortune is not large enough to allow me to do nothing. Here I am, here I must remain. I don't say I find no pleasure in my life, or no interest in my work; nevertheless, it is the last profession in the world that I should choose had I my life to go over again."

"Have you been shipwrecked often?"

"So often, that now I really hardly mind it; it is an excitement like any other, and breaks the monotony of life; but there, too, it is always accompanied by so much sorrow, so much misery, that one shrinks from thinking of it, and one feels a brute to wish any change that would bring such terror on the poor passengers. Yet, for my part, so calm and uneventful a voyage as we have this time is wearisome to a degree."

Though we were not far off our journey's end, we were fated not to accomplish it without a disaster bad enough to satisfy even my friend's desire for change. We remembered our conversation afterwards and referred to it.

A pretty sharp storm came on the day after our talk, and a good deal of damage was done; the *Hurricane* plunged and bounded immensely. The two ladies retired to their cabins, but the captain and I endeavoured to eat our dinners as usual, the stormy wind in noways affecting our appetites. The difficulties were, however, very great. When I tried to raise my glass of ale to my lips, it would pour over my right shoulder; another effort, and my left shoulder would receive what my open mouth was waiting for. I nearly put out an eye with a fork when, giving up the attempt to get a drink as hopeless, I tackled the chicken on my plate, and was deciding to use my fingers, when crash came in the skylight, followed by an immense deluge of water, which swept me from my seat, and sent me floating around the dining saloon before I had time to call upon the proverbial Jack Robinson, as is usual in all such cases.

What a scrimmage it was! Though not a little frightened—"tell it not in Gath!"—I could not help laughing at the sight we presented, such drenched specimens of humanity. Captain Johnson recovered himself first, and got on his feet, with water pouring from him. Without heeding me he dashed up on deck, where I heard him shouting out orders above the roar of the tempest.

The storm stormed itself out, and the *Hurricane* once more wended her way through calm seas. At this time, a huge whale nearly ran into us, but evidently thought better of it. He insisted, however, on politely escorting us for some miles, and so closely as almost to touch the ship. The old sailors were very much frightened, for they knew the danger but too well. The wreck and loss of many a fine vessel can be traced to those monsters of the deep. We (the passengers) were merely greatly astonished at his bulk. He appeared to be larger than the *Hurricane*, and she numbered three hundred feet. Maybe our amazement at his great bulk and his close proximity added magnifying power to our eyes; still, of a surety he was, as a Pat said, "a rale monstrous baste intirely."

Many flying-fish appeared to have a keen desire to improve our acquaintance, for quantities of them flew on deck, one nearly blinding the steersman by darting into his eyes, attracted by the binnacle light. They were all caught, and swam in the sea and flew in the air no more, for—they are very good to eat!

And now the long-wished-for land was near, and a busy time it was for the crew—scraping the masts, painting, and otherwise refitting the vessel and making her clean. The damage done by the storm was repaired, only the boats lost could not be replaced until we got into port. The passengers were much occupied preparing for shore, and the female part, needle in hand, were touching up their finery—I suppose to astonish the natives by and by.

The night before we entered "The Heads," the pilot came on board and took command of the ship. I was amused to see how Captain Johnson, giving place to the autocrat, seemed to become almost a nonentity in his own ship.

Next morning we entered Hobson's Bay. The sea was rough, but though the wind was brisk it was not boisterous, and the sky was blue and clear. Having made all my arrangements I went on deck, observing everything with the greatest interest. On the starboard could be seen the quarantine buildings, imposing by virtue of their size, and Dromana; while on the port side, the fine city of Geelong was clearly visible.

What happened then was so sudden, so unexpected, that even after this lapse of time my heart beats faster as I recall those scenes—we were wrecked in sight of land!

The coast about here abounds with dangerous reefs that, like some beast of prey, lie in ambush to catch some unwary vessel as it sails proudly by on the sparkling waters. So was the good ship *Hurricane*, with white sails set, gaily floating on to that port that even now opened before her.

A sudden crunching sound, a quivering that shook the vessel, a momentary stop—that was all, but the *Hurricane* had received her death-blow.

A loud cry, "She has struck," was followed by the captain and his officers, who came on deck, and firmly and quietly calmed the panic-stricken passengers.

"Is there any danger?" I asked Mr. Farleigh, in a low voice.

"Yes, she is lost," he answered, in the same tone.

"But she is sailing just the same," I said, in amazement; for beyond going a little more slowly there seemed to be no difference in her progress.

"Come and help at the pumps; that is our only chance of keeping her afloat a little longer."

I went with him. The crew were already working as strenuously as men could work. I took a hand at them, when Mr. Farleigh touched me on the arm and pointed forwards. The bows of the *Hurricane* touched the water and began to sink. The men looked at each other significantly, but worked bravely on; very soon it was useless, we were driven aft by the rising water. The order was given to prepare the boats; only two, it will be remembered, were on board, the rest having been washed away in the storm. I went below to acquaint my sister of what had happened, and to bring her quietly on deck, for no time was to be lost if we would save ourselves. Without waiting to secure anything, we hurried on deck, where an indescribable scene met our eyes. The passengers were all crowded together, and though in great excitement and fear, behaved very well. Captain Johnson told them briefly that, being so near the shore, their lives were not in danger. He then ordered the two boats to be lowered and the women to enter them; luckily there were very few on board, and room was found for me in the second boat.

Both boats, heavily freighted, were kept in the

lee of the ship, which served as a sort of breakwater; and from them we watched the vessel settling down in her watery grave. Captain Johnson stood with folded arms and white, stern-set features, while his wife sobbed bitterly. Presently came a thundering sound; the deck of the *Hurricane* had blown up, and she sank rapidly, remaining on even keel, her masts perpendicular, her white sails spread, and about twelve feet of water over her bulwarks. A groan broke from the crew, which the captain stopped with a gesture, as, not allowing himself the comfort of one word of sorrow or regret, he told those who could swim to leave the overcrowded boats and get into the rigging of the wreck. This was done, and they remained there until taken off by a steam tug, which was despatched from Landridge to our rescue. So near were we to land that the people at Geelong saw what had happened, and assembled in crowds on the quays and wharves. Some of the authorities telegraphed the disaster to Melbourne.

We remained a long time floating aft of the wreck, being prevented from drifting away by a rope attached to the spanker-boom, for although only two or three miles from shore, we dare not attempt landing, owing to the reefs that abounded and our ignorance of the coast, let alone the overcrowded state of the two boats. To add to our misery we were surrounded by enormous sharks, who, scenting misfortune, came in shoals, swimming about with their huge jaws yapping and their small eyes fixed on us until our blood fairly curdled in our veins. Mr. Farleigh very nearly fell a victim to one of these voracious brutes. He was swimming to one of the boats, when a great lanky shark darted at him, his snout almost touching him; but while the monster turned on its side to seize him the men dragged him into the boat, where he viewed his would-be devourer with anything but affection. The sea for a long distance around us was covered with thousands of candles and millions of boxes of Cockle's pills, and I could not help wondering how, the latter especially, would agree with the fish. Pounds of candles, dozens of boxes of pills went down a shark's capacious throat each time one opened its jaws, and it afforded me a somewhat fiendish glee when I pictured to myself the sad astonishment of those monsters of the deep at the new, and most likely unpleasant, sensations that would shortly pervade them.

After some dreary hours of anxious waiting, the tug returned and took us on board. Captain Johnson, who had mounted the rigging of his vessel, was with difficulty induced to forsake her, and came on board at last in gloomy silence. His wife prevailed on him to go down into the cabin with her, and we all felt that if any one could comfort him it was the woman he loved and who loved him, and who had been with him in more than one time of peril and sorrow. The tug took us to Geelong, where we were hospitably entertained by the authorities. After which we re-embarked and steamed to Landridge Pier, and from thence to Melbourne.

I may state here that nothing was saved from the *Hurricane*, the accident was too sudden, and she sank too rapidly for anything to be secured. Personally, with the exception of a telescope, which was somehow or other thrown into one of the boats by a sailor, I lost everything I possessed. All my scientific and chemical implements, my canvas and colours, tools for sculpture, a fine collection of valuable books, jewels, family plate, &c., &c., things too numerous to mention; and, greatest loss of all, my manuscripts, certificates, and testimonials, none of which could be replaced. My sister fortunately had a cheque on the Melbourne bank safe on her person.

Thus I landed in the New World, half clad and penniless, with life to begin over again, when I thought I had just attained ease and comfort.

A man in such a condition is not always welcomed even by his nearest relations; on the contrary, "near of kin, less of kind" has been proved too often to need comment. The rat who leaves the sinking vessel is a true type of humanity. A poor relation is such a very unpleasant thing; he gives the rich members of the family an uncomfortable feeling that something ought to be done for him, as blood is thicker than water, and there is still supposed to exist such a feeling as natural ties and family affection. The wild beast respects its own species, but man is superior to the wild beast, and respects no one but himself. Why should he be burdened with that worst of all unpleasant objects, that wearisome incubus—a poor relation ?

Seeing my sister comfortably settled in her new home (she had come to Australia to be married), I felt myself to be one too many, and sought for employment in all those branches in which I was proficient. But without testimonials, and minus a single implement necessary for my profession, it was, I suppose, little wonder that I was received with suspicion, and my story of the loss of everything in the *Hurricane*, with scarcely veiled sneers.

In a very short time I saw it was hopeless. No one seemed to care, I was getting past middle age and useless; only young men were needed, and those who could work not with their heads, but with their hands. What did it matter, one man more or less who breaks down in the struggle for life? After all, it was no one's concern half as much as my own, and if I would live, I must shake myself out of the state of lethargy into which I was tempted to sink, and putting aside all idea of making my living as painter, sculptor, or professor, endeavour to put bread into my mouth by the labour of my hands.

Feeling it was wiser to leave Melbourne, as I had connections there, and had no wish to distress them with my presence, or let them know to what a state of poverty I was reduced, I managed by a chance piece of work (copying it was) to get together the price of a passage to New Zealand, and landed at Wellington.

There I found things somewhat worse than in Melbourne. Literally no work to be had. There was a great rush at that time to the Thames gold-fields, where large nuggets of gold were reported to have been found; so, finding I could do nothing here, I went also to try my luck at gold-digging. One morning I landed at Graham's Town and Shortland, half towns, half mining camps, the possessor of a pair of blankets, a few shillings, and a heart somewhere in my boots.

I looked around for a few days, "taking stock," and looking, looking, looking for work. At length, when my last penny had gone, I succeeded in finding employment in a mining office connected with the Thames gold-fields, at a high salary. Barely a week had I enjoyed this happy state of things, and had hardly come to feel safe for the future, when crash went the whole goodly edifice; the gold-fields were declared a sham and a swindle, the mining stockbrokers broke, hundreds of men thrown out of work, a cart-load of scrips for sixpence, or, if you hadn't a sixpence, for nothing.

Well, I had no sixpence, and, what was worse, no work; for work means bread, and starvation is decidedly unpleasant. If any one doubts it, let him try it. For my part, I know I would have sold all my illustrious long line of ancestors for one good square dinner if I could. How like Esau I felt! for whom I have ever since had a brotherly feeling instead of the scornful wonder with which I used to regard him and his act of selling his birthright for a bowl of porridge. But I am getting rather gloomy. Let me alter my tune to something of a livelier strain.

I will relate one of the many stories—true ones all—that were afloat in Shortland at that time, showing how men outwitted each other, and would sell their souls if they could for gold. There was a man who dwelt in Shortland—now there is nothing very extraordinary in this, as very many men dwelt there also; but this man was what is called in Shortland phraseology "a strange cuss." He was once a clerk to a broker, and when he learnt full understanding of the business, calmly swindled his employer and set up for himself with the stolen money, and rapidly became a wealthy man. He offered a clerkship to his late master, which was indignantly refused; the poor desperate man in a fit of despair blowing his brains out in the office in the presence of his usurper, who pronounced the following brief oration over the body: "Well, now you've gone to h—l, I'm safe, and all's well." He paid for the funeral expenses—an act of generosity he was never tired of recounting with a naïve astonishment in his own goodness that was a curious thing to hear. Months passed on, and he became richer and richer; everything prospered, every mine he had to do with succeeded, and every mine he turned from failed. It was like magic.

One day a poor miner who had "started out" a mining "claim," finding it did not succeed, wanted to dispose of it, and for this purpose placed it in the hands of our afore-mentioned friend the broker, stating his price—£500. A few days later this miner rushed into Mr. —— (I cannot think of the fellow's name—no great loss, certainly), into Mister's office, crying out in great excitement, "Och! Aare an' ages. Has your Honour sould my mine?"

"I can't say," answered the broker, "I have sold so many since you were here. Why do you ask?"

"Och, an' you have. I'm ruined, so I am, ochone. Oh! for marcy sake, your Honour, will you aise me heart, and tell me you have not?"

"Shut up your blarney, and clear out of this! Come to-morrow, and I'll see if I have sold it; but be sure of one thing, it hasn't fetched £500," said Mr. Broker.

"Oh, murther! murther!" wailed the miner. "See here, yer Honour, the pure gould I've struck in fair handfuls; and now yer go and tell me you have sold me mine."

The broker carefully examined the sample of gold-dust, which was besprinkled with a few little nuggets, and seeing that they were genuine, hastily decided to do a good thing for himself.

"Wait a moment, my friend," he said to the miner; "I will go and see whether your claim is sold or not. I rather fear it is."

Going into his inner office, he returned presently with a cheque in his hand. "I am sorry to say it is sold, and here is your money, £500, less my charges, which are not much."

Language could not paint the grotesque despair and strange antics of the poor Patlander. He signed the cheque, dashed from the broker's office to the bank, grinned a horrible and ghastly smile as he pocketed the cash, and—vanished.

Now comes the best part of the story. Mr. Broker brought some of his friends, two days after, to see the splendid "grab" he had made, for needless to state that on seeing the nuggets he had bought the claim himself. When they reached the spot they found a little earth removed, but of gold ore not the smallest trace! Thus for once was the sharper outwitted by a poor dirty Irishman; and, what he felt almost more than the loss of his money, the story got about, and he became the laughing-stock of every one.

To return to myself. In company with hundreds of others—I used the numeral "hundreds" advisedly—I prowled the streets and lanes, the camps and mining districts, in the weary and ever vain search for work. A chance job now and then enabled me to buy my daily rations, which consisted at that time of a ship-biscuit and cold water in the forenoon, ditto in the evening, when I was rich enough to afford it, which happened by no means every day.

There is a story of a young gentleman in some

old play, whose name I forget now, who, on his servant's lamenting the emptiness of his larder, tells him, "There is a page turned down there in Epictetus that is a feast for an emperor." True, such diet is not likely to induce nightmare—a decided advantage, and about the only one it possesses. Alas! I have proved it *ad nauseam.*

My home was a manikin bush, or rather grove, and, although it was winter, the weather was not unpleasant. I rolled myself up in the one blanket I had not parted with, laid down at the foot of a tree whose roots formed a sort of hollow, and generally slept very well, unless prevented by the pangs of hunger. It is really wonderful how little a man can live on—perhaps exist would be the better phrase. I had almost forgotten the taste of meat, and found that my strength did not diminish to the extent I had thought likely, on a biscuit a day for all nourishment.

An election came on, and I got myself enrolled as a special policeman to help to keep the polling-booths intact. "Ah," said I to myself, "this day I will get something better than air and water to sustain me." · What a fool I was! All day long I wrestled with a mob of Irish blackguards, and at night crept into the root of my tree without having broken my fast; nor was I paid for that day's work until a fortnight had passed.

With some clay I modelled a church, which I offered for sale from door to door. A common miner, flush with money, gave me five shillings for it because it reminded him of his village church in Cornwall. After long and serious thought I expended most of the five shillings in getting a stock of newspapers, and selling them; but the young boys beat the old one, and I found I had half my papers on my hand to do what I pleased with.

But enough of these details. The very recollection of this time makes me feel sick and weak. It was a terrible state of things, and no one to blame. Without friends, without money, without the knowledge of a trade; in a country overrun with strong, able-bodied men seeking work—work to which they had been born—how was I, a gentleman, therefore a useless article in the market of life, to get food enough to keep the life in me? Often did I desire to die; fierce were the temptations that assailed me to drop into the sea, and end the intolerable burden of life.

Well, the weary days went on; constant starvation began to tell upon me; my clothes hung on my wasted body like sacks, and with my long, uncut beard and hair I made a sorry figure indeed. One morning, as I was mooning about listless, weary, not seeking for work, not caring what might happen, hardly even thinking, some one touched me on the shoulder, and a voice that seemed to reach my ears as from a dream, said: "Dunbar, old fellow, is it you? are you alive?"

Turning my head, I saw the sergeant of the

Hauraki Rifles, with whom I had had a slight acquaintance on first coming to Shortland.

"Great Heavens, what a scarecrow you are!" he cried, with more frankness than politeness. "Have a glass of ale and a talk?"

We went to a small inn, where I was accommodated with some bread-and-cheese and beer, the sergeant sitting gravely smoking and watching me until, the keen edge of my appetite blunted, I could listen to him.

"Will you volunteer to go to the front?" he asked. "Te Kooti is out again with his How-Hows, and a hundred men must leave at daybreak to-morrow."

"Go! I believe you!" I answered.

"All right; then when you have finished your grub, run as fast as you can to the captain of the corps; say McRugall sent you. You will find him at the armoury; he will be sure to take you. Be lively."

And lively I was—that is, as lively as I could be under the circumstances, saw Captain Kurton of the 1st Hauraki Rifle Volunteers, was accepted, sent out immediately on parade; that over, was ordered to be at the armoury by daybreak the next day to embark for the seat of war. So I slept for the last time in the root of my tree, and before daybreak shouldered my "swag," went to the armoury, and was reviewed with the other volunteers.

Oh, holy and blessed-looking mob! Had I my

Shakespeare at hand, how appropriately could I bring in certain quotations, to my great honour and glory, about Falstaff's immortal ragamuffins, and make sundry comparisons which Mrs. Malaprop would stigmatize as "odorous"! Certain it is that Falstaff's corp of gallow-birds was as the Coldstream Guards compared to us.

Let me try to give you a faint idea of what we looked like. A few, a very few, had dingy uniforms; these were the Haurakis proper, if I may use such a term; but the new volunteers, how shall I describe their rig out? One man had curtailed the tail of his coat, leaving the raw edge, with a sublime indifference to appearances. I wore mine in fringes, with elbows out, for ventilation sake, minus a collar, and with but one cuff.

Now for the other volunteers. Some had coats, some paletots, some jackets; all were fragmentary, and not a little picturesque, waving in every breeze, and giving a weird and flibberty-gibbet appearance to the whole crew almost impossible to depict. As to the nether garment, I really dare not venture to describe what is indescribable; I will only say that some came to the knee, some lay in folds over the boots, trying with a sort of charity to cover a multitude of faults and deficiencies; some, whose proud possessors could work a needle, were patched all over with pieces of cloth found in the dust-heaps, and were as many coloured as Joseph's coat. Hardly a vestige of a vest among the lot, but instead Crimean shirts in every stage of decadence. But the crowning glory was the headgear! Oh, Paddy! thou who erst dwelt in that "Garden of God, the wild Connemara," mightest have been able to produce a specimen worthy to vie with the coverings that hid the heads of the Volunteer Corps of the 1st Hauraki Rifles. The collection taken just as we stood would have rendered a museum immortal. There was the stately chimney-pot, mangy, battered, and brimless; the mushroom-shaped wide-awake, as green as a stagnant pool in summer; the Turkish sanguinary fez, minus the tassel, and faded as to colour; the dapper cheese-cutter on the cranium of a gaunt man of some sixty years;—such were a few of the head adornments of some of our *sans culotte* corps.

At the blast of the bugle we shouldered our "impedimenta," and fell into rank and file, and proceeded by the really good band of our Haurakis, we marched through Shortland to the pier at Graham's Town.

Our queer and ragged appearance did not excite any comments in either town as we passed through. The floating populations of these mining districts are accustomed to sights stranger and even more grotesque than the hundred tattered and torn recruits of the Volunteer Corps of the 1st Hauraki Rifles. The Government troopship, the *Stuart*, was waiting by the pier, in readiness to start as soon as we went on board. In less than an hour we saw Graham's Town receding from our sight, and I think none of us felt anything but unfeigned thankfulness at the chance that enabled us to turn our backs on a place where we had one and all suffered such misery. Once shaken a little into our places, we began to take stock of each other, and here I met Gilbert J——, like myself, as miserable a looking object as starvation and rags could make him, but nevertheless unmistakably a gentleman. Good birth will assert itself under the most adverse circumstances. We fraternized at once, and have been fast friends ever since. Sorrows and privations we have often suffered together, but misfortune has but drawn us closer and riveted our friendship more securely.

To return to my narrative. After an uneventful voyage, if so short a distance can be termed a voyage, we landed at Auckland (of which town more hereafter), and for the first time for many days had a good dinner—an important fact that has remained in my memory with a faithful pertinacity of which I ought to feel ashamed; the very *menu* springs before my eyes with an unforgetable clearness. Oh, Brillat-Savarin! with what scornful wonder wouldst thou have viewed the mountains of fat boiled mutton, the cartloads of boiled turnips and carrots that burst upon the delighted vision of a hundred hungry men! We needed no *Sauce à la Béchamel*, being all provided with that best of all sauces—hunger. And we ate gravely and silently, like men fully impressed with the importance of that unusual event, a decent, sufficient, sit-down, knife-and-fork dinner!

After being supplied with this interior ammunition, we were given arms and clothes. Here is our costume. No coat or vest, instead thereof a woollen shirt of bright colours; no trousers, but a large plaid shawl, fastened by a strap around the waist and coming to the knees, like a Highland kilt; socks and shoes; a small dark blue cap, around which was wound a white puggery, with the gold and crimson fringed ends hanging gracefully behind—altogether a wild and picturesque costume, a decided improvement on our civilian habiliments, and, like Norah Crima's robe, "leaving every beauty free." I confess the effect was rather startling when first we broke upon one another's gaze, and my friend greeted me with a shout of laughter, while he pointed to the yards of bare bone that emerged from my kilt, and which he vowed gave me the appearance of a Highlander on stilts. He being a short man, with hands and feet of womanish smallness, had an advantage over me as far as looks went, for my six-foot-one of ordinary height was seemingly increased by my appalling thinness, while, like Lady Godiva's lord, I wore

"My beard a foot before me, and my hair a yard behind."

Our arms were the Enfield rifle and bayonet,

far too long for bush fighting, and which placed us at a great disadvantage with the enemy, who was well supplied with "repeating arms." How did they procure them? That is a question we could never satisfactorily answer. The craftiness and cleverness of the savages were truly Machiavelian.

Thus equipped, the transformed corps of the 1st Hauraki Rifle Volunteers (I always like to put it down in full, it is such a delicious mouthful) embarked again for Tanronga, our destined field of operations. There we in due time landed, and pitched our tents behind the town, in the direction of the Inden Ford, and near an entrenched camp of friendly Maoris. Fine fellows they were as to physique, tall, well made, and brown. As to their costume, well—

> "Except a shell—a bangle rare—
> A feather here—a feather there—
> The South Pacific Maoris wear
> Their native nothingness."

We were supported by two ships of war, which were anchored in front of Tanronga.

Tanronga is situated on a promontory, surrounded with beautiful scenery, and the land very fertile. It was once a very thriving city, but war and its many attendant blessings (?) had pretty well ruined it. At the seaward end of the town was a fortified fort, which we had to man. Two Armstrong field guns in good order, with the necessary ammunition, were placed here. The

RIVER SCENERY—NEW ZEALAND.

bay in front of the town is the estuary of the Waimapu River, and behind the town at about half a mile is another bay, which can be forded at low water, and which we were obliged to guard at a spot called "the Inden Ford," and at the other side of this bay the enemy lay in ambush.

We were kept pretty busy; what with sentries, videttes, pickets, scouts, drill, heat, and mosquitoes our time was fully occupied. At sunset all lights out; at 2 A.M. parade in strict silence, waiting, like spectres, for a foe who was too wise to come. For two tedious hours there we stood motionless, with blue or grey blankets wrapped around us, no pipes allowed, no word above a whisper, for fear of betraying our presence, and drawing upon us the fire of an invisible foe.

The Maoris always make their attacks at the weird and uncanny hours before daybreak. During the day we were tolerably secure, but darkness is the time for savage beasts—and no less savage man—to enjoy themselves; so we were kept always on the *qui vive*. The inhabitants of the neighbourhood all around Tanronga flocked into the town every evening for greater security, returning to their homes and occupations at daybreak.

Hard by, in the centre of the Inden Ford, was an island "taboo" by the natives (*i.e.*, forbidden to, or not to be violated by, white men). On this island were dozens of peach-trees, which, at the time we were there, were loaded with large and delicious fruit. Some of us would steal out at night with empty sacks, wend our way with infinite caution to the sacred island, cram our bags full with the forbidden fruit, and steal back again to our camp, where captain and men feasted upon them, and felt none the worse for the sacrilege. It was, however, a very dangerous undertaking, as the enemy was ubiquitous, although seldom seen.

On Sundays we had church parade. Standing in a hollow square, our captain would read the Church of England service—somewhat shortened, it is true. In the evening some of us were allowed to attend the missionary station at Tanronga, where Archdeacon —— (I will not give his name) held the service and preached. He had been asked to give us a service in our camp, and had refused emphatically unless paid so much *per capitem*. An old Maori chief thus spoke on English missionaries: "The Pahĕhă (white missionary) came unto us; we welcomed him, we gave him land and pigs, we built a house for his God, and lo! he took all and nothing gave us in return, though many moons have passed by; so now, if God wants more land, or pigs, or houses, God must pay for them." Their eyes are opened now, and they can distinguish piety from covetousness.

Many missionaries, be it spoken to their shame, under the pretence of religion have "land-grabbed" to no small extent, but, as the Yankee says, "It can't be did no more." Mr. Maori now knows the value of land, and holds his rights very tenaciously, all the cajoleries of the white man—the "Pahĕhă" particularly—leaving the noble savage unmoved and immovable. Their cleverness and keenness is such as often to surpass the white man in the rapidity with which they make their fortune. Take the chief Tapari, for instance. He lived at the Thames, and was owner of the whole town of Shortland; his rents brought him in somewhere about £8,000 per annum. Formerly, like Diogenes, his dwelling was a cask, and he lived on the smell of the liquor it had once contained. "See what a rent the envious Casca made!" Pardon this quotation: I could not resist the temptation, although I have always held that a man who could perpetrate a pun ought to be strangled. While speaking of Shortland I may as well relate an anecdote proving the value of knowing the language of the natives in your intercourse with them. I was one day standing in the gallery of Smaile's Building talking to his janitor, when two Maoris came up and asked him in English what the hour of the day was.

"Good, good," replied the janitor. "Clock strikee, strikee, one, two," at the same time frantically twisting his right hand in a circle above his head; then, turning to me, he remarked with becoming modesty, "When first I came to Shortland I could not speak one word of Maori, and now you see I get on swimmingly."

I certainly did not see it, and as to the poor natives, they stared at him a moment bewildered, then slunk away, doubtless saying to themselves, "The white man is either mad or a fool."

The Maori language is soft and sweetly harmonious, something in sound like Italian, but more liquid, having many vowels. It is very figurative, and abounds in picturesque allegories and beautiful similes.

As I have said before, the Maori is, generally speaking, a noble-looking man, straight and well built, tall and strong, lithe and graceful, and walks like a king. Among their tribes they dress in their "native nothingness," but in civilized places they give in to the white man's weakness for clothing, and wear loose trousers, woollen shirt, and a coloured blanket worn like a Roman toga. They don't seem to care about headgear, but are very proud of a new hat, the only awkwardness being that with one on the head the Maori considers himself full dressed, and any other article of clothing superfluous.

To describe the gentler sex is more difficult. They are tall and well made, but walk as if carrying a burden. I will venture to depict a "belle" as she walks, or rather sails, down the one street in Shortland, a dazzling meteor of all violent colours, the bonnet a "love," the parasol a "delight," and sucking away at a short black pipe! She meets a friend, they both squat down on their heels in the middle of the street, rub noses and have a "corero" (talk). The Maori women make most excellent wives, are faithful, good, and very clean. Some half-castes we saw in Auckland were very handsome women, splendidly made, of so rare a

MAORI BELLE.
(*After a Photograph.*)

beauty that it was a real pleasure only to look at them.

But to return to our camp at Tanronga. We remained here some time, but the enemy never showed. The days were passed in hard drilling, and we were really a very proficient corps when the order came to move forward to the Gate Pâ.

This place was celebrated in the earlier part of the war by the crafty and clever escape of the enemy. Gate Pâ was built in the narrowest part, on the neck of the peninsula, and consisted chiefly of underground works, built with no inconsiderable skill. The English troops stormed the place, hurled upon it shot and shell, and finally took it. But on entering Pâ no one was to be seen; the place was literally deserted, not a Maori remained. The whole tribe had vanished, no one knew how or where, yet sentries were posted all around, and declared that not a single native had passed or been seen. The whole thing was a mystery that was never solved.

When we got there we found some of the shells which our men-of-war had thrown into Pâ, unexploded.

The same evening we arrived a sad accident happened owing to the foolish carelessness of some of the men. The captain had told us all to go to the one small inn the place possessed to have a drink after our long and hot march. Some of the men found an unexploded shell as we were returning from the inn, and began to amuse themselves by extracting the powder, placing little heaps of it on the ground and igniting them. A fine, handsome young soldier called Burrows went up to them, warned them that it was dangerous play, and then having lit his pipe, threw the lighted match by accident into the half-emptied shell. There was a frightful explosion, and when the row and smoke died away three men lay on the ground. One was my friend, and I rushed to him, finding, to my great joy, that he was absolutely unhurt, a part of the shell having simply knocked him over as it passed by. The second man was a good deal injured about the shoulders and stomach, and poor Burrows was dead. Half his head was blown off, and pieces from various parts of his body torn out. It was a sickening and horrible sight, those bloody and mutilated remains of what a minute before had been a strong, stalwart man. We laid him in a blanket, and the wounded man in another, and wended our way sadly back to the camp. The next day we were all marched in Tanronga, where we buried our comrade in the cemetery there, with military honours. Then we returned to our tents at Gate Pâ.

Pâ is a very tiny place, the only buildings being a miniature fort fairly well constructed and supplied with ammunition, and the afore-mentioned inn, where, however, you could get nothing to eat, and only beer to drink. Some of the men, particularly the Irishmen, thought this a great hardship, and pined for their dear whiskey.

Many expeditions were sent in boats up the

Waimapu River, with stores to be conveyed to the front. This was always done by night, and was attended with much danger and discomfort. Our work was to convey the stores to a certain point half way to the front, where the principal fighting was going on. So as night came on eight privates, with a sergeant and lieutenant would take our places in a boat, in the bows of which was a mounted gun, loaded. Four men at a time took the oars, which were always muffled, as we could not be too cautious with such a crafty enemy as the Maoris near us. We were all supposed to be sailors that were picked out for this work, but I knew of one who most certainly was not, and didn't know one part of a vessel from another. It generally took us all night to get up the river, and glad enough we were to see the lights from the small fort, and to know help was near, for had we been attacked whilst on the water we ran the pretty certain risk of all being killed before any assistance could reach us.

At the fort was stationed a small body of troops well armed, to protect the stores. We usually remained at the fort for a day's rest, returning in the night to the camp, and starting again the following evening with more stores, and so on until all sent on from Auckland was safely packed away in the fort.

One morning a special parade was called, after which the captain informed us that a company of constabulary with surveyors and engineers were away in front of us surveying roads; they had with them a troop of soldiers to guard them; unfortunately they were running short of stores, and it was necessary that relief should be taken to them as soon as possible. "I will order no man to go," he said, "for it is a most dangerous undertaking to march forty miles through the enemy's country. I will therefore take only volunteers to the number of fifty." He might have had twice that number had he chosen, for we all seemed fired by the chance of excitement. Fifty were quickly chosen, including five corporals, two sergeants, and a lieutenant. My friend and myself went as privates.

Our first work was to reach the afore-mentioned fort, where we procured the necessary supplies, which were packed on horses, of which there were twenty-five. We left the fort at three o'clock in the afternoon, and hoped to reach a very high point of land some twenty miles distant before darkness set in.

The guide, a Scotchman, who had been here before, went first with the lieutenant; then came an advance-guard, followed by the pack-horses, and finally a rear-guard. Gilbert and I were in the rear-guard, by no means the pleasantest position in the world, as we were liable to be cut off from the main body at any moment. It was so dark we could hardly distinguish one another. Strict silence was enjoined, and no smoking allowed. On we groped our way in the gloom and silence, when suddenly the stillness was broken by unearthly and discordant sounds of clattering of hoofs, kicking, and loud cursing. A halt was called, and it was discovered that the disturbance was caused by a young colt, who doubtless, not appreciating the slow, silent mode of proceeding forced upon him, thought he would show us what he could do, just by way of diversion. His first act was to kick down the man who was leading him, and then, by plunging and starting, get rid of the burden on his back with the greatest despatch possible, and, before he could be prevented, bolted away from us with great speed and in the wildest spirits. It was useless to think of going after him, so we were obliged to pack his burden on one or two of the other already overloaded animals; and, seeing the man kicked down was not hurt, only furious with rage against "that d— hoss," we once more proceeded on our silent way.

After two hours had passed, it was discovered that we were off our track. The guide, having fallen asleep whilst walking, had taken us at least three miles out of our way. The darkness was so great that it took us several hours to find the track again, the ground being covered with short bushes. Finally it was discovered, and once more we set off, and marched on until we came to a river, a branch of the Waimapu River. Here we had to unpack all the stores into a boat, and swim the horses over, which was accomplished in safety;

then, re-packing our stores, we partook of a hasty meal consisting of meat, biscuit, and a glass of grog, and, without resting, resumed our march in Indian file as usual. We arrived within sight of "Hancock's Point" about two o'clock, it having taken us half a day and a night to get thus far.

The Point was at the top of a tremendously high peak. The order was given to ascend. As you may imagine, it was no light work, for we had on our full accoutrements, sixty rounds of ammunition, two days' provisions, our blankets, and a heavy Tower rifle.

We began the ascent, and made our way but very slowly, owing to the steepness and the want of a beaten track. The Point loomed up straight before us like some huge and unattainable giant, who seemed to look down on these struggling human flies with calm and cold indifference. On we went, stumbling at every step, clutching at every branch or twig, steadying ourselves against every tree, for full well we knew that if we lost our hold it was all up, for a deep precipice yawned at the bottom; once slip into it, and death would be instantaneous. We were a good three-parts of the way up, when suddenly we received a volley from a band of How-Hows, native rebels, who were lying in ambush, and had doubtless been quietly waiting until we were within range of their rifles. Three of our men were shot, whether killed we could not tell, for they rolled over and over, one I saw rebound several feet into the air, then they disappeared into the abyss below. The horses got wild with terror, and it took half the men to attend to them and prevent their dashing down the mountain side with all the stores on their backs. The remainder of us extended ourselves in skirmishing order, and advanced with caution. The How-Hows had the advantage of us, for they were under shelter, while we were exposed to their view, and they could pick us off at their good pleasure, while we could only fire more or less at random. A second volley—two more men killed, and the horses becoming more frantic. Our lieutenant, who had never been in action before, lost his head and gave the insane order, "Every man to cover," and forthwith ensconced himself behind a large stump of a tree. The trees were few and far between, and the low bushes were but a poor shelter from the foe. We crouched down according to orders, feeling very much as if our death warrant had been passed upon us, for lying here many were sure to be killed, whereas, if we had continued our march, we might by firing have kept the enemy at bay.

For some ten minutes, that seemed like ten days, all was quiet; then the How-Hows let fly a volley in our very midst. Gilbert, and two other men, were lying to my right, close to the rotten stump of a tree. Jack Ward, one of the men, a former mate of my friend's, remarked, "This is hot," when a bullet struck him, took off the top of his skull, scattering his brains all over

Gilbert, and filling his pannikin that was on the top of his kit. "Dunbar," he called to me, "for God's sake, wipe this off! I feel sick!"

I crept over to him on all fours, removed the body of poor Ward, and forced a little grog down my friend's throat. He looked ghastly, and I was afraid at first that he was wounded. That, however, was not the case, and after a few moments he got all right again. Ward was not the only man that we lost, by a good many, owing to the lieutenant's mad order.

Another volley from the enemy—more killed, more wounded, and the horses wild with terror. At this point of affairs, the coloured sergeant, finding the lieutenant had completely collapsed behind his tree, sprang to his feet, shouting, "Now is your time, boys! On to them before they can reload."

We all darted to the bushes, firing as we ran; but on entering the scrub—no one. Again the How-Hows had vanished, leaving no trace behind but one dead man we tumbled over. I sent that one spinning into the precipice to get rid of his ugly phiz.

Such is guerilla fighting.

Our enemy had disappeared as though he had never been, and although we searched all that part, we saw nothing whatever of any one of them.

The How-Hows generally fire from the hip, making sure of killing something or somebody.

In tackling an encampment, they fire first on the ground to get at the sleepers, next volley at a quarter of a minute's interval, a little higher, for the roused men sitting up, and the third volley for the standing men.

Finding all was safe for the time, our lieutenant crawled from behind his stump, and feebly asked if any one was hurt. He was a cowardly cur, and it seemed a pity the How-Hows' bullets had spared him. His former profession was that of a ship's carpenter; but more of him hereafter.

Night coming on, we took possession of the shrubbery deserted by the How-Hows, fastened the horses, and had a meal, of which we stood greatly in need. All but the sentries then rolled themselves up in their blankets, and were soon fast asleep.

I was one of the four sentries placed on guard, one at each corner of the hastily-constructed hut. Our orders were to lie on our stomachs, with full-cocked rifle, and to fire on anything we saw moving, *without* challenging. It was pitch dark, and as I lay flat I fancied I heard a movement behind me, as if some one was crawling on the ground. I listened, rifle in hand; all was still. After a few moments I heard it again. Thinking it might possibly be one of the men, I challenged in a low voice. The object took no notice, but kept crawling closer. It was not more than ten or twelve yards from me now. Again I challenged low, fully determined, if I received no answer, to fire, when I heard a voice faintly whisper, "Don't be a fool; it's me!"

"Me" turned out to be one of the sentries who, feeling frightened and lonely, had risked being shot in order to hear a human creature's voice. I should have been fully justified in shooting him. Luckily for both the man and myself, his little nocturnal visit was not discovered, or both he and I would have got into trouble. In another two hours we were relieved.

At daybreak we started again on our climb upwards to the Point, and after some four hours' struggling through the scrub we began to near our destination. We were disagreeably surprised, as we came within sight of the encampment, to receive a volley of bullets, followed by a second, before we perceived that our lieutenant had neglected to hang out the flag of peace, so the natives who were friendly to us and were protecting our white men at the Point, mistook us for How-Hows.

That little matter rectified, we reached the camp in safety, and were received with the deep joy which starving men give to those who rescue them. The commander, however, was horrified at the smallness of our number, and severely censured our captain for sending such a handful of men through the enemy's country.

After a few hours' rest and some refreshment, we set out on our return journey. The pack-horses being left behind, we got on much faster, reaching the scene of our late conflict in the evening. There being no signs of any How-Hows, we camped there for the night, some of the men, chiefly the large heavy ones, being completely fagged out. The night passed in peace, the enemy doubtless supposing that we would remain at least a night at the Point. At daybreak we were on the march again, taking a new track, which obliged us to scale some very steep mountains—no joke, heavily loaded as we were, and worn out by the last two days' exertions. Some of the men lagged miles behind, in spite of our lieutenant's vigorous cursing at them and threats of punishment.

Being still somewhat thin, I got over the ground very well, while my friend was as fresh as a lark, and actually appeared on parade the morning after our arrival, which I must confess I did not. Some of the men were laid up for weeks, being attacked with a sort of low fever, brought on by exposure and fatigue.

After this expedition to the Point we were sent on no more for the time, but continued at Gate Pâ, passing the days in the usual routine of military life.

At this time the senior captain, Frazer, died at his residence at Tanronga, and we were all marched in to bury him. His body was placed on a gun-carriage and drawn by a party of soldiers to the cemetery. The Archdeacon read the burial service of the Anglican Church over the remains (being well paid for it, no doubt), and the body being consigned to the earth, we fired the regulation volley over the grave, and were then marched back into the town for refreshment previous to our return to Gate Pâ. It was a march from a funeral to an orgie. Most got elevated, not excluding our officers. As is usual on such occasions, the scum rises to the surface, and it was a pitiable spectacle to see our superiors (?) stumbling about, finding a resting-place in a dirty gutter; and, worse still, to hear the language that might have put to the blush a Billingsgate fishman, come from the lips of English soldiers and officers.

I have reason to remember Captain Frazer's funeral, for I nearly lost my friend, who narrowly escaped being killed by our drunken comrades. The few of us who were sober made the attempt, when the hour came, to collect the men in order to march back to Gate Pâ. Unfortunately many of them were so far gone that they only became furious at our interference, and, being armed, some fired and others used their bayonets, until a free fight ensued, during which our efforts to disarm them met with but partial success. Gilbert was in the act of tearing a rifle from the hands of a private, when the man with a stroke of his bayonet cut clean through his cap into his skull, on the very place where, some time before, he had received a similar wound during a riot in Eden Gardens, Calcutta. When I saw him fall I ran to his assistance, kicking aside the brute who was swaying to and fro over him, half-sobered and whimpering, "I say, mate, get up; I didn't mean no hurt."

I lifted him up, and with another man's help carried him to the soldiers' quarters. Before doing so, however, I bound up his head as well as I could with my puggery. It was an ugly gash, and the blood kept oozing through the bandage. The surgeon sewed it up, and though faint from loss of blood, and the pain also, which was severe, the plucky fellow insisted on marching back to camp with the rest of us later on in the evening. I am sorry to say, though, that ever since he is liable to constant attacks of illness that preclude all possibility of his ever doing much head work.

Some weeks after the death of Captain Frazer we received orders to move some miles further on to the front, where the chief fighting was going on, and where we had been told our work would be varied by constructing roads. So behold us one morning, having been supplied with all requisite tools for road-making, marching on loaded like pack-horses, having, in addition to our usual *impedimenta*, bars, axes, shovels, spades and picks.

" John Brown's body lies a-mouldering in the grave,
But his soul goes marching on,"

was chanted more vigorously than euphoniously, ably accompanied by the squeaking and rumbling of the wheelbarrows, one of which I trundled along filled with our rifles. I must say that we were at this time a most creditable body of soldiers, had been well drilled, and were in excellent condition. No wonder we felt quite veterans, and shouted lustily—

"We'll hang Jef Davis on a sour apple tree," &c.

On we went, over the sandy roads, or, more strictly speaking, tracks, mere sheep tracks most of them, now in a compact body, now in Indian file, which last style of marching we much affected. Turning to the left we crossed a plain, on the other side of which was a camp of the militia, composed of settlers, under the command of a Captain Tovey, a one-eyed veteran; but I'll say this for him, his one small grey eye made up in sharpness and cunning for any two eyes of an ordinary man. We only stopped for a few minutes to allay our thirst, then on again to the edge of a swamp covered with beautiful rushes and shrubs. The Rapu, similar to our English bulrush, the Typha latifolia, and the New Zealand flax (Farmium tenax). I deserted my barrow in order to observe these shrubs more closely. We crossed the swamp in an easterly direction, and very weary work it was, and having traversed it found ourselves at the foot of a steep bluff. This we were obliged to mount. The summit of it was quite level, forming what the Californians call a Mesa Land. On the other side of this bluff ran the Waimapu River. We hastily pitched our tents on the neck of the Mesa, as hastily took some refreshment, for so tired and jaded were we from our long and fatiguing march that we only longed for rest.

All could not, however, seek "Balmy slumber, sweet repose," for we were obliged to keep our weather eye wide open, the hostile How-Hows being known to have a partiality for this place. So sentries were posted, silence enjoined, all lights extinguished, and those men not on duty rolled themselves in their blankets and slept as only tired men can.

The next day the camp quickly assumed its usual orderly appearance, and we began to make a road right across the swamp, in order to facilitate the bringing up of heavy guns, military stores, &c. This road-making was not altogether unpleasant work. There were some disagreeablenesses, such as wading into the swamp to cut down the hard manntean bushes, which were used to form supports for the road, and were covered with sand, which we excavated for that purpose from the side of the hill. Our orders from the captain were as follows: "Keep moving, my boys, keep busy, let there be no actual idleness, for Tovey (the captain of the militia) has his eye on us. Still, don't overwork yourselves."

Needless to say, we took his advice, yet we did very good work, and felt a real pride in the fine road that soon began to cross the swamp. In our leisure hours we built ourselves huts, thatched with needles from the rapu rushes. Gilbert, another man, and myself constructed a fine little house on the summit of the Mesa overhanging the river. We slung up three bunks and lived there very comfortably, having a most beautiful view of the Waimapu River and the surrounding country. Nor were we entirely without sport. The wild duck abounded there, and we often made a raid upon them, for they were by no means to be despised as an addition to our ordinary rations. Fish, too, were very plentiful in the river, vast numbers of kauai (pronounced cow-eye) came up with the tide. When the tide falls they return to the sea, observing which we took good care to be on the spot when they arrived, and welcomed them warmly, as they were very good to eat, and had a most delicate flavour.

Of course we had our usual parade, picket and sentry duties to perform, for the How-Hows had a trick of appearing when least expected, and kept us always on the *qui vive*. But altogether we had a very good time of it, and were just busy enough to banish *ennui*. Some of the men would sometimes steal out of the camp at night, cross the country to the Gate Pâ in order to procure whiskey, and would be back again before parade, the love of drink overcoming all fears of the enemy or dread of punishment. One of these men, an Irishman called Murphy, commonly known as "Spud Murphy," a truly comical scoundrel, would return sometimes very drunk, and on reaching the top of the Mesa would let himself roll over and over into the river, where he would swim about until sober, "cooling himself off," as he graphically expressed it—a very necessary operation. That he never came to any harm on his dangerous nocturnal walks can only be explained by a belief in the old proverb, "Providence protects children and drunkards."

One dark night I was on guard on the neck of the Mesa, and after passing the usual hours on duty was glad enough when I was relieved, and turned into the guard hut to enjoy a pipe before going in to my own shanty. The sergeant was there, and he and I were chatting *sotto voce*, when suddenly he rose up, saying: "I must go and look after that confounded sentry to the right, he has not passed for the last ten minutes, the wretch must be asleep or dead."

"Wait, I'll go with you," I cried; and, seizing our rifles, we hurried out.

At the place where the sentry of that point was supposed to be keeping watch we could discover no one, and it was not until we had poked about in the dark for no inconsiderable time that we discovered our friend "Spud Murphy" lying under a bush fast asleep and gloriously drunk.

The sergeant took away his rifle, rolling him over with his foot as he did so, but Murphy was not disturbed by such a trifle, and only gave a prolonged and triumphant snore as his head settled more comfortably in a tuft of grass. I begged the sergeant to say nothing about it, and to let me go on duty in "Spud's" place. After some hesitation he consented, and I began pacing up and down in the darkness waiting for Murphy to awake. After about an hour he did so, and, missing his rifle, was in a great fright.

"Oh, holy Vargin," he prayed, coming towards me, "only but show me whereiver I placed me rifle, and niver again will I touch whiskey, the evil cratur."

It was very dark, and he was very drunk, but even so to take me for the Virgin was, to say the least of it, odd, and I hardly knew whether I felt more embarrassed at the implied compliment, or wounded in my *amour propre* at being taken for a woman.

"Keep silence, you idiot!" I whispered to him, seizing him by the collar of his shirt, and shaking him with a force that effectually proved to him that he was in no woman's grip. "Go into the guard-house. A nice mess you've got yourself into!"

Thoroughly alarmed, he stole into the hut, where I joined him when my self-imposed watch was over, and begged the sergeant not to report him, as no harm was done, and no one knew of it but our three selves. The sergeant pretended to refuse to give in for a long time, but finally, having reduced poor "Spuds" to a limp state of abject misery, he consented to pass it over.

Such conduct on the part of a sentry deserves the most rigorous punishment, the lives of so many being dependent on his vigilance. Murphy did not make us repent of our lenience towards him, as although I cannot say he never touched the "cratur" again, he certainly never did when on duty.

On another occasion, after we had all retired to rest, and the entire camp was wrapped in silence and darkness, we were all disturbed in the middle of the night by the sharp report of a rifle. In a very short space of time we were all under arms, fully expecting an engagement with the enemy, ever ubiquitous, yet seldom seen. What resolutions to perform heroic deeds sprang suddenly into our martial breasts! How many undeveloped heroes stood side by side, determining at all hazards to win their laurels, to exterminate by various acts of transcendent bravery these cannibalistic savages who even now were preparing to pour their deadly fire upon us! What nodding of heads à la Jupiter! What metaphorical clapping of wings! What compressing of lips—lips somewhat pale, it is true—but then the night air produces sometimes strange effects! And after all, it was but a false alarm, a "schiser," as gold miners say. One of the sentries being a little under the influence of the "cratur," mistook a bush for a Maori, "both being black," as he explained, and having more valour than discretion, fired accordingly. Before discharging his gun, however, he drew out his bayonet and cast it aside. Why? Ah! that remains a mystery unsolved to the present day: he either could not or would not give an explanation of so singular a performance. The whole corps stood there armed and ready for action, called up by his over-zeal; so having not even one cold native to show up for breakfast, our sentry looked rather foolish, and muttering something to the effect that he could not help it, if the "darned bush looked as black as a darned Maori," slunk back to his interrupted duty.

We, on the other hand, gathered ourselves up, feeling at least one cubit higher in stature for all the Maoris we had not killed, and with a glow of pride burning within us, returned to bed.

The wonderful and intimate knowledge "some of ours" displayed in the use of firearms was a marvellous sight to see. Another private, the greatest—no, I will not say the word—I will only say the most fearfully nervous man I ever came across—had a sort of Maori-phobia, and on the night of our false alarm, having the advantage of standing near Somers, I observed him with great interest and no little wonder. In a *fearful* state of excitement, he crammed cartridge upon cartridge into his rifle until the poor thing could hold no more.

"I'll have a shot at the black brutes anyhow," he said to me, his teeth rattling in his head, and his whole body trembling violently.

"You had better keep your bones quiet," I said, rather wickedly, "for the How-Hows can hear the breathing of a fly."

" Black devils, I'll—I'll——Oh, what's that?" howled my brave comrade, his eyes opening so wide that I really feared for him or them, while his hair standing up with fright gave him a weird and awful look. I have never before or since seen any one terror-struck, literally beside himself with fear.

"It's nothing," I replied to his cry, "only the sentry returning to his duty. But, Somers, the How-Hows are not black, they are a lovely clear brown, and are by a long shot better built men than we Europeans."

Somers gave a grunt of disgust, and with the words, "Brown or black, they are worse than the devil," sought his bunk like the rest of us. The next day, at the roll call, he did not answer, having absconded at daybreak. Some time afterwards I met him in Auckland, selling riding whips in the streets. What a work it was unloading his rifle!

A dozen more privates were sent over from Gate Pâ to increase our little body. Among the new comers I recognized a man who had played me a scurvy trick back in my Shortland days. It had happened thus: the episode is worth relating, although I go back to that horrible time with considerable repugnance.

One dreadful day, dreadful only to such a starving unfortunate as I was then, for the weather was simply perfect, I was roaming about like a certain gentleman (sable as to his exterior) seeking what I might devour. Suddenly a cheery voice hailed me, "I say, Auld Misery, will yer gie us a han' wi' this 'ere chist?"

I turned and saw a decently-dressed man standing by the side of a seaman's chest. Without further parley I took one end of his box, and he the other, and between us we managed to carry, drag, haul, and pull it on board a sloop which lay high and dry on the beach, waiting for the incoming tide.

"Here, tek this, and do for the Lord's sake git yersell a blow-out, for yer doant look human," he said, giving me five shillings. Feeling quite rich, I did allow myself a meal, and then started for Auckland, hoping to obtain some employment there. This cost me two shillings, one for the dinner—fearful extravagance!—and one for a lift on the long journey to the town. I therefore had three shillings left, which I calculated would last me three weeks. Lodging *al fresco* cost nothing, and light meals are conducive to quiet repose.

I reached Auckland, and going to a newspaper office, requested permission to look over the advertisements, in the hope of finding an engagement suitable for me. While so employed I heard a man telling the editor a long and highly-coloured yarn about the gold-mines at the Thames, how many miners were at work, the heavy wages given—in fact, showing that everything was flourishing, and depicting a little paradise of prosperity, wealth, and happiness.

"Draw it mild, my friend," I said, going up to

the enthusiastic talker, " I am a miner myself, and I have just come from the Thames. My experience is that all the mines, with the exception of three or four outside Shortland, are ' bust up,' and hundreds of men are out of work."

" All bosh and gammon!" cried the man ; " why, I will employ any number of men I can get ; aye, and pay them £2 10s. a week. I want them, I do."

" Will you take me, and pay me that amount ? " I asked.

" Most certainly I will, and what is more, will take you over to Shortland in my boat on Wednesday next ; but mind, you must pay your passage."

" Agreed ! " said I ; " I will pay you out of the first wages you give me ; and pray where shall I find you on Wednesday ? "

" I lodge at the ' When-you-Appear ' Hotel ; my name is Jones. Ask for Captain Jones. Good morning."

Having nothing better to do, I went off to find the " When-you-Appear " Hotel. No one could direct me. Some grinned, some laughed outright. At length, by mere accident, I came in front of a largish building, with the name " Winyard Pier " Hotel written over it in immense letters.

" I've been done brown by a Jones, at a temperature of 212 Fahr.," I muttered to myself, as I entered the bar room.

" I say, boss," I called out, " does Captain Jones lodge here ? "

"Captain Jones! Let me see. A Captain Jones was here some months ago. A rum cuss, sure enough. I heard that he sailed for the west coast yesterday; gone to Taranaki, I think."

"Are you sure that he sailed?" I asked.

"Oh!" was the answer, "no one is sure of Captain Jones. Why do you ask?"

I mildly suggested that a balloon would be the most appropriate means to reach that country, whereat "mine host" haw-hawed vigorously, and colonial fashion insisted that I should have a drink. Nothing loth, I drank the ale, and felt revived, for the beer was good; then I left the hotel in a mixed state of mind between gratitude for this slight kindness and the desire to punch Captain Jones's head.

So now, seeing this worthy among the volunteer privates, I went up to him. "Ah! *Captain* Jones, I think? How about the numbers of miners you needed to work the gold at £2 10s. a week?"

"Were you one that I had promised it to?" asked the rogue, quite unabashed; "I promised it to so many (in a tone as if he had acted most generously) that I really forget their faces."

"Well, I promised myself that if ever I came across you again I'd punch your head," I remarked, suiting the action to the words, and sending "Captain Jones" to embrace Mother Earth. The poor wretch was so weak from starvation and misery, that having knocked him down, I felt compelled to help him up again, and see that he was taken care of. In a very short time he became an excellent soldier and a good comrade, although always apt to draw the long bow. One glorious morning we were on dress parade, making a fine show in our picturesque costume, when for a little change we were ordered to fire a few rounds. Some of the men, as I have before hinted, were better known for their zeal than for their knowledge of arms. I was standing side by side with my friend, when the man in his rear suddenly raised his rifle, fired, and missed shooting Gilbert by a hair's breadth.

"What are you about, you blasted fool!" cried my friend, with pardonable indignation, as he set his cap straight, that the air from the passage of the bullet had blown aside. The private seemed rather disappointed that his shot had not done some greater execution, and boasted tremendously of the near shave Gilbert had had.

And now our military career draws to a close. Our lieutenant, the same worthy who had shown himself so wise and brave when we went to carry provisions to the Point, having come across a deserted settler's house, had given orders that the furniture therein should be carried to his own hut, in order that he might be more comfortable, and arguing that he was quite justified in so doing, as all that district was in military occupation, and therefore everything found there might be used by the officers and men. However, a great row was made about the matter; it was reported to headquarters with a good deal of exaggeration, and the upshot of it was that we were recalled.

We knew well enough that the real reason was, that so many troops quartered in different parts of the country were a heavy expense to the Government, and the road having been made, troops could in case of need more easily get to the scene of action. The enemy, too, appeared to have deserted this part, or so we were told, although we were always coming across them, and knew that they were only waiting an opportunity to massacre the whites. However, one excuse is as good as another, and this one was gladly seized hold of by the authorities to "reduce the expenditure."

It was not without regret that we dismantled our huts, and turned our backs on the Mesa, where we had been so happy. We marched along the fine road we had made, paused to salute the one-eyed captain of the militia, who leered at us horribly, and seemed to find the reason given for our recall a source of infinite amusement, for we left him grinning from ear to ear, in spite of the angry face of our captain, who naturally did not see the joke, and resented Tovey's untimely mirth.

On we marched to Tanronga, thence by easy stages to Auckland, and finally to Shortland, which town we entered in grand style, and in such good trim that it was difficult to believe we were the same body of ragged starving creatures who had left some months before. We were not disbanded at once, being ordered to do military duty until our pay came. Every one made a great deal of us, and treated us in fact as though we were veteran heroes of a thousand fights. To hear some of the men talk you would imagine that to kill Maoris was the daily occupation, and that we were always steeped in the blood of the rebel How-Hows. " Captain Jones " in particular had some wonderful adventures that he was never tired of relating. I heard him once, when he did not know I was near, and really it was as good as a romance of the stirring deeds of ancient days. I marvelled at the fellow's imagination. When I tackled him the next day, and asked him how he ventured to concoct such a tissue of lies, he said with a wink and a grin, " Those gulls would swaller anything; they likes it, it pays me, and besides, it might have 'appened!"

Many a hero has no better foundation for his glorious fame, so let me too clap my wings and cry, " Cock-a-doodle-doo."

Pay-day came, and with our pockets well lined, and some complimentary words from our captain, Gilbert and I turned our backs on the armoury, and ceased to be members of the First Hauraki Rifle Volunteer Corps.

III.—AUSTRALIA AND 'FRISCO.

Sic transit gloria—Tuesday! It was on the third day of the week that Gilbert Jenkins, Dane

Stuart, and myself ceased to be members of the First Hauraki Rifle Volunteer Corps, as the Government, being eager to cut down expenses, had seized upon a misdemeanour of our lieutenant's as a sufficient excuse to recall and disband us. It was not without real regret that we laid aside our picturesque costume—it was so becoming—bade good-bye to our captain, who was a true, good fellow, and turned our backs on our soldier life. We each had a good round sum of money in our pockets, and having determined not to separate we adjourned to a neighbouring tavern, called for ale and sat down to a "palaver" concerning our future plans. I was the patriarch, and, like many patriarchs, was far more ignorant than my younger comrades. We talked long and earnestly, and with the gravity befitting the occasion, weighed the boot trade against the book shop, the butchering business against the baker's, the bush life against the costermonger's, and so on. Two hours' hard and heavy talk brought no results beyond formidable appetites.

"What shall we do?" cried Dane in despair, brushing up his sandy locks until they stood upright, giving him a comical resemblance to a Scotch terrier.

"Eat," said Gilbert, dryly, disgusted that so much talk should lead to so little result.

We followed his sage advice, and with eating, a luminous idea occurred to me. Yes, I can take all the credit of the notion to myself; indeed, as it failed, neither of the others would thank me to name them as instigator of the plan that turned three late privates of the First Hauraki Rifle Volunteer Corps into pedlars! At the time, however, it seemed to promise well. We put our money together, and rented for a small sum a vacant house outside Auckland. The house was very much out of repair, the doors in most rooms being conspicuous by their absence, and those that were there could never by any amount of coaxing or force be induced to move an inch either way, from the half-opened position in which they had been placed. True, it saved us the trouble of opening and shutting them, nor were we ever driven to frenzy by their banging in a high wind. The windows—well, there were window-frames, and there had been panes of glass, but here, as in old England, a deserted house is an irresistible target for every passing boy to have a shy at, and judging by the holes, some of them were good shots, so the panes were few and far between. Still, the four walls of the house and the roof were solid and water-tight, and we neither of us felt anything but a pride in our mansion. Was it not our own? We very quickly got the absolute necessaries, turning aside with Spartan firmness from the smallest of luxuries, and installing ourselves in state one evening, had another two hours' hard and heavy talk on the "stock" we thought most likely to sell, and having settled that knotty point retired to rest with hopeful hearts, all undaunted by past experiences, and in merciful ignorance of future troubles.

The verb "to sell" can be conjugated in many different ways; we were not long in finding that grammatical fact out. The stock we bought had been guaranteed by a fairly honest tradesman; not that we trusted to him entirely. No, we put our common sense also to bear on the subject; nevertheless, we failed, which looks as though the common sense of the three of us, and the guarantee of the fairly honest tradesman, were no match for the wiles and wickednesses of the people of Auckland. Certain it is that we laboured much, and talked more, peddling our goods through the country, but all to no avail. We were afraid of the women. I think they saw that and took unmerciful advantage. They would help themselves, paying what they chose, and treated us generally as though we were two (one of us always stayed in our house to look after things and cook the dinner) nicely-spoken, harmless imbeciles. So we found the goods going out and no money coming in. The wandering through the country was very pleasant, and one picture of marvellous beauty remains in my memory even in that scenery where all was lovely.

It was Dane's turn to stay in the house, so Gilbert and I set out "dock digging," as it is called. We were not in very good spirits, for we saw, although we had not yet acknowledged it to each other, that our present trade was a failure, so we jogged on in somewhat gloomy silence. It was a perfect day, neither too hot nor too cold, and as we went on through the balmy air, and noted the luxuriant growth of trees and flowers, our hearts grew lighter, our tongues unloosened, and we admitted to each other that we had been "sold" once more, and it would be wiser to try some other line of life before our last pound was swallowed up in our present losing business.

So we stepped on more briskly, and in turning the corner of a lane we came upon a most wonderfully beautiful sight. Picture to yourself a cloudless blue sky, a golden sunlight, green and profuse vegetation, and under the shade of an immense tree a small cottage, entirely covered with the scarlet passion-tree. It was in full bloom, and these marvellous flowers peeped in at the windows and over the door, and twined themselves around the chimney, and even threw out tendrils to the overhanging branches of the tree above. To complete the picture a young half-caste Maori woman, superbly made and of rare beauty, stood at the door, her only clothing a piece of white linen around her waist, which did not hide the graceful contours of her shapely limbs. As she stood there, in the act of picking a branch of the passion flower, her pose was so graceful, her beauty so striking, that all the artist spirit rushed back upon me, and I would have given a kingdom for a canvas, brush, and colours. The Queen of Sheba was a dairy-wench compared to this soft-eyed, lovely

Maori maiden; and even ox-eyed Juno would have been put aside in her presence.

So our last " dock digging " expedition has always remained in our memories with pleasure, for having decided to abandon that noble profession, we lost no time in selling what the women had kindly left us of our " stock " to the self-same fairly honest tradesman from whom we had purchased it. He asked how we had got on, and having extracted various details from us as to our manner of selling, &c., gave vent to his feelings by a shrill whistle that would not have disgraced a steam-engine or a schoolboy.

It does not take long in this country to turn from one trade to another, or to free yourself from the encumbrance of a house. Our arrangements were quickly made, and with the money left us from our unlucky attempt at "peddling," we resolved to try our fortunes in Australia. There, at least, we could procure food by hunting, and live retired in the bush, "away from the world's cold strife," which, by the bye, is all bosh. One has quite as much anxiety there as everywhere else on the surface of this fractious, fretful little earth of ours.

We went into the town of Auckland, that beautiful city, where all is beautiful, but one gets heartily sick of so much beauty with *res angustæ domi*, and taking our passages on board a sailing vessel, landed without accident or adventure in Sidney, New South Wales. Beautiful city too, but I recollect it best by the fact that we were nearly devoured by the hotel "tooters," who pursued us all over the town, hoping to make some money out of us, for we were all three well dressed, and carried ourselves with the soldierly bearing learnt during our life as privates in the First Hauraki Rifle Volunteer Corps. So the "tooters" had their labour in vain, for, as the Yankees say, "we could not be did." Baffled and disgusted, they at last got weary of following and pestering us, and slunk off one by one in search of easier prey.

We finally got lodgings in Erskine Street, near the wharf, and looked out for a boat bound for Melbourne. We were not long in finding what we wanted, and having secured our berths, went on board the dirty, dingy little vessel, feeling fairly hopeful as to our future.

A few days after we landed in Melbourne, another beautiful city, but one whose ostentations and pompous show of wealth is somewhat crushing to the hundreds of poor, homeless, penniless exiles who throng her portals in search of food and shelter.

Dane Stuart had an aunt living in Melbourne. I, too, had relations there, but we neither of us made any attempt to visit them. *Cui bono?* We had passed out of their lives, they out of ours. For my own part I shrank from the sorrowful memories this city brought back to me, and drove away the fast recurring thoughts of the *Hurricane*, wrecked within sight of land, carrying down with her all I possessed in the world.

We were all three eager to begin our new life, so only remained in Melbourne long enough to procure tent, rifles, blankets, knives, and some other things absolutely necessary for bush life. This done we packed up our baggage and migrated to Lillydale, a town about twenty miles north of Melbourne, with nothing of note to mark it from any other ordinary town. From thence we journeyed on foot near to the Dandenmy Mountains, which abounded in game of all sorts and sizes, kangaroos, bears, opossums, &c., &c. Our first capture was a great rat, which we thought was a bandicoot. Now the bandicoot is the best of all the bush "varmin" to eat. So our joy was great as we skinned him, prepared him for the spit, and roasted him before a clear wood fire just outside our tent. We ate him with great complacency, and could not sufficiently admire the exquisite flavour and great delicacy and tenderness of his white flesh. We determined to keep our eyes open and try and catch some more of the same species.

A day or two afterwards a sporting gentleman passed by our camp, and seeing the skin and head of the animal nailed up to dry, questioned us about it.

"It's a bandicoot that my friend shot the other day; we kept the skin because it is so handsome, but we ate the brute, and very good he was," I answered, a faint doubt springing up into my mind as to whether he was so very good after all.

"Faugh!" cried the sportsman, "why you've eaten a beastly bush rat, and found it very good. Ha! ha! ha!" His laugh had all the melody of a sow undergoing the operation of having its teeth filed. No matter—it was not the last queer thing we devoured, and we had also learnt the difference between a bandicoot and a bush rat—a good thing in its way. No harm was done, for our stomachs made no difficulty in digesting the mistake.

Our next exploit was shooting a bear. The particular species that live in these mountains are very curious animals. They are not bigger than a large dog, brown in colour, with rather a pointed muzzle, and their paws and feet provided with very terrible claws. On the whole they are quiet, harmless brutes, and make good and affectionate pets. Gilbert and I discovered one high up in a tree, lying at full length sunning himself and lazily licking his paws. We forthwith opened fire upon him. Our first shots took no effect; I think he winked. Thirty shots, that is to say, thirty times we fired at him, still no change in his attitude of unruffled composure. At last in despair I went back to the tent for a rifle, with which Gilbert brought him down dead at the first shot. The day before had been very wet, and pools stood about everywhere on the sodden ground. Into one of these pools Mr. Bruin fell with a flop, covering us with mud and water from head to foot. But the joy consequent on our victory overbalanced all such trifling inconveniences. We cut a long and strong stick, slung our prize upon it, and went on our way rejoicing, seeking other conquests. Soon we lost our way, having neglected to mark our passage by notching the trees as we went along. We wandered on and on, neither finding anything to kill, nor our lost road either. Night began to descend upon us. We were in a regular fix, for we were hungry, the ground was wet, and we had not even a blanket with us. Sheer weariness at last forced us to call a halt, and we determined, bush fashion, to "make a camp." Choosing a large tree whose thick branches had somewhat protected the soil beneath from the rain, we hastily collected wood, and stripping the leaves from the branches, soon lighted a fire, around which we crouched, and wished for day. But a couple of hours of this warm but cheerless comfort was enough for Gilbert, who had doggedly set his mind on finding the right track, and the moon having risen, we left our fire—somewhat to my regret, I must confess—and shouldering our *bête-noir*, set out once more. Very shortly we stumbled right upon a road, but here was another difficulty—which way ought we to go to reach our tent, to the right or to the left? The bush is all so much alike, and we had been foolish enough to leave our compass in the camp. Not that it would have been much good to us, for, having so lately settled down, and never intending to wander far as yet, we had taken no notes as to where we had encamped with regard to the town. Once at Lillydale or on the road, we knew we should eventually reach our tent, as it lay in a straight line. Undecided, we spent some minutes, I in trying to prove that the right must be right, and Gilbert voting with equal vehemence that the left was sure to be right. We were just going to settle the knotty point by tossing up a penny when we saw the gleam of a fire in the distance.

Leaving Gilbert sitting on Mr. Bruin to watch by the road, I started off in the direction of the fire, hoping to find a camp of wood-cutters who could direct us. But on reaching the spot I found it deserted. A party of men must have been there but a short time before, for the fire burnt brightly, and there were relics that showed they had cooked their supper there. Nothing eatable remained, though I searched carefully, hoping to find if only a bit of biscuit with which we might still the imperious cries of our empty interiors.

So I returned to Gilbert, whom I found in the same posture, nearly asleep in spite of his hunger. We had another consultation, which resulted like the first—in nothing but talk. We were again going to have recourse to the mystic aid of " heads or tails," when we heard the clanking of a horse's hoofs coming towards us.

We sprang out upon the road, and, stopping the horseman, inquired the way to Lillydale. The man simply pointed behind him, and digging his spurs into his horse's flanks, vanished from our sight like a flash of lightning. He was evidently in great terror at seeing two men with firearms, and suspected that we were two of a band of bushrangers, such gentry being not uncommon in these parts.

Again we shouldered our bear, and dragged on wet, weary, and horribly tired. Bruin seemed to get heavier and heavier, but we were too proud of him to leave him behind, and had not sufficient *nous* to skin it, so we endured all sorts of discomfort for the sake of this, our first big prize.

After what seemed to us a long and toilsome way, we were suddenly agreeably surprised to hear close by us a "coo-ēē" in Dane's shrill, clear voice. A few steps more around a clump of bushes, and there we were at our camp. Stuart had been very uneasy at our prolonged absence, had imagined all sorts of evils, and had pictured every possible and impossible accident as having "arrived" to us, as the French say. Unable to sleep, he had prowled around the tent, a prey to the most lugubrious thoughts, when he heard our voices, and, as I said before, "coo-ēēd" to us both loud and long.

How rejoiced we were to get in, dead beat, and as hungry as Arctic wolves! We left the skinning of our bear until we had had the rest of which we stood in great need, placing him, however, inside our tent for safety's sake.

A few days after we moved our camp further into

the mountains, to a place called "The Two Sisters," a savage, wild, but lovely spot, that kept one always in a state of rapturous wonder at the ever new, ever varying beauties of nature. Immense quantities of kangaroos lived there, and it was a curious and interesting sight to see a band of them go bounding along in "Indian file" at an incredible pace. The females are called "flying does," from the speed at which they travel, more resembling a bird than an animal. It is very pretty to see the little ones with their heads poking out of their mother's pouch, looking out into the world with large, soft, wondering eyes.

One morning Gilbert called me to come out from the tent where I was cooking our breakfast. On going out I joined him on a small hillock, from whence we saw a very astonishing sight. A "mob" of kangaroos, comprising some hundreds, were crossing the country. They were headed by a deer, who acted as general of the forces, and whose leadership they all followed. On went the deer with stately, graceful movements, and after followed the kangaroos, springing and bounding in the most grotesque manner imaginable. We fairly laughed aloud, and watched them until their "general" led them out of our sight. Whether the deer continues to live with the herd after having piloted them in safety across the country I do not know, but strange as it appears, the fact remains that the kangaroos prefer the guidance of a deer to one of their own tribe.

Some very unpleasant ants, about an inch long, also lived near us; their sting is very painful, and their tenacity in sucking blood, and never letting go, has gained for them the name of "bulldogs." Their habits and customs among themselves are said to be interesting to study. I confess I preferred to give them a wide berth, and the only anxiety I displayed was to kill as many as possible. Scorpions, centipedes, and iriantilopes also abounded; the latter is a giant spider, who seemed to possess the misanthropical character of his European brothers to a great degree. His sting is also very painful, and one generally avoids his advances to a nearer acquaintance, particularly as he possesses no great beauty to attract one to him. The sting of the scorpion every one knows is very agonizing, but here they are not necessarily fatal.

At night various members of the above insect races, accompanied by cousins and friends, would crawl, creep, or fly into our tent, get upon us, and proceed to inspect our anatomy with exhaustive care. I discovered that by not vexing them, *i.e.*, flinging the arms about, and using forcible language (to which latter insult they appeared to have a great objection), they would not molest us, but after crawling cautiously over any part of us that happened to be uncovered, would make tracks elsewhere, their curiosity satisfied, leaving us secretly glad at their departure.

I must not forget to mention the snakes, which

GUM TREES.

were infinite in number, snaky in their habits, which I suppose is not astonishing, and most of them poisonous. But of these our natural enemies I will speak more fully when we get to the Yarra-Yarra River.

Here at "The Two Sisters" we lived a real Bohemian life under the shade of the great Eucalypti. I use the plural, as there was a great variety of species. Here, too, are varieties of pines, and I think among them the Sequoia Gigantia, that celebrated giant pine of California, reported to be the biggest tree in the world. This, however, is a mistake, for some of the Australian Eucalypti (gum-trees) far exceed them in height, and are quite as large in other respects.

To a "new chum" the varieties of the gum-trees are often a matter of perplexity and much wonder. The red gum, whose wood never rots, the white and the blue, which latter is largely planted in California; then there are the peppermint, the box, the apple, the stringy bark, the iron bark, the bull's wood, and so on *ad infinitum*. These, like all the Australian trees that I am acquainted with, are evergreens, of rather a dusky, sombre hue, and have an aromatic smell, which, besides being very pleasant, tends to repel disease, and renders the living among them healthy and invigorating. The foliage of the Eucalypti, like that of the majority of their compatriots, is placed vertically. I mean the edge of the leaf is towards the branch on which it grows, which is occasioned by a slight twist in the petioli; they shed their bark annually, and not their leaves, which are constantly growing and constantly dropping off.

From the gum-trees one is led naturally to speak of opossums, a genus of marsupiate carnivorous mammals, as the dictionary tells us. Vast numbers surrounded us; they would leave their holes at night to feed on leaves, climbing the trees for that purpose, and after a while, wishing to vary their repast, would descend to the earth and nibble at fresh grass or any other dainty herb they could meet with. For cleverness in thieving, give me an opossum. We found to our cost that they much loved potatoes, while bread put them into ecstatic raptures. I wonder where they got their taste for it, for Mrs. Opossum can know nothing of bread-making. They would walk into our tent at night cool and confident, seeking what they might devour, and although they generally fell victims to their kleptomaniac tendencies, that did not in the least deter others from trying the same game, with the same results.

We killed immense numbers of these "marsupiate carnivorous mammals," many by snares, more by shooting them through the head with a very small bullet. Gilbert was extremely skilful, and never a 'possum escaped his shot. We would all three of us go out on a moonlight night, for 'possums are sentimental, and love to "pose" by the light of the Queen of the Heavens, and station ourselves each one on the shady side of a large gum-tree. Looking up through the branches, we were sure to see one or more, sometimes a whole family stretched out, I was going to say " sunning " themselves in the moonlight, for they looked as though the rays of the moon were as pleasant to them as the rays of the sun is to a cat. We would then pick them off one by one with a rifle; down they fall dead, and when cold were skinned, and the skins dried. This was done by pegging the skin flesh side out, like Brian O'Lynne's breeches. These same skins, when properly prepared and sewn together, make very fine rugs, being both light and warm—one seven feet square weighing only five pounds—and on that account are invaluable to hunters and bushmen. We often got thirty skins in one night, both Stuart and I being fair shots, while Gilbert's aim was certain death. Great skill is requisite in shooting them, for if wounded anywhere except in the head the pelt is of no value.

The flying-squirrel has also a beautiful coat that fetches a good price in the fur market. We got many of them, shooting them as they sprang from tree to tree. They leap an amazing distance, being supported by the skin stretching between their fore and hind feet. I saw a handsome little fellow one day high up in a gum-tree; he wanted to get to another tree some distance off, and was evidently not quite sure whether he could manage it. He seemed to measure the distance with his eye, ran to the extreme tip of the branch he was on, then back again. Gilbert and I watched him with interest.

"I tell you what," said my friend, addressing the squirrel, who was undecidedly scratching his head, "if you jump that I won't shoot you, but if you funk it I will."

That decided our little friend: giving us a long side glance from his beautiful sharp eyes, he swayed himself a moment to and fro, then paf! in one graceful, mighty leap he shot across the immense space between the two trees, and alighted safely on a branch. We could not help crying "Bravo!" to the brave little leaper, who, hearing us shout, disappeared swiftly high up in the tree.

Skins of all sorts, and from every kind of animal, we prepared simply by drying. When we had amassed a large quantity of them Stuart took them into Melbourne to sell.

We wished him at the same time to see a doctor, for he was not at all strong, and gave way to fits of melancholy and irritation sad to see in so young a man. We made him promise also to see his aunt. At this time we knew nothing of his past life, for, although we had lived together many months, he had not been communicative concerning himself, the freemasonry of good birth only drawing us three together.

Gilbert and I passed the days of his absence in the usual way, killing many 'possums and other "varmin," and looking forward to a nice round sum of money from the furrier at Melbourne. But some ten days after Dane returned with a much smaller sum than we had been led to expect, as the skins were all good and properly prepared. We were told afterwards by an old settler that we should have manufactured them into rugs ourselves, for which we would have been handsomely paid.

"Did you go to your aunt?" I asked, as, having spoken of the furs, Stuart seated himself in the corner of the tent, and proceeded to smoke in gloomy silence.

"Yes," was the encouraging answer.

"Wasn't she nice?" demanded Gilbert; "didn't you give her those best opossum skins? I should have thought they would have softened the heart of any living woman."

"She was very kind to me, and wishes me to live with her," was the unexpected answer.

"By Jove!" cried Gilbert. "What reply did you give to such an astonishing request?"

"I said not yet," answered Dane, more to himself than to us, as he pushed his rough sandy hair back from his brow—a trick of his when at all perplexed or annoyed.

"Well, at any rate it's nice to know that you have a place you can go to if you are not strong enough for bush life," I said; when to our surprise he started to his feet and cried passionately, "I'm as strong as either of you, and can bear bush life better; but if you want to be rid of me, I can go and camp alone."

"Don't be a fool!" said Gilbert, before I could find my tongue; "you had better have supper and go to bed; there's nothing like a sleep to chase away the blue devils. Did you see a doctor?"

"Yes."

"Well?"

"What?"

"What did he say? Why it's harder to drag words out of you than to get gold out of a gold mine," said Gilbert, impatiently.

Dane Stuart gave a short laugh as he answered, "You won't be much the wiser than I am by the idiot's opinion. He told me I might live or I might die, and on my suggesting that every one was in the same box, he further added that while there was life there was hope." Seeing that Stuart either could not or would not say anything more on the subject of himself and his health, I turned the conversation, and no further reference was made to him.

But I began to observe him more closely, and came to the conclusion that whatever was affecting him was more mental than physical; his fits of irritation were followed by moods of profound melancholy, one as trying to bear with as the other, and often I had some difficulty in preventing hot disputes between him and Gilbert, the latter having a very impulsive, quick temper.

Months went by, and we shifted our camp some miles further on, to the banks of the Yarra-Yarra River, in order to take advantage of the fishing season. We pitched our tent on a lovely spot under the shade of our old friend the Eucalyptus tree, near the banks of the river, and what sport we had! Old Isaak Walton would have been in a continuous state of rapturous delight. I wonder if he ever had the chance of real good fishing, such as these majestic Australian rivers give.

Our chief quest was for the "black fish," a most delicious piscatory tit-bit, which always fetched a high price in the fish market, large and small being paid for at the same rate per pound. We used to place them in a large box that we had sunk in the river, with holes to admit the water, until we had captured enough to send into the next town. We were getting on in the world now, and bought a horse to carry our *impedimenta*, for when we had fished out one place we moved farther up the river to another spot.

A strange-looking party we were, not unpicturesque, I take it. Our coloured shirts made a bright spot among the bushes, and with our rifles, high boots, and slouched hats, I flatter myself that we should have been looked at again if we had been walking down—Regent Street, let us say. Magog, our horse, must not be forgotten; he was a monster of strength and ugliness, but of a gentle and retiring disposition, bearing any burden put upon him with cheerful patience and meek submission. He had one absorbing passion—perhaps I ought to say two absorbing passions—love *for* Dorcas, a cat, and love *of* bread. In finding out where the latter article was packed or placed he was nearly as clever as the opossums, perhaps even more so, given his great bulk and consequent difficulty in stealing. It is only fair to him to state that his former master was a baker, and he must have contracted this habit when in that line of life. Dorcas was a large, a very large, cat, grey with black stripes, and had been found when a kitten in the stable with Magog. How she came there is not known—like Topsy, " 'spects she growed." She was no expense to any one, catering for herself, and being the mother of sixty-eight children to the knowledge of Burton, the man we bought Magog from. We never thought of taking a cat into the bush, nor did Burton wish to part with her, for she was the best ratter for miles around; but on going out to see Magog the morning after our purchase of him there sat Dorcas on his back, cleaning her face, and evidently intending to remain. We were afraid she would be a dreadful nuisance, so Stuart rode her back on Magog; but he might have spared himself the trouble, for he had not been but four miles on his way back to the camp before a "mew" caused him to turn round, and there was Mrs. Dorcas scrambling up Magog's tail, and, seating herself on his broad back, proceeded to clean herself, not condescending to notice Stuart in the least. So we kept her—in fact we could not help ourselves, and soon grew alarmingly fond of her, for when one loves much one suffers much, and we were always afraid some accident would happen to her, for she always accompanied us on our shooting expeditions, and seemed, unlike the generality of her sex, to love the sound of a gun. No dog ever was so useful in bringing back the game. Often I have felt terribly nervous when she has sat with her green eyes fixed upon me, for I dreaded her contempt if I missed my aim. On such occasions she would calmly walk back to the camp, curl herself up on a blanket and go to sleep.

On one of our moves up the river we came upon a settler who was building a shanty, and intended to settle down altogether. We helped him to choose a suitable spot and remained with him some ten days or so to aid him. He intended having his wife and two children out as soon as he was settled.

One morning Gilbert, Stuart, and the settler (I forget his name, if I ever knew it, for one uses the terms "mate" or "boss" with strangers generally) were standing near an immense Eucalyptus tree, when suddenly an awful thunderstorm came on. The noise was deafening, like a charge of artillery, and the glare of the lightning, so continuous and brilliant, was simply appalling. I ran out from the tent to call them in, when at that moment a thunderbolt struck the tree, catching it on fire and smashing it to pieces. Gilbert and Stuart came running in, how they had escaped was nothing short of a miracle. The settler was killed, nor could we find anything of him to bury but a very small portion of calcinated matter.

We looked over his papers, and sent them and the money and anything of value into Melbourne by a man chancing to pass our way. He undertook to forward them to England to the poor widow. Then we moved our camp from the half-built house with its sad association, and went further up the Yarra-Yarra.

I was one day keeping camp, Gilbert and Stuart having gone fishing, and had thrown myself down in the tent door, mending some fishing tackle, when, looking up, I saw a huge black snake deliberately coming along with the evident intention of paying me a visit.

"Come on, my friend," said I, putting down the net and taking up a large stick.

The brute eyed me stedfastly with sparkling eyes, and came on undaunted and unafraid. I raised myself on my elbow, and when he was within half a yard of me I brought my stick down upon his head and killed him on the spot. I then hung him up to show the other two when they returned; he was of great length and very thick. Dane had a womanish terror of snakes: it was useless to point out to him that they generally avoid you, and if they do not are very easily killed; also that their power of springing and throwing out their poison is very limited; stand one quarter of an inch beyond that short distance, and they are perfectly harmless. He never saw one without turning pale, and all his nightmares had a snake in them,

We killed multitudes of these reptiles, for the bush abounds in them. The hideous and deadly tiger-snake, banded with dirty black-and-white stripes; the beautiful carpet-snake, of varying colours; the death-adder, whose bite is instantly fatal; and a host of all sorts and sizes, down to the whip-snake, which lies coiled up in the branches of the shrubs. Look out as you pass by, for if they dart their head out and prick you on the hand—for it is little more than a prick—you may make your peace with God, for death will infallibly result.

We skinned a great many of these reptiles, and kept them, as they were not without beauty. They are also good eating, so I have been told, and have always been content with that knowledge from hearsay; for, although I don't mind meeting the devil, I decidedly object to eating him, and so incorporating him as it were into myself. Gilbert also had no wish to try the taste of them, while, as to Stuart, I believe he would have killed us if we had attempted to palm off a snake on him instead of a dish of stewed eels.

There was another living animal, or rather insect, that we never tried to eat, though we had abundance of them, and I have read somewhere of a starved traveller becoming fat and jolly on them —the wattle-grub, a grub as large as a large man's largest finger, nearly square in shape, of a fine clean cream colour, very fat and soft, not by any means a disgusting-looking thing if you happen to admire that style of thing. When roasted they are remarkably good, and have a flavour of almonds—at least, so I have been told; for, as I observed before, we avoided them, our tastes not having been educated up to wattle-grubs. We got them by splitting up the bark of the gum-trees that were somewhat decayed, where they lived and bred in vast numbers, thriving and fattening on the gum that they sucked. We used them for bait when fishing, with great success, the fish evidently looking upon them as a rare tit-bit, even worth dying to get a taste of.

A party of "sports" met once near Danderong, to enjoy an outing in the woods, and to "do" the bush generally. These were Melbourneites, and tolerably verdant. It was not often that they indulged in such wild extravagance, so were determined to have a good time of it, being highly elated at the prospect of slaughtering "'possums," bears, bandicoots, &c., and being able afterwards to "swagger" to their less fortunate friends at home, boasting of their wood craft, and detailing hairbreadth escapes from the loving hug of the bear, or the poisonous breath of the snake.

Among them was a young man who had never been in the bush before, and would neither know a bear nor a snake if he saw one. On the strength of this, he took upon himself to act as cicerone and general adviser to the rest of the "greenies." Hiding from them the fact that his knowledge of bush life was the result of very cursory reading of some traveller's experience, he depicted himself as an old experienced hand, whom nothing could astonish, still less alarm. The others, quite as ignorant but more modest, gave in readily to their self-elected leader, and followed him with all the gravity and want of sense peculiar to a flock of geese.

A gentleman, an old settler, came upon the party, and joining them in the free and easy way of bush life, took the measure of the bumptious greenhorn in a moment, and determined to have some fun at his expense. He secretly procured some of these nice large cream-coloured grubs, which he concealed in his pocket; then, returning to the party, he entered into a lively conversation with the "cicerone," agreeing to all the bombastic nonsense he talked, pretending to believe all the impossible stories of adventures of which he had been the hero, and otherwise flattering him up, until, like the frog in the fable, he was ready to burst with pride, or rather self-conceit. Every now and then, during the talk, the gentleman made a pretence of turning his head aside, of slipping something into his mouth, and munching it with infinite relish. The other's curiosity was much excited; he watched his flatterer more closely, and seeing a large, soft, creamy-looking substance apparently being popped into his mouth, said, "May I be allowed to ask what it is you are eating?"

"What!" exclaimed the settler, with uplifted

eyebrows, "do you, an old experienced bushman, not know the celebrated and delicious wattle-grub, that greatest delicacy in the bush?"

On hearing this the rest of the party gathered round the two with eyes, mouths, and ears wide open.

"Oh, yes, I know it well," cried cicerone, quickly. "I didn't see distinctly, many a hundred I've eaten, and enjoyed above all things; they are indeed a real luxury."

"Have some," said the wily one. "I can spare you a few; here's a nice one," handing him one nearly as big as a sausage."

The poor wretch took it, and with a tremendous effort put the smaller end of the soft fat live thing into his mouth, when, faugh! he was seized with an internal earthquake, and he nearly fainted. The whole starch was taken out of him; he completely collapsed, and was mute, crestfallen, and wretched for the rest of the day.

The settler, after seeing the salutary effect of his lesson, cheerfully wished the party good-day, and returned to his shanty with another good story to add to his list.

Another shifting of our camp brought us further up the river, near a bend of which we pitched our tent, after having ascertained that the spot met with Dorcas's approval. She was, like all her sex, very capricious, and if we were luckless enough to settle down anywhere that did not please her, she would render night hideous and sleep impossible by her yowls. Her great objection seemed to be the close proximity to large trees, whether from some recollection of the terrible thunderstorm we had passed through I cannot tell, for she kept these things secret in that "dark place where cats keep their thoughts."

The Yarra-Yarra is of all the rivers I have ever seen the most extraordinary. It winds about in every possible and impossible direction. One mile, as the crow flies, makes many miles of the stream, along the banks of which are numerous lagoons, the habitat of all sorts of water-fowl, notably among them that gigantic crane, the "Native Companion," a solemn and stately-looking bird, who always reminded me of one of the proverbs of the Sheviri, "The crane stands upon one leg, in heavenly meditation, but all the while is looking sharply after his fish." Also the small and handsome "Nankeen crane," so called from its colour, such a knowing-looking little fellow, and so very beautiful. The diminutive flying squirrel, called "Turan" by the natives, were very numerous here, lovely little animals, and easy to tame. Stuart kept a baby one, whose mother he had shot, for some little time, but Dorcas eyed the wee thing with such jealousy, and evidently had such difficulty in keeping her claws from it, that he thought it better to separate the two. At first he intended to set it at liberty, but when he put it up a tree the little thing sprang on to his shoulder and would not leave him. Luckily for "Dot," just as we were going to move on, a settler asked Dane to stay with him a while to help him fence his shanty around. So Gilbert and I, Magog and Dorcas started off, leaving him to follow us when the fencing was finished. Bears, opossums, bandicoots, &c., were very plentiful—in fact game of all sorts; but, being summer, their fur was of no use to us, being too thin and faded at that season to fetch any price in the market. So we only killed what we needed for food, such as deer, of which there were a large number, the bandicoot, and wild fowl.

We continued our fishing with great success, for we got well paid, and began to put by money towards buying a ranche, which was the ultimate aim of all our toil and all our hopes. One day we discovered a "bee-tree," a huge gum-tree, in which a swarm of bees had taken up their abode —a very valuable find, as sometimes there are several hundredweight of honeycomb. The difficulty was to get at it, the only possible way being to cut down the tree, and as this one measured at least five feet in diameter, and was of great height, it was no small undertaking for two men. Nothing daunted, however, we set to work, Gilbert being a very good hand at wielding the axe, while I, on the contrary, can hardly use it. We worked away many hours, and succeeded in cutting a pretty deep gash on one side, when, night coming on, we had to adjourn till next day. Dorcas, who always accompanied us on our fishing expeditions, finding that we stayed all day by the side of her *bête noir*, a tree, had left us in disgust, and, we concluded, had returned to the tent to sleep off her vexation after her usual manner. On returning, however, no Dorcas was to be seen. Feeling very uneasy, we went out and called her loudly. A faint " mew " answered us, and in a few minutes Dorcas appeared, bleeding and wounded in many places. She manifested such an evident desire to show us something that we followed her before attending to her wounds. She led us to some little distance, and there lying side by side, dead, were seven enormous rats. Her pride was immense; she limped all round them, purring and rubbing against us, as much as to say, " You have killed nothing all day, but see what I have done." That the victory had been hardly won her numerous wounds plainly testified. We carried them back to the tent, took care of her, and she soon purred herself to sleep in the midst of her slain.

The next morning Gilbert was obliged to row down the river to Lillydale with a " swag " of fish, and I made some feeble efforts to enlarge the gash we had made the day before in the " bee-tree." While thus engaged, a party of " bee-hunters " came along, eyed me a moment in silence, then one said—

" Honey there, mate ? "

I nodded.

" You here alone ? "

I nodded again.

At a sign from him the others threw down some bags and ropes they had, and drew their axes, while the man that had spoken before turned to me and said, "We will save you the trouble of cutting that tree down. You will never do it alone."

"My mate will be back to-night," I answered. "We found the tree, and therefore it is ours. Kindly go on your way."

The fellow laughed aloud, and simply called up two more men who were behind with a couple of horses, carrying buckets and kegs for honey. In a few minutes the five of them were working away vigorously with their axes, making the chips fly in every direction. I said no more, what was the good? In this case of might against right, who was likely to win? So I lit a pipe, leant against a neighbouring tree, and watched them.

All day long they worked in a blazing sun, stopping only at midday for some food, to which they politely invited me, and I as politely declined.

Early in the evening Gilbert came back, and was furious at the sight that met his gaze—the "bee-tree," his "bee-tree," nearly cut through by a band of robbers, who had come provided with every convenience to carry off their ill-gotten gains. But his righteous indignation was of no avail; the kegs and buckets were placed in readiness, and shortly the mighty giant of the forest fell with a crash like thunder, and lay quivering on the ground. The men rushed forward to cut out the honey, when, to their infinite disgust, they found hardly a single pound, the bees having only commenced their settlement.

The disappointment was great. After all their toil under a burning sun; after playing a shabby trick, too, to get—nothing. The language that ensued was more forcible than polite. I confess I was Christian enough to feel savagely glad at their discomfiture. " I wish you good evening," I remarked, as they began re-loading their horses with the empty kegs, " and may the same good fortune attend you the next time you attempt such a scurvy trick."

A fierce growl was the only reply, and Gilbert and I returned to our camp, and had supper, feeling quite a glow of virtuous satisfaction at this unexpected example of " grab " and its reward.

For the first time since we had lived in the bush we came across some of the aborigines, or rather, they came across us, a party of them passing our camp. Some one or two were rather handsome, but for the most part they were frightfully ugly and intensely black, the women seemingly having an extra dark tint.

"God's image carved in ebony,"

says some one.

" I hope some day she may become one,
The present image is a very rum one,"

as Brinston Steevens says. The men call their wives "gyns." Strange how closely allied to the ancient Greek word γυνη, which, written in Roman characters, would be Gynē.

I did not hear them speak, for they went by in solemn silence, so cannot say what their language is like, but if the formation of the mouth has anything to do with the enunciation of a language, theirs must be something truly extraordinary. They are very good shots, ride half broken-in horses fearlessly and well, are exceedingly expert in the use of their wooden missile, the boomerang, and throw a spear a long distance with unerring and fatal aim. Altogether they are gentry one would rather read about than meet, and we were not sorry that they passed us by without even condescending to betray by a glance that they were aware of our presence. If they consider themselves handsome, what frightful monsters must we "whites" appear in their eyes!

Gilbert shot some of those strange animals, the Platypus, or Arnothoryneus, feet webbed like those of a duck, the broad bill of ditto, and a tail like that of a beaver; their fur is soft and close and very valuable. Dorcas was much perturbed in mind on first seeing this animal, and walked around it and on it, touching up its head and tail with her paw, spitting and, I fear, swearing badly at the poor dead Platypus.

At this time Gilbert got one of his sudden illnesses, to which he had been subject since the second bayonet wound he had received from the drunken soldier in Auckland. Whether he had neglected to put on his hat when in the burning sun, or had overworked himself, I cannot tell, but he came in one evening complaining of headache, and before morning was delirious. Luckily I knew what to do and had the remedies at hand, but it was a week before he could venture to face the sun again; and I had a great fright, fearing a relapse, on account of an unfortunate incident that happened directly after his recovery.

It was one cool evening, the day after he had been out for the first time since his illness, and he thought he would like to do a little fishing. So we got into our small flat-bottomed canoe, having left Dorcas and Magog in charge of the tent, for I would not let Gilbert go alone, fearing he would commit some imprudence. As after events turned out, all my precautions were useless—I had counted without Dame Nature. Well, we rowed some distance up the river, intending to have a pleasant night's fishing for " black fish " and eels. We had provided ourselves with a lantern and candles, and anticipated some good sport. Not without some difficulty we piloted our canoe safely past snaps and large pieces of broken timber with which the stream is much encumbered, until we reached a favourable place: here we fastened our craft securely and proceeded to fish. We were repaid for our toil up by catching a fair amount of the much-demanded " black fish," and a large quantity of long, slimy eels; not but what the "black fish" is just as viscous as the eel, and the latter when well cooked are almost as good to eat. The Yarra-Yarra eels are devoid of that oily and objectionable rancidity peculiar to the eels of the Old Country, which so disagreeably affect delicate digestions. Night, which falls quite suddenly in Australia, caused us to light a candle, and so engaged were we in hooking and landing our victims that we failed to perceive that the sky was black with clouds, our first intimation being a downpour of rain, which at once put an end to our sport and drenched us within three minutes. Here was a nice state of things, lashing rain, and so pitch dark that we could not venture to return down the river because of the mass of broken timber floating about, nor could we seek shelter on shore for the same reason, the light of our lantern being insufficient to show us a landing-place, and, worst misfortune of all, no wraps, and Gilbert only just recovered from a serious illness. There was nothing for it but to possess our souls in patience; so there we sat, Gilbert in one end of the canoe, and I in the other, through all the hours of the long black night, as wet as the fearful torrents of rain could make us, keeping up a fitful conversation on the most lugubrious topics possible, until daylight, forcing its way through the gloom, allowed us, or what was left of us, to return to our camp.

How glad we were to get into dry things, drink some hot grog, and lie down for a few hours' sleep!

Much to my astonishment Gilbert was none the worse for his wetting. Such an incident is one of the amenities of bush life; but unpleasant though it undoubtedly is at the time, is seldom followed by any bad consequences, that part of Australia enjoying so healthy a climate.

The aborigines think a few branches thrown against a tree, with a good fire in front, a comfortable shelter, and wish for nothing more; they call it a " Miomi."

After a good many such trivial adventures we found that we had fished that part of the river very thoroughly; and not caring to go further up without Stuart, resolved to return to our old camping-ground and pick him up before seeking pastures new. So we struck our tent, packed all our belongings on Magog, and marched slowly along, carrying Dorcas by turns, her ladyship for some reason or other refusing either to walk or to mount on the back of her friend Magog.

"Oh, hang it all!" cried Gilbert at last, putting down Dorcas and wiping his heated face, "I think you might walk a bit now."

Dorcas thought otherwise, and seating herself on the grass, began slowly to clean her face, while, hot and perplexed, we held a hasty consultation as to what was best to do. Her mind was made up, and we poor, weak mortals might fuss and worry as much as we liked, that in no ways affected her equanimity; she knew she would get her own way, so was content to bide a wee. On our road we had shot several birds and some bandicoots, which we were obliged to carry ourselves, as even Magog's powers of endurance were taxed by the heavy tent, canoe, and all the fishing paraphernalia that he had on his back.

So we rested a short time under the shade of a Eucalyptus tree, and then by bribing Magog with slices of bread, got him to carry our game and rifles. Dorcas watched the preparations with unblinking eyes, showing no shame at her good friend being so loaded to please a whim of hers.

"Come along, old woman, I'll carry you," I said, when all was ready. But without condescending to notice me, she sprang into Gilbert's arms and began purring and rubbing herself against his face in the most coquettish and irresistible manner possible. Of course he liked it, and of course he carried her, while I walked along feeling rather left out in the cold, but pretending I did not care, which pretence I am convinced deceived neither Gilbert nor Mrs. Dorcas.

In due time we regained our former camp, and found Stuart heartily glad to see us again. The fencing was nearly finished, and we agreed to stay there a few days to complete the work, and we also wished to make inquiries about buying some land, for we had put aside a fair sum of money for that purpose, and Gilbert had come into a little on the death of a relative.

Mr. Lydgar, the settler, whose ranche we were all assisting in fencing around, was the son of the

State surveyor, a singularly handsome young man. Having led too gay a life, his father had sent him to the bush to cool his ardour, and restore his health, somewhat impaired by late hours and fast living.

He told Gilbert that he had some land he would sell him situated in Gipp's Land, near the Tarwin River, a wild and almost uninhabited country, but exceedingly fertile and with unlimited fishing. The climate of that part is well known to be the most salubrious of that portion of Australia.

You may be sure that we made many and minute inquiries before Gilbert closed with the bargain, and became proprietor of some thirty-five acres of land, a large vineyard occupying ten acres of it, a small shanty ready built, and a fine orchard. The river Tarwin ran past the ranche, and a steamer passed occasionally, which would take our fruit, fish, &c., to the near towns to sell.

Pending all these arrangements, we remained near Mr. Lydgar, leading our ordinary lives of fishing and shooting. Stuart camped with us again, and out of deference to Dorcas's dislike to, or perhaps it would be more correct to say, too great a liking for, "Dots," he had given his pet to Mr. Lydgar, who was very fond of it. Dane had seemed much more cheerful at first, and appeared really glad to see us again, but Gilbert's talk of buying a ranche irritated and depressed him, though he would give no reason for it, and, indeed, denied that the proposed change had anything to do with his state of mind. Gilbert and I took it as a matter of course that he would come with us, and always consulted him before deciding any point with reference to our move.

One Sunday evening I was walking along the bank of a lagoon, quietly smoking a pipe and thinking and pondering over many things, when I saw the figure of a man coming along swiftly and silently, looking back every now and then as though he feared being watched. I drew farther back under the shelter of the large tree against which I had been leaning, and attentively observed Dane, for it was he.

On he came, in the same swift, silent manner, until he reached the edge of the lagoon, on the opposite side of where I was. He went so close to the water that his boots were covered; he hesitated, looked at the gloomy, dark swamp, seemed undecided, then, retracing his steps, went a little further on, where there was a sort of small beach. Here he began rapidly filling his pockets with the largest pebbles he could find. There could be no doubt as to his intention.

"What are you doing, Dane?" I cried, sharply, emerging from behind my tree.

He started; then, unaware that I had been watching him, said, "I thought I would have a bathe."

"What, *here?*"

"Yes, here if I choose," he cried, hotly; "I wish you would go away, I hate to be spied upon and followed."

"I was here before you," I said, quietly.

He started again, opened his mouth as if about to speak, changed his mind, and remained silent with the colour coming and going in his cheeks.

"When a man, who can't swim a stroke, prepares to go into the water with his pockets weighed down with stones, it can be but for one purpose—to end his life. What the sorrow or sin is that has tempted you to such an act I do not know, nor do I wish to force your confidence, but believe me, nothing, absolutely nothing, can justify a man taking his own life."

"I don't agree with you," he muttered, "you don't know. In some cases it is the only course possible. We are told in the Four Gospels that Judas Iscariot hanged himself, but in neither that he was wrong in so doing; the act is passed without comment. Yes, I was going to end a life that has long been unbearable to me. Why did you prevent me?" And he turned such a look of reproachful misery on me that my heart ached for him.

"Can you not tell me what the trouble is?" I asked. "Force yourself to speak of it; I assure you it will help you, if only a little. Come, I am old enough to be your father."

"I cannot speak of it."

"Does your aunt know?" I asked, struck by a sudden thought.

"Yes."

I felt greatly relieved, for if she knew of it, and still wished her nephew to live with her, it could not be, as I had feared, some crime that he had committed himself.

"I will only ask you one more question," I said. "Does your aunt think you have cause for thus despairing?"

"No."

"Yet she knows all?"

"Oh, yes."

"Then come, Dane, be a man. Every one has trouble, some more, some less, but no one escapes. If you can do nothing in this matter to better it or prevent it, do not at least add worse to what is bad. Promise me you won't attempt it again."

He hesitated a moment, and then said, "If you will promise to keep this to yourself. One day I will tell you all, and you will understand then what now seems to you so strange."

Poor Dane! when afterwards I did know, his life was ended. It is in looking at lives like his that one fails utterly to comprehend the mysteries of sorrow, sin, and death.

I will relate his story in its place. For the present it is enough to say, that having given me his promise not to attempt his life again, we said no more on the subject, but talked of hunting and fishing as though nothing more serious had occupied our minds so short a time before.

The next day he and Gilbert went into Melbourne to settle the business of buying the ranche. Without telling my friend anything of yesterday's scene, I gave him a hint to be forbearing, even if

Dane proved extra irritable. Gilbert laughingly promised to take care of my sandy-haired baby, and give in to his every whim; which promise he faithfully carried out.

I, seizing upon the fact of my being alone as a reason for a holiday, left our tent with Magog and Dorcas under Mr. Lydgar's care, and placing sufficient food for a day in my wallet, took my rifle and started off on an expedition which had for some days been my great ambition to undertake.

About half-way between Lillydale and where we had encamped ourselves, lay to the right a tiny village or settlement, chiefly inhabited by charcoal-burners, a harmless, quiet set of people. Rumours had lately got about that one of these charcoal-burners—Fisher by name—claimed to be the Saviour. Various cures, miraculous, of course, had been performed by him. His preaching was pronounced wonderful, and his followers numbered not a few, considering the sparse population for miles around. A settler passing our camp a few days before, had told us about this man Fisher, and said he was to be seen and heard in a little hut on the outskirts of the charcoal settlement, where he carried on his work as charcoal-burner when not preaching. My curiosity was aroused, and I much wished to see a man who not only could dare to claim to be the Christ, but could get people to believe that he was so. For ignorant as bushmen and settlers of all sorts often are, it is well known that the life so much alone with Nature brings

Nature's God nearer to them, and makes them far more religious than they would be had their lives been spent in the towns.

I was not above two hours reaching the tiny settlement. It seemed deserted; I walked past several shanties and down a steep incline, at the foot of which I perceived a small group surrounding a figure taller than the rest.

"I'm in luck," thought I, "Fisher is preaching." I quietly approached the little band, keeping, however, at a certain distance, from whence I could both see and hear distinctly.

Fisher, a tall man with a long beard, and hair falling over his shoulders, was clothed in a blanket, worn not ungracefully. His eyes flashed out from his thin, white face with the glare of madness in them. His preaching consisted of a string of texts from the Gospels, and an exhortation to repent and believe in him as the Christ. As he went on he became incoherent, and finally subsided into mere mutterings at intervals. His listeners remained respectfully silent and quiet until Fisher suddenly diving into his hovel, they quietly dispersed. I entered into conversation with one of them, who said, I remember, among other things, "I don't mean to say he's the Christ, but he tells the words of Christ, and I likes to hear them." So I suppose the poor half-witted creature did some good.

I returned to my camp and found some settlers with Mr. Lydgar, who, on hearing where I had been, expressed a wish also to hear the prophet.

They went the next day, but Fisher had disappeared. I heard after that he went to Melbourne, proclaiming himself as the Messiah. There some believed in him—if such a thing can be credited—but the "larrykins" of Melbourne (colonial name for roughs) were too many for him, and squashed the Messiahship out of him by having a street brawl, in which Fisher lost his life. Whether the man was a knave or a madman is not known. From the little I saw of him I am inclined to believe he was mad.

Gilbert and Dane, when they returned from the city, brought with them a waggon and a team of horses; so I knew before we were within speaking distance that the deed was done, the papers signed, and the property bought. In the work and excitement that necessarily followed I was glad to see that Dane was much brighter, and threw himself into the spirit of the thing with real pleasure. He and Gilbert were more friendly, and appeared to work and talk together with a feeling of true good fellowship.

At Melbourne we bought all the necessaries for our new life, sending on the heavy baggage, such as a plough, other implements of husbandry, utensils for house, and so on, by a cutter which went to the Tarwin River. Dane undertook to go with them, and it was wiser so, as we were told we had probably a journey of no little toil and difficulty before us, and his health was none of the strongest. So we saw him off, and at the last moment decided that Dorcas had better go with him also. Luckily she made no great objection, though the sailors did at first.

Dane told us afterwards that it was wonderful the way she walked all over the cutter, inspected every part, and catching a rat in the hold, killed it and brought it up on deck, returning for more. She won the hearts of all on board, and when Dane reached the Tarwin he was obliged to watch her closely for fear of her being stolen.

Meanwhile Gilbert and I started overland in the waggon, with a team of horses headed by Magog, to whom we gave a whole loaf of bread, in order to console him for the temporary loss of Dorcas. He ate it very mournfully, and I think would have wept had he known how to shed tears.

It was now winter, the creeks all full of water, and the roads in many places flooded. The second day of our journey we were crossing a river when we stuck fast, and should most assuredly have been obliged to abandon our waggon, had it not been that providentially for us a number of men were working near, who, seeing our difficulty, came to our aid. After great labour they succeeded in extricating us from our unpleasant and perilous position, and we once more proceeded on our journey. After three or four days of hardship we reached the Bass, a town called after the Bass Strait, near to which it is built. This channel is about forty leagues wide, and separates the south extremity of New South Wales from Tasmania. It was discovered quite by chance in, I believe, the year 1798, by a surgeon of the name of Bass, who was in an open whale-boat.

With the Bass Strait we had nothing to do, remaining only in the town for a couple of days. Here we were obliged to leave the waggon and continue our journey on horseback. We were fortunate enough to come across two men who were going our way—no slight advantage to us, as they knew their road. One of our fellow-travellers was a gentleman, Frazer by name, who was doing good business as horse dealer: he had a large number with him now taking to his settlement, which was situated about twenty miles beyond the Tarwin. The other was a strange character, a thorough bushman, commonly called "Cranky Jack." He rode ahead, steeplechase fashion, not caring what obstacles might be in his way, and always came out right. Foolhardy to a degree, and imbued with a strong love for adventures, he appeared to pass his time in getting into dangers for the simple pleasure of getting out of them. He had been wounded by the natives, generally smashed by various accidents, ought to have been drowned several times, and burnt oftener. Prairie fires and wild beasts, thunderstorms and fell diseases, poisonous reptiles and cunning natives, each and all had had a try at squashing "Cranky Jack," and each and all had failed. Here he was, at fifty-five, hideous by reason of his many scars, and surly enough to frighten any one not used to his ways; but strong as Hercules, tough as the toughest leather, and an invaluable companion in the bush. If that man's life and adventures could ever be extracted from him, they would form a volume of marvellous interest.

But to return to our journey to the Tarwin. The roads in this part are invisible to one not used to them, and wind about through the bush in a most bewildering way, losing themselves on the banks of creeks, which at this time of year are full of water, and very generally overflowing. Bridges are a luxury almost unknown, so swimming is the only method of crossing, at times a difficult and dangerous one. Many a life has been lost in trying to ford these turbulent streams that rush through the country at their own sweet will.

We rested some little time in a grove of "honeysuckle" trees to refresh ourselves and horses. "Entertainment for man and Baste" is often to be seen gibbeted on an Irish mud-built sheekeen in the Green Isle (the "m" in man always small, and the "B" in Baste very large!), but in the wilds of Australia our entertainment was drawn from our haversacks, while our horses procured theirs in the rich kangaroo grass which abounded here.

While we were camping for a rest, the horses all hobbled so that they might not stray too far from us, a party of natives passed, and "Cranky Jack" speaking to them, I was enabled to observe them more attentively than had been the case when a troop had passed us on the Yarra-Yarra River. They were entirely naked, painted with various colours, and ornamented about the head and shoulders with beads and shells. The men seemed active and vigorous, although many of them were very stout, and one of the fore-teeth in the upper jaw was wanting in most of those present. Several women were with them, and " Cranky Jack " called my attention to the fact that they had all cut off the two joints of their little fingers, but he could not tell me the reason for such an act of mutilation. They spoke, and their voices were soft and pleasing, while the men's, on the contrary, were harsh and rough. They carried some of their canoes with them, which were made simply of large pieces of bark tied up at both ends with vines. Considering their slight texture, the dexterity with which they are managed, and the boldness with which they venture out to sea in them, is truly wonderful.

Some time after, we came across some of their huts, which consist of pieces of bark laid together in the form of an oven, open at one end, very low, but long enough for a man to lie at full length. I couldn't hear much about their habits and customs beyond the facts that their women were not without modesty, and that they burned their dead.

Having rested ourselves, we remounted, and led by " Cranky Jack " (who was in the employ of Mr. Frazer), we went on as fast as we could ride, hoping to reach " Archie's hut " before nightfall.

"Archie" was once an English jockey, and had won not a few races, although a bandy-legged and rather deformed little man. Now he has a herd in this wild region, though what had driven him to so solitary a life was not known.

We reached his hut late in the evening, but Archie was away. However, we took possession of his dwelling and made ourselves as comfortable as we could. He returned at daybreak, and was no ways disturbed at finding his hut occupied by four strangers.

We breakfasted together, and bidding him farewell continued our journey. About midday we reached a stock-yard on the top of the hill, and there, to our delight, saw the Tarwin River lying beneath us. The cutter was riding at anchor, and Dane was rowing our boat up the river, filled with stores.

We were soon on the bank of the Tarwin, exchanging warm greetings. Dorcas looked handsomer than ever, and sprang upon Magog's back, walking up and down him as though she were on quarter-deck, the horse quivering with delight.

The first talk over, I left my horse with Gilbert and got into the boat to help Dane row her up to the place suitable for a landing. Gilbert, Frazer, and "Cranky Jack" had an awful job swimming the horses over, for the river is very deep, and the banks swampy and slippery to a degree. Several of the horses were nearly lost, being so exhausted in the many ineffectual efforts to gain a footing, as to be nearly unable to swim; but Australian horses are like cats—have nine lives, all naturalists to the contrary notwithstanding. After terrible efforts and many wonderful deeds on the part of "Cranky Jack," the whole lot were safely landed, and stood dripping and trembling with fright on the dry land.

We soon reached our destination, and surveyed "Jenkin's Ranche" with beating hearts. The house was a very small, poor business, having one room only, which we found filled with men working for a Mr. Black, a settler not far off. It is not bush etiquette to turn any one out, even of your own house, so that night we were packed like herrings in a barrel, or a tighter simile still, like Chinamen in their sties at " 'Frisco."

The next day these men camped at a little distance from us, using a large sail for a tent, leaving us in quiet possession of our own possession.

With what pride we surveyed our vineyard, which had at least 6,000 vines, of which only a hundred or so were dead; our orchard, with its peach, apple, and plum-trees; the place in front of the shanty where we meant to have a flower garden; the place behind where we intended to rear poultry; even the miserable little one-roomed hut, ten feet by eight wide, seemed to us delightful, because it was our own.

Mr. Frazer and "Cranky Jack" bade us goodbye, and started off, with all their horses. We never saw either of them again.

For many days after we were very busy settling in and putting things in order. We built up another room, laid out a vegetable garden, and gradually settled down into our irregular groove.

Months passed by; we laboured, hunted, and fished, particularly the latter, for the Tarwin which flowed past our dwelling was full of fish, all large and good. These we salted and exported to Melbourne by the same cutter that had brought our heavy luggage, and which called occasionally, taking our goods into the city. Vaughan, the owner of the cutter, was a pleasant spoken young fellow, and seemed honest and above suspicion, so we fully trusted him—indeed we could do nothing else, for his was the only cutter that passed up the Tarwin River. We began to have our eyes a little opened when time after time he brought back so little money, with a separate excuse and reason; but still, knowing the difficulties of navigating so rapid a river, and the depression in trade that happens sometimes from one week to another, we could say nothing, and only hope for better days.

So we improved our place, fenced it all around, built a kitchen, planted some pear and fig-trees, raised plenty of melons, squash, potatoes, carrots, and parsnips, not forgetting onions, which grew to an astounding size, the smallest weighing two pounds; the carrots were also giants, the very largest I have ever seen.

Hunting occupied all our spare time; we had abundance of wild fowl, ducks in particular, geese, and swans, curious-looking black birds with red bills and feet, uttering a singular cry like the sound of an Eolian harp. The breast fried is somewhat in flavour like a beef-steak. Every morning we would examine our nets, which were generally well stocked with all sorts of the finny tribe. We breakfasted always on fresh fish, and became expert cooks in roasting, boiling, and otherwise cooking them. Our guns gave us all the meat and fowl we required. A small sort of kangaroo called the wallaby is very delicious, its flesh being like tender venison; it is particularly wholesome, but is entirely without fat. "Paddy-melon" is also a species of wallaby; its fur is marked somewhat differently, having a dark stripe down its back and another across its shoulders. They are equally good to eat, and it is a meat one does not tire of. We found also large quantities of opossums, whose pelts are most valuable, chiefly by reason of their tail, which is very long, bushy, and of a splendid glossy black. We have eaten them when hard up for animal food, but they taste too strongly of the gum-tree to be agreeable; still, when one has nothing else, they are not bad, and one quickly becomes accustomed to the flavour.

One day Gilbert and Dane went down to the bay to shoot swans, and wading out to retrieve their birds, got entangled in the rushes and mud, sinking to their waists at every step. The water was not deep enough to swim, and they had the almost certainty of a horrible death in the marshy lagoon, into which they had entered. By cool, cautious efforts—for frantic ones would but have sucked them in with a deadly, irresistible force—and using their guns as props, they managed to extricate themselves, and reached land exhausted but safe. Their escape was nothing short of miraculous. Dane's fits of depression began to overwhelm him again, and he suffered greatly from his heart. Gilbert and I did all we could to cheer him up and make him take an interest in our life, but it was all useless. He would sit for hours in the boat, unconscious that a fish was caught; or, taking his gun, would go hunting and return empty-handed, with unloaded rifle. I became seriously uneasy, and never let him be without Gilbert or myself, though he showed no signs of wishing to repeat the mad act he had attempted on the banks of the Yarra-Yarra River.

Dorcas seemed his greatest comfort; her cool, calm, independent character seemed much to attract him, and when she went out hunting with him he was sure to bring back something. He dared not face her contempt.

One lovely morning we were all three in our large boat, a captain's gig, with full sails on, intending to sail down the bay to Screw Creek, so called from its corkscrew-like conformation, in order to pass a pleasant day shooting and fishing, and to amuse ourselves generally. We were in good spirits and good health, our affairs were prospering, and we had a much larger cargo of fish and furs prepared to send by the cutter when next it called, than we had ever hoped to amass. Dane was the brightest of the three, and seemed to have thrown care to the winds, joking and singing snatches of Scotch songs in his really good tenor. The day passed on; we had caught fish, had shot opossums and wild fowl, and, night falling, let ourselves drift down the river, steering our boat by the light of a new moon. We somehow began to talk of our different childhoods and early life. Mine was an ordinary enough case, my father having a longer pedigree than a purse, and struggling to bring up his large family on a stipend that a footman would despise nowadays. The Emerald Isle was my native place, and there I spent all my early life. Gilbert was born in Nova Scotia, the eldest of seven, and having the misfortune of losing his mother when quite a boy, a mother to whom he was passionately attached, passed the sad life so usual, alas! when father or mother is called away, and the little ones are left to battle with life as best they can. His father died, too, when he was just entering manhood, and there was little inducement for him to return to England, where death continued to make havoc in his immediate family.

When we two had spoken I looked at Dane: would he tell us something of his life, I wondered? and hardly thought so, when, without our saying a word, he began, in a curious, dreamy voice: " My father was a Laird, the only land he held being a* desolate moor and a ruined house near which stands a small but deep lake. The ruins of an old chapel are there also, and we have our ghost," he added, with a ghastly smile.

"Don't talk about it, old fellow," said Gilbert. But Dane took no heed of him, and went on in the same dreamy voice: "When any misfortune is going to happen to us beautiful sad music is heard in the ruined chancel of the church that passes over the lake and dies away in the water, whose surface is then, and only then, agitated and dashes against the sides with fury. My two brothers and I as boys were always drawn to the lake by some mysterious attraction. They were much older than I, for five sisters had been born and died between them and me, but we loved each other, we three."

Dane stopped suddenly, looked around almost wildly as he said, "What matters it to you how they died? They are gone—all—I only am left. There, let us talk of something else." I remember we talked of those mysterious warnings that sometimes are given to people, Dane's mention of the music that heralded a death in his family probably giving rise to the topic, and it was astonishing how many different cases we had heard from various people.

We reached the ranche, and while Gilbert was fastening the boat, Dane asked me to walk awhile with him; he was restless, and could not sleep. It was a lovely night, the young moon was setting over the Tarwin, and all looked still and beautiful.

As we paced up and down Dane told me the story of his life.

A sad story, but alas! not an uncommon one. The father, brooding over his poverty and supposed wrongs until scarce responsible for the wild acts he committed. The mother, taken from a large bright family and isolated in the gloomy ruins of her husband's ancient home, drooped and pined. One by one her little girls died, and she became a mere shadow of a woman wandering around the house silent and heart-broken. More money difficulties, more trouble, for the father's body was found in the lake; he had drowned himself; the second son, who had evidently attempted to save him, lost his life at the same time. The grass trampled down and broken bushes testified to a struggle between the two men. Under this blow the mother sank, and the eldest and youngest of the family lived together, and it seemed as if peace at last and some happiness was to be theirs.

Not so, however. When Dane was just grown up his brother married. The bride, a handsome, self-willed woman, soon made the life unbearable to Dane, but her husband was infatuated. To satisfy her whims and extravagances everything was sacrificed, and all the improvements the two brothers had made when alone were left unfinished; all the money put aside for rebuilding the old home was used in gifts for the woman who had so fascinated the Laird. Then, when there was no more money, she became fierce and intolerant; her husband, heavily in debt, could do nothing more. Bitter disputes arose. One day she left him, having forged his name to a cheque, leaving debts in every direction. Dane said his brother told him all the story with the manner of a man frozen with grief. He left him, saying he would go into Edinburgh to see what could be done to keep at least the dishonour from becoming public, and he begged Dane to stay at the Keep until his return. Some days after he was asked to come and identify the body of a man which had been found in one of the deep ponds with which the place abounded. In the corpse with its face distorted with agony he recognized his brother. "I always see it before me, it never leaves me," said poor Dane, shivering so violently that once the story told I tried to soothe him, and speak to him of hope; he was young and in fair health; a strong effort of will would help him to get rid of what was after all but a great nervous shock.

"It is no good," he said, in a tone of hopeless despair, "I shall end as they did, I cannot help myself, the temptation is at times quite irresistible. A power within me stronger than my will pushes me on. Whenever you hear I am dead you will know I couldn't help myself. Don't mention what I have told you to any one until my death frees you; it cannot matter then, for I am the last of the race."

"But your aunt, she seems to have been kind to you."

"She is my mother's half-sister—yes, she is kind,

but I hardly know her, and have neither the wish nor the right to cast a gloom upon her life."

" But you promised me not to attempt to take your life," I reminded him.

" Yes, and I have kept that promise, and mean to keep it as long as I have the power."

We talked a little longer, chiefly about the beauty of the night, then Gilbert called us in. Actuated by some impulse, I shook hands with Dane, and we all retired for the night.

We never saw him again.

He must have got up when we were both asleep and slipped out of the tent. On the table he had placed a bit of paper with these words : " Don't trouble about me, I am going to my aunt for a change, and will write to you from there if I don't return in a month."

Though I felt a little uneasy, still we agreed that a change was the best thing for him, and there was nothing extraordinary in his going off suddenly like that. It was only in thinking it over that I noted how he had never told me his aunt's name, nor what profession her husband was, so we could not trace him if we wished. Whether the name he went by was his own I do not know for certain, but I have sometimes thought that his curious Christian name might be his surname, for he answered to it much more readily than to Stuart.

It was three weeks before we knew for certain what had become of him. Then some settlers coming past our ranche brought us the sad news of his death. They had met him going to Melbourne, and as they were also bound for that city, rode on together. Dane had taken one of our horses. The morning before they reached Melbourne they missed him, but finding his horse with theirs, waited a short time, thinking he would join them. As he did not do so they searched around for him, and came upon his dead body floating in a lagoon. Not knowing his name or anything about him, they buried him there, and went to Melbourne, where, having done their business, they returned to their settlement some forty miles beyond ours. They called at our ranche to return the horse, poor Dane having said that his horse belonged to a settler called Jenkins, on the Tarwin River.

"He must have got caught in the swamp grasses," said the man who told us the story, "and although he must have shouted for help we were too far off to hear him. Very hard, poor young fellow, to be cut off suddenly like that."

I knew better; it was no chance or accident that had ended Dane's short life. One of those hereditary morbid fits of depression had evidently come over him, and as it were forced him to take his life. I reproached myself bitterly for not watching him more closely, yet he had never been so bright and cheerful as on that last day he spent with us. From what I could extract from the three settlers he had been a pleasant and cheerful companion the days they spent together, but had mentioned neither his name nor where he lived, only saying the horse was ours, so that we might get the animal again, but not telling his fellow-travellers that he had lived with us.

Poor Dane! his sad, troublous young life was ended. From the day of his birth to the day of his death a curse had seemed to lie upon him and overshadow him until the burden of life was greater than he could bear. Let us not judge. God's ways are not our ways, and all we, in our poor human judgment, can say is, that the poor lad was more sinned against than sinning.

We afterwards tried to see his grave, but we found that the floods had been out and swept away the rough wooden cross that the three settlers had placed above him, so we could not be sure of the spot.

Gilbert and I went on our usual way after Dane's death, waiting for the cutter to take our really valuable cargo to Melbourne. We increased it daily either with skins or fish. At this time I built a small boat, pointed canoe fashion at both ends, very light and easy to manage, and from which we caught many fish.

The cutter still not coming, Gilbert packed a large quantity of fish, flour, fruit, &c., on Magog and started for the nearest town, the Bass. He was a long time away, as he had forty-nine miles through a wild and uninhabited forest to pass through. With endless swamps and streams and rivers to cross, often he found himself in great peril and difficulty, and being quite alone, got depressed and unhappy. But Magog was a fine beast, and carried him safely through all dangers, swimming a river or trotting on contentedly under a burning sun, asking for little and contented with less.

Arriving at Bass, Gilbert went to the one hotel, and renewed acquaintance with Mr. Laycock, the proprietor, who "ran" the hotel at that time. This gentleman, an Englishman, had only lately married, and hearing so much from Gilbert of the beauty and healthfulness of the Tarwin, determined to return with him and give his bride an idea of life in the bush.

Nothing could have been more delightful. We gave up the one bedroom to them, and did all in our power to make it agreeable to Mrs. Laycock, who was a delicious young English girl, devoted to her husband, and delighted with everything. We spent our time in picnics up the river in out-of-the-way places, where we found beautiful plants, and all sorts of lovely flowers, tropical in their rich luxuriance, returning in the evening to our camp and having music or readings. They brought many books, and, what is more, left them for us, so we passed a very happy few weeks — a bright spot in our lonely existence.

As soon as they left us, Vaughan came with his cutter and took our valuable cargo on board. Even estimating the value low, we calculated to make enough money to enable us to buy the adjoining land, and hire men to help in the work on the farm.

SCENERY—GIPP'S LAND.

One day, pending Vaughan's return, Gilbert went down in his boat to Screw Creek, about twelve miles off, to fish, and on coming back the boat stuck fast on a sandbank in the bay, and was soon high and dry, so rapidly did the tide go out. The gig was too heavy for him to push off, and there he sat for the whole night cold and hungry, with endless sandbanks rising in every direction. This place, called "Anderson's Inlet," is a large reach of sandbanks with a narrow channel winding about in a most tortuous and, as Pat would say, "serpentine" manner. It was early morning before Gilbert could get off. He said a pelican or two came and looked at him, but walked away when their curiosity was satisfied.

It is very comical to see these gigantic birds standing in the shallows, with their wings extended, watching for their prey. An unconscious fish passes by, Mr. Pelican snatches him up, and you see the poor victim descending the immense skinny bag with many a leap and flounder, until with a final gulp it disappears. The pelicans here are not white, nor yet pink, but beautifully pencilled about the shoulders (you can see by this feeble description that I am not much of an ornithologist); they stand about four feet high, perhaps even a little taller. In 'Frisco I have seen them very little larger than a goose, and quite white.

Screw Creek is full of fish, and there is first-rate seine fishing. The tremendous stringarees, or sting-ray, abound here, a large flat fish with a serrated spine and whip-like tail, with which he can inflict a terrible and, as we have been told, fatal wound. These are the "devil-fish" of some authors, and the name is not altogether misapplied.

About a mile from our ranche were several lagoons, where we used often to go and shoot wild duck. Standing under a ti-tree the ducks would alight almost at our feet, and they would continue to come in immense numbers, not in the least deterred by our firing, until we got positively sick of such wholesale slaughter. Had there been a market near, or any regular communication by steamboat with the nearest town, we should quickly have made our fortune; and we thoroughly enjoyed our mode of life, for neither Gilbert nor I cared for the pleasures of city life. This Bohemian existence, far "away from the world's cold strife," was far more to our taste than the gayest and most luxurious life modern Babylon could offer to us.

As you walk along through the bush you are startled by the sharp sounding lash of a whip, and to your amazement you find it is produced by a little scrap of a bird, who seems to enjoy your confusion immensely, and lashes away as though he had a carter's whip four feet long in his possession. The lyre-bird is a wonderful creature. Whistle a tune and he will take up the air note by note with faultless accuracy. He is a fearful mimic; nothing escapes him. Cocks and hens crow and cackle all around; you would think the whole district a vast poultry-yard, the *raison d'être* being a few fowls around your hut, whose amorous conversation is the subject of gossip all over the country by these busybodies. The barking of a dog, the singing of the bull-frog, is faithfully reproduced. Dorcas has been driven to the very borders of frenzy by hearing her own words repeated in her own voice from the top of a mimosa or a gum-tree. I have taken out my violin sometimes and played a tune. After a moment's silence a dozen Paganinis scrape and fiddle around. The effect is weird in the extreme. This lyre-bird—panura, I think, is its family name—is a sort of pheasant, at least in look, of a bright brown colour, with a most magnificent tail, which tail, when spread out *à la* peacock, resembles an ancient lyre—hence its English name. These same tails, alas! are much sought after, and fetch a high price in Melbourne.

Numerous and extraordinary are the creatures of all sorts and sizes that one comes across. I stooped down once to pick up a twig to clear out my pipe. Seeing a nice straight little branch about six or eight inches in length, I took it up, when lo! the thing came to life and wriggled out of my fingers! How I started, dropped my pet little black pipe, which smashed to pieces!

The praying insect (mantis religiosus) is another marvel in the insect kingdom. It walks along with its lengthy thorax at a right angle to the rest of its body, its nun-like head raised aloft as if waiting an answer to its prayers, and its fore feet elevated high in piteous supplication. Hypocrite! it is only on the look-out for some victim to rend in pieces and devour; those pious hands so tightly clasped are powerful and merciless saws. Insatiable, inexorable, cruel, and false, the mantis religiosus goes on its baneful way, leaving desolation and misery wherever it passes. Did you ever meet a human mantis religiosus? They are not uncommon. I shall speak of one shortly.

These praying insects seem to be a large family, and vary in size from one to six inches in length, some never exceeding one inch. Their wings are like green leaves, and their eyes sparkle with snake-like brilliancy.

We were now daily expecting Vaughan to return, and building up many *châteaux en Espagne* with the golden harvest that was to be ours after our hard toil and patient labour. Fools! we should have learnt ere now how useless it is to plan for the future, the expected rarely happens; only of misfortune and sorrow can we be sure in this world. And so we found it.

Vaughan sent us a letter by a messenger, saying a frightful misfortune had overtaken him, and with him we too were ruined. His steamer had become a wreck, and all our valuable cargo had gone to the bottom. He expressed a hope that we knew where to look for help, to bear our troubles patiently, the Fountain of Life, in whose waters he himself intended to dip in, or wash himself in—I forget which expression he used.

"All lost!" said poor Gilbert, staring at the messenger of woe.

"Is Mr. Vaughan much broken down?" I asked, wishing to turn the current of his thoughts.

"He has lost everything, he says he is ruined." The man grinned as he replied, "The boat's gone down fast enough."

"What's there to grin at, you idiot!" cried Gilbert, irritated by the fellow's untimely mirth.

"Not so big an idiot as some one I know," was the answer. "This child would never trust a sharper like Vaughan with a rich freight, not he!"

"He couldn't help the steamer's being wrecked," I said.

The man grinned again. "In course he couldn't help it after she was run on a reef, but there's some wrecks as is accidents, and there's some wrecks as isn't."

"Look here, my man, just speak out plainly, will you, if you know anything," I said, quickly, for I saw Gilbert was getting in a state of irritation bordering on frenzy.

"Well, the truth is that Vaughan is a d—— scoundrel. He's just wrecked the steamer hisself, having first heavily insured the cargo—your cargo—in his own name. The boat, in course, was insured. Lots of the skins and kegs of fish and fruit were floating about; these he had hawked about Melbourne streets, and made a nice little sum. You see, you are the only settlers down this way now, so it 'tain't worth his while to steam here any longer. The boat was old, and being well insured he's lost nought; indeed, he's gained a mint o' money."

"But surely," I said, "we can get some redress?"

"Can you? I should likes to know how. No, no, you're done, and if I were in your place I'd clear out of this as quick as I could. You might get a little money for it now, you won't in another month or two. You see, with Vaughan's cutter your only chance of export trade is gone."

"Do you know where Vaughan is now?" asked Gilbert, who had been very quiet while the man was talking.

"I left him in Melbourne, playing the martyr, bemoaning your fate, and selling the skins for a fair price, as he said the money was for two mates of his, who had all their fortune in his cutter. Has he sent you any money?"

"Not a penny; he simply says that he as well as we are ruined."

"Well, I'm real sorry for you," said the man, preparing to go, which recalled me to the duties of hospitality.

He remained with us the night, and left the next day to return to Melbourne.

"If you come into the city at any time, you can come to my diggings if you like," he said, telling us where he lived.

"Yes, we shall be in Melbourne soon," replied Gilbert, to my surprise, for we had settled nothing yet. "I mean to see Mr. Vaughan."

"Lor', it ain't no good; you won't git a penny out of him."

"Nor do I wish to ask him, but I don't leave Melbourne until I've seen him and horsewhipped him in the public streets," was the quiet answer.

The man looked at him thoughtfully; he was evidently comparing the somewhat stalwart frame of Mr. Vaughan with my friend's slight make and small stature.

"If you do, I hope I may be there to see it," he remarked. Then, mounting his horse, he was swiftly out of sight.

Here we were once more face to face with ruin, once more to begin climbing the ladder again, the top of which we had so nearly reached. Well, it was no good sitting still and cursing our fate, which I was more disposed to do than Gilbert, who seemed seized with a feverish desire to settle up everything as quickly as possible in order to get to Melbourne. His determination to punish the scoundrel who had ruined us became stronger every hour, and every delay but added fuel to the fire of his wrath. All my attempts at changing him being useless, I could only hope Vaughan would leave Melbourne before we entered it, for I feared in the tussel that must inevitably come if the two men met, that Gilbert would get the worst off. He, however, seemed to have no doubt not only that he should meet Vaughan, but that he would horsewhip him in public.

It was a sad few weeks that followed. The ranche

was disposed of to a settler who did not care to export his skins and fish, but only to rear horses; and one morning we packed our remaining baggage on Magog's back, put Dorcas on him, and sorrowfully turned away from our pretty ranche where we had spent so many peaceful days. Not without great toil and difficulty we reached Bass, and remained there three or four days to rest. I could hardly persuade Gilbert to so much, for his eagerness to reach Melbourne had now assumed all the strength of a mania. I perceived that a small but exceedingly powerful horsewhip never left his possession.

At length we reached Melbourne, took Magog and Dorcas to their old master. He bought back the former, paying a fair sum for him, and was enchanted to have Dorcas back again. We grieved sorely at parting with her, and hurried away from her, fearing to trust ourselves to another look or word. My last sight of her, she was sitting on Magog's back cleaning her face in a slow and thoughtful manner. I have known cats before and since, but never have come across one to compare with green-eyed, grey-coated Dorcas. But to less pleasant topics. We lodged with the man who had brought us the tidings of woe, and from him we heard that Vaughan was in Melbourne and had set up large stores, and had every prospect of doing well.

Gilbert's eyes—large green-grey ones—dilated and grew black, like Dorcas's when she saw a foe.

I made one last attempt to dissuade him from carrying out his intention, but in vain.

The next morning he asked me to look out for a ship going to Sydney, and to bespeak two berths. He then went out with Hogg, the man at whose house we were lodging. I went down to the wharf, found a vessel that would start in a fortnight's time, one having left the day before, took our berths, and returned to our lodgings as quickly as I could. I had not been long there when Gilbert and Hogg entered, flushed and excited.

"There, I've done it," cried the former, letting himself drop into a chair. "Now we can leave Melbourne as soon as you like."

Hogg was eager to tell the story. They had gone straight to Vaughan's stores, who, on first seeing Gilbert, changed colour and looked uncomfortable, but recovering himself after a moment, greeted him as though he were a dear friend. Finding Gilbert quiet and polite enough, and seemingly not disposed to bear him any ill-will, he proposed going to a neighbouring tavern to have the usual "drink." Hogg, of course, was also invited. No sooner were they in the public street than Gilbert pulled out his whip and struck Vaughan across the face, following the blow up with a rapid succession. So quick had he been that Vaughan, amazed and stunned, was some seconds before he could defend himself. He drew out a revolver, but it was knocked from his hand by a man standing by, while cries of "Shame!" were heard on all sides.

A large crowd had collected, several policemen among them; but these guardians of the peace, beyond taking a keen interest in the matter, made no objection.

"Niver enjoyed myself so much in my life," wound up Hogg, wiping his heated brow. "You wouldn't 'ave thought he had so much strength in him, but he was like a wild cat. Vaughan won't lose those marks in a hurry, I bet."

It was lucky our ship did not leave for a fortnight, for the worry consequent on his loss, added to that day's excitement, brought on one of Gilbert's illnesses, far more serious than the one he had last had on the banks of the Yarra-Yarra River.

All night he was delirious, his talk being solely and entirely about Vaughan and the loss of the ranche. All his pent-up anger seemed to find vent in passionate invectives against our pretended friend, and he struggled violently with Hogg and myself in the fancy that he had not yet meted out the punishment due to that scoundrel. After a while he quieted down a little, and at daybreak Hogg went for a doctor. Gilbert fell into a heavy, uneasy sleep, and I nearly dozed by his side when the door of our room opened, and what I took to be an "old clo'" man entered.

He was tall and thin, with baggy trousers in the last stage of shabbiness. A long coat with three capes, all green with age and more or less torn, was kept on his spare limbs by one large button.

A chimney-pot hat surmounted some thin, straggling locks of grey hair, and a pair of keen, dark eyes looked sharply out from snowy eyebrows. Dirty, unshaven, and fierce-looking, my uninvited visitor was decidedly unprepossessing.

"You've made a mistake, my man," I said, rising and going towards him, and speaking in a low tone for fear of rousing Gilbert. "I don't know you, and my friend there is ill."

"Move aside," said this strange object, trying to push past me as I barred his way.

"But who are you? What do you want?"

"Sent—Hogg—doctor——"

I fell back in astonishment before this weird disciple of Hippocrates, who, taking advantage of my involuntary movement, advanced towards the bed and stared fixedly at Gilbert.

Fearing I had to do with a madman, I left the door open that I might call in help in case of need, and put a thick rug handy to smother up the "doctor" if he showed the least signs of mischief. Then I stationed myself on the opposite side of the bed, which, being a small iron one, I could quickly get around.

The "doctor" took no notice whatever of me, but appeared profoundly interested in my poor friend, whose eyes he opened, pulse he felt, tongue he examined with an indifference to the man whom he thus manipulated that was curious to see. Then, without looking at me, he asked me many questions about Gilbert, telling me sharply once that he didn't need any surmises on my part, but simply answers to his questions. The cicatrice in the head appeared deeply to interest him, and he could hardly tear himself away.

Finally he asked for paper and pen, wrote down his ordinance in a singularly firm and beautiful handwriting, and muttering, " Shall come again this evening," shuffled out of the room.

The chemist to whom I took the prescription glancing at the signature, said, " You are in luck's way, if you want to save the life of the person who's ill. But how did you get at him?"

I explained, and then asked some questions about the doctor. The chemist informed me that Dr. Fernnoh was as well known for his great skill as for his great eccentricities. Any dangerous or singular illness always attracted him, and he would stay night and day watching and attending some hopeless case that other doctors had given up. He had snatched so many from the grim hands of Death that no one despaired if he could only be induced to undertake the case. But there lay the difficulty: he cared for no one, for nothing; money, fame, and honour were offered him in vain; if the malady happened to be one that did not interest him all prayers and entreaties were useless. Without apparently either heart or feeling, seeing the most atrocious sufferings with coldness, performing the most terrible operations with a *sang-froid* that could only come from an utter want of sensibility, Dr. Fernnoh's presence was as much feared as desired in many cases. But he went where he chose, and sometimes where he was not wanted. The chemist told me of a case where a poor woman was suffering from cancer complicated with heart disease. Her one prayer was that Dr. Fernnoh might not be told, for she dreaded his cruelty, and preferred to die in peace. He scented her case out as a cat scents a mouse, came to her, and, utterly indifferent to her prayers and entreaties, took her in hand, forced the other doctors to leave, as he always did by his intolerant insolence, cut out the cancer, strengthened the heart, and, in a word, cured her.

Thanks and abuse were alike indifferent to this strange man ; his one passion was the curious and extraordinary in his profession. No one knew anything about him or his family. He was supposed to be of Danish extraction, although no reason could be assigned for the supposition. He lived alone in a huge, bare house with an old man and an old woman, who were as taciturn and odd as their master. Some said he was a millionaire, others that he had not money enough to buy his daily bread. In fact, nothing was really known about him, except the fact that he was very clever as a doctor and very singular.

I paid for the medicine and went back thoughtfully to my friend. I found him in the same position, and the woman I had left in charge said he had not moved. I looked at him with interest. What was there peculiar in his case that called the attention of so curious and clever a man as Dr. Fernnoh ?

While I was standing there Hogg came in.

" Has the doctor been ? " were his first words.

" Yes, but why did you get such a man as that ? "

" Because he's the cleverest doctor anywhere by a long shot. Why, was he angry ? Isn't the case serious ? " asked Hogg, anxiously.

" Serious enough, I dare say," I replied, gloomily; " he's coming again this evening."

" Then he's safe," said my landlord, looking at Gilbert, who began to toss and mutter angrily, as though protesting against any interference.

I did not know what to do. With the help of necessary medicines I had brought him round before, and I somewhat resented his being taken out of my hands in this cool way. In spite of what I had heard of Dr. Fernnoh, I resolved to tell him that evening that I would cure my friend myself, pay him what I owed, and be free. I found that I had counted without—Dr. Fernnoh.

He came again early in the evening, and sitting down by Gilbert's side began to talk to him. The medicine he had ordered had been almost miraculous in its effect, and my friend was calm and nearly without fever.

The old doctor, with great skill, got at all our past lives, and Gilbert's, before we had met, of what nationality he was, who were his parents, in what station of life—in fact everything that could in the least help his understanding of the illness.

The talk ended, the doctor took from his pocket a small case of instruments, which he opened, and ordered me to bring a basin of warm water.

"Now is my time," thought I; and not without a tremor of nervousness I asked what he was going to do.

A broad stare and an imperious repetition of the order was all the answer I got.

"Because," I said, hastily, "now that my friend has so far recovered there is no longer any need for a doctor's attendance. I have seen him like this often, and know what to do. So if you will kindly tell me your fee, and go——" I finished lamely, disconcerted by the fixedness of Dr. Fernnoh's sharp, dark eyes, which seemed to gauge my very soul.

"A basin of warm water at once," he hissed out, tossing back his grey locks and flourishing the steel instrument in his hand as though he would like to stick it into my heart.

Gilbert, who had been silent until now, raised himself up and said, "Dunbar is right, doctor. I don't need any operation of any sort, and what's more I won't have it. By to-morrow I shall be all right."

Dr. Fernnoh picked up his old hat and walked out of the room.

"Thank Heaven!" I ejaculated, piously; but my gratitude was premature. In less than a minute the doctor returned with a basin of warm water in his hands.

In spite of my angry protestations, and Gilbert's more feeble ones, he reopened part of the wound and sewed it up again with wonderful dexterity and quickness; then giving the patient a few drops of some opal-coloured liquid in a glass of water, he said, "Go on with the medicine. Will come to-morrow," and shuffled away as before.

Gilbert was feverish and uneasy all night, but undoubtedly the wound had been clumsily sewn up by the army surgeon; it rapidly healed now, and before five days were over he was out of all danger.

The old doctor had come morning and evening, had changed the medicine, had chatted pleasantly with Gilbert, and treated me with a contemptuous scorn that made my blood boil.

On the evening of the fifth day he said to Gilbert, "I shall not come again—you are cured;" adding, in a tone of regret, "I thought the case would have been more interesting."

"Will he be able to travel in a week's time?" I ventured to ask; but he turned his back on me, and said to Gilbert—

"You are cured, for the time, but you will always be subject to attacks of fever following any excitement or worry. The sea voyage next week is good," and he began to shuffle out of the room, when Gilbert said—

"As I may not see you again, may I ask what I am indebted to you?"

"Nothing," was the short reply.

"But I can't allow——" began Gilbert, when he was stopped by an outburst of rage from the doctor, who fairly danced with passion—a grotesque figure he cut, too, with his ragged clothes and old hat.

"At least let me thank you," said my friend, struggling to keep from a burst of laughter.

Dr. Fernnoh spat out a volley of obscene and blasphemous words and left the room; nor did we ever see him again. I heard some years after that he had died of blood-poisoning, caught in attending some bad case, which he had treated in a new way. The remedy cured his patient but killed himself.

The days passed on. Gilbert recovered with wonderful rapidity, thanks to Dr. Fernnoh. We bought some necessary clothes, packed them in as small a compass as possible, and one fine morning bade good-bye to Hogg, not without regret, for he was a good, honest fellow, a *rara avis* that one seldom comes across, and went on board the *Arrow*, bound for Sydney.

We did not intend to stop there, having decided to try the Sandwich Islands, though what line of life we meant to follow we had as yet no idea. One advantage in being Jack-of-all-trades, no work, of whatever sort it might be, could come amiss to us.

The voyage was a pleasant little time of rest, during which we tried not to allow our thoughts to dwell too much on the past, but looked forward with hopeful hearts to the future. The weather was lovely, the sea neither too rough nor too calm, but fresh and sparkling. No adventure of any sort happened, for which I must confess I felt glad. One gets somewhat weary of adventures as time goes on, and were it not for the occasional "rests" on the road of life, would find it a difficult matter to get up even a semblance of interest over a wreck or a shark or an encounter with a rattlesnake.

One interesting and amusing incident came under my notice which may be worth relating. Among the passengers was a young lady who was going to Sydney under the care of her guardian and his son. Everything gets known about everybody on board ship, and it was soon an open secret that Miss Merton was engaged to young Mr. Tullock. She was a tiny little thing, with large, round, blue eyes, and short, yellow, curly hair. Every man on board was at her wee feet—or would have been had she not been so safely and jealously guarded by Messrs. Tullock, *père et fils.*

Mr. Tullock, senior, was immense, tall, broad, and stout; he carried his sixty odd years very well, but he was decidedly ugly and painfully nervous, while his awkwardness when attempting any little act of courtesy towards his ward would make the proverbial bull in a china-shop blush with spite at being so much outdone. Mr. Tullock, junior, was also tall, broad, and stout, ugly too—but there the resemblance between father and son ceased, for if the one was conspicuous by his diffidence and modesty, the overweening conceit and vanity of the other was a thing to marvel at, given to him, perhaps, for the perfecting of his ugliness. It was curious to watch the three, the young man on one side of his lady-love talking in a loud, self-satisfied tone, generally about himself, the old man the other side, carrying the stool and shawls and cushion and all the rest of the paraphernalia without which a lady seems unable to admire the view of sky and sea on board ship.

Gilbert soon made friends with Miss Merton, and, despite the scowls and frowns of Mr. Tullock, junior, contrived to pass some very pleasant hours, and found out, or thought he did, something about the state of the little lady's heart.

"I'm sure she doesn't like that great hulking lump of conceit," he told me one day. "I believe it's a simple plot got up by the father and son to force her to marry the young one in order to keep the money."

"Mr. Tullock, senior, has no look of the cruel or wicked guardian about him," I protested, looking across the deck where the old man, laden as usual, was walking by his ward and gazing at her with open admiration and affection, which she appeared to take very much as a matter of course.

"Of course he would hide it," persisted Gilbert. "It's my firm opinion that she is frightened out of her life between the two of them," and my friend, who is rather inflammable, sighed deeply.

At that moment came to us distinctly, in Miss Merton's clear, bird-like voice—

"Most decidedly not; I won't have it!" and the old man's meek reply, "Very well, my dear, as you like, of course."

I looked at Gilbert, and we both went off into a fit of laughing. The little lady heard us, called us up, and requested to know the reason of our mirth. You may be quite sure we neither of us intended to tell her, yet somehow before five minutes had passed she had got it out of us. I beat a hasty retreat when I found I was losing, leaving Gilbert to get out of it the best way he could. Mr. Tullock joined me, and began to talk of his ward: she was an orphan daughter of an old friend of his; that his son should marry her had always been understood.

"Are they engaged?" I asked.

"Yes, they always have been?"

"It is a love-match then, I suppose?" I went on, feeling very wily and fox-like.

"No one could know May without loving her," said Mr. Tullock, with such fervour that, looking into his face, I read his secret. He, too, loved his ward. Poor man, my heart ached for him.

Now, Miss Merton had a pet dog, one of those toy terriers, with eyes darting out of their head, and always shivering and whimpering. His digestion was bad, which affected his temper, and he snapped and snarled at every one who went near him. Still, as it was the only way to his mistress's smiles, all the men on board (I except myself) made great asses of themselves, and got up a fervent interest in Beau's state of health that forced them to be always inquiring for him. I excepted myself. I should also have excepted Mr. Alexander Tullock, between whom and Beau existed a deadly and deep hatred. This unchristian-like feeling he dared not show before his lady-love, for she had a way of flashing out a look of scorn or anger from her blue eyes that made even the great Mr. Alexander Tullock feel small.

One morning the little lady came on deck early, her guardian only with her, as Mr. Alexander was doubtless engaged in donning one of the wonderful nautical suits wherein he loved to array himself. The old gentleman having comfortably settled her, took up the dog to place on her lap, when, how it happened no one can tell, perhaps the sudden apparition of his hated enemy in all the glories of a blue and white costume was the cause, but Beau sprang out of Mr. Tullock's arms and went plump into the sea.

What a commotion! Miss Merton screamed. I shouted "Man overboard!" without thinking, the cry was repeated, the man at the wheel brought the *Arrow* to a standstill, and all was bustle and confusion.

"Save my dog! oh, save my dog!" cried Miss Merton, rushing distractedly to the side of the vessel.

"He'll be saved all right," said her lover, drawing her away; and turning to one of the sailors said, in a tone of haughty command, "Save the dog."

"Sha'n't for your telling," said the man, moving away to where a boat was being lowered to pick up the struggling Beau, who was frantically beating the water some little distance off.

"He's drowning," shrieked Miss Merton. "Oh, do make haste, some one, and save him!"

A sudden splash was heard. Mr. Tullock had jumped in after the dog—Mr. Tullock, senior, not Mr. Tullock, junior! That worthy was engaged in the sweet office of trying to soothe the young lady, who on hearing the plunge and learning who had attempted the rescue of her pet became more wildly excited than ever.

Now comes the cream of the story. There being not the slightest danger, for the boat was quickly lowered and manned, we could enjoy the grotesque sight of the huge Mr. Tullock sporting himself in the water like some mighty porpoise. But the comedy nearly turned into a tragedy. The poor old gentleman had not long finished his breakfast, and the sudden plunge into the sea gave a shock to the nervous system and brought on a sort of fit. He was hauled into the boat with the dripping and exhausted Beau, and both were laid on the deck.

I happened to be standing near Miss Merton when it was seen that Mr. Tullock, for some reason or other, was sinking. She saw it too, and sprang forward with a cry.

"Don't fear, darling," says Mr. Alexander, "I am near you." But she turned upon him, a very Titania of furies, and, stamping her tiny foot, cried passionately—

"Go away. I hate you!"

And I must say for her, that she looked as if she meant it.

Observing that I had both seen and heard this little incident, Mr. Alexander muttered something about nerves out of order, and moved away towards where the boat was coming with his father and the cur on board. Miss Merton and I followed, but when Mr. Tullock was lifted on deck and she saw he was insensible, she flew to his side and, throwing herself on her knees, sobbed out, "Richard, if you are dead, I shall die too!"

The reader has doubtless remarked that Mr. Tullock, junior, was named by his godfathers and godmother, Alexander. I sought my friend's eye, and we exchanged a significant glance. Mr. Tullock soon recovered, and retired to his cabin to put on dry clothes; his son sulked in a chair on deck, while Miss Merton, wiping and drying her restored pet, talked nervously to Gilbert and me.

Soon old Mr. Tullock appeared, and, after we had congratulated him on his heroic deed, Gilbert and I discreetly withdrew.

The next day it was known that Miss Merton was engaged to Mr. Tullock, senior, having asked him herself—so said rumour. At any rate they were simply a delicious couple to see, their happiness in each other being so very apparent.

"I cannot realize it," said the old gentleman to me one evening as we paced up and down, smoking. "I feel as if it were wicked of me to allow her to sacrifice herself so, but she will, and what can I do?"

"Nothing," I answered, quoting those lines of the old poet, who tells us—

> "That man's a fool, who thinks by force or skill
> To stem the torrent of a woman's will."

Mr. Alexander Tullock did not seem to enjoy the new state of things as much as his father and future mamma, which perhaps is not astonishing. It was highly diverting to observe the little airs of wisdom, and to hear the sage pieces of maternal advice that she employed towards her future son. One thing is sure, although it is, I know, the custom to cry out against the union of May and December, the little lady had a far better chance of happiness from the large-hearted, kindly old man than she could ever have hoped for from the selfish, vain, and conceited young one.

This little domestic drama made a very pleasing diversion in the monotony of life on board ship; beyond that nothing happened of any interest, and in due time we entered the harbour of the great city of Sydney.

We had plenty of time to become well acquainted with that city, for we found we were obliged to wait two months, as the new line of boats had not commenced to run to San Francisco.

I shall not describe our stay in Sidney, or our voyage to 'Frisco, as nothing of particular interest happened.

We landed at 'Frisco, and were immediately taken possession of by a "Looter," who brought us to the Marhattar House, a lodging-house in the part of 'Frisco that went by the name of the "Barbary Court." This said "Court" is the habitat of all sorts of bad characters, night birds of the worst sort; but the house was clean, a good table was kept, and the beds not more densely populated than is usual. Being travellers, we could not well object to these nightly companions, so there we stayed, spending the days seeking employment, which was as hard to find as is water in the Sahara.

With the recollection of our New Zealand experiences, we husbanded our little hoard, not spending even what was necessary, and searching for work with a feverish desire quickened by despair.

It was useless striving against fate; again one day we found ourselves utterly destitute. No work, no money, hungry and thirsty, our souls fainted within us, wandering to and fro, with that great gaunt spectre Despair ever accompanying us. Oh, those weeks that followed!—let me pass them over with as few words as possible. We haunted the wharves, and now and then, by a rare stroke of luck, got a little work in unloading; on those days we could buy a ten cent loaf of bread, and seek some silent place to eat it, washing it down with water from a horse trough. Again and again we have frequented the quays to gather up some grains of Indian corn lying about, in order to satisfy our hunger, for in that city we and hundreds of others were literally dying by inches of starvation. We would have worked day and night; but no, the Chinese were preferred, the Europeans rejected. No wonder the workmen hate these yellow, crooked-eyed vermin, with their clever cunning and their merciless cruelty.

I applied to the F. and A. Masons, in the hope that some of them would give or get me work; they could not; all in their power they did, which was to give me lodgings for four weeks.

During that time Gilbert went dish-washing in a hotel in 2nd Street; his fellow-washer was a French count! But the constant dabbling in hot soap-suds blistered his hands so terribly that in a very short time he could not use them at all, and was obliged to give up a business that, as he confided to me with some irritation, more disgusted him than anything he had ever yet undertaken in his chequered life. His next work was window-cleaning; but all he had ever done or thought of doing paled before the revolting and disgusting business that was offered to, and of course accepted by, me. Oh, long line of illustrious ancestors, how would your venerable hairs stand upright on your venerable heads could you but see your unfortunate descendant in a pork-packing factory, cleaning out the shoots which were filled with the guts and offal from the slaughter-house! These had been accumulating for over twelve months, and the odour emanating from the putrid mass had better be neither described or imagined. Allow me a moment to fill my pipe, or I cannot continue. I always hated swine, but since that time the sight of a pig is enough for me; never from that day to this has a piece of pork entered my lips, and, if I know myself, it never will.

Soon the pork-factory "bust up," the men were discharged. Thank God I was free again, with some dollars in my pocket. I persuaded Gilbert without much difficulty to leave his enchanting work of window-cleaning, for I had heard of more congenial employment which was to be had, although at a great distance. This was no other than road-making, and was not unknown to us as we had helped in the making of one when privates in the Rifle Corps in New Zealand.

We did not decide without careful consideration, for the road required was over in Tennesse, and led to, or rather was to lead to, the Knoxville quicksilver mines. We were of course an immense distance off, and it would take nearly all our money to get there; yet, as nothing turned up in

'Frisco, it seemed wiser to risk our all for a certainty than to remain here where we might expend every cent we possessed before having a chance of adding to our store. Besides, it was healthy work in the open air, and we were neither of us long penned up in a city without pining to be free. Placards posted all over certain parts of 'Frisco stated that numbers of able-bodied men were required to make a new road to the well-known quicksilver mines near Knoxville.

Accordingly we turned our backs on the City of the Golden State which had treated us so shabbily, and, with that hope that paints the future fair, set out for the Napa city in Tennesse.

It took most of our cash in hand to reach Napa. Arriving there, we were told that our destination was a two days' journey farther on, and we determined to do it on foot, although much pressed by the driver of a coach that had been set up expressly to bring people to the quicksilver mines. We thought the charges exorbitant, and much preferred "footing" it.

It being early morning when we arrived at Napa, we only went far enough into the town to find an eating-house, where we replenished our wallets, and, without caring farther to inspect a town that looked like other towns from the cursory glance we bestowed upon it, asked our way to Knoxville, and set off at an even pace of four miles an hour.

The weather was beautiful, and the country

after we had left the town was fertile and very picturesque. Far away in the distance we could discern the peaks of the Alleghany or Apalachian Mountains rearing themselves against the bright blue sky; a branch of the river Clinch, I believe, ran along by the side of the road we were following; it was not much more than a stream, but clear and limpid, its continuous murmur and occasional babbling being delightful to hear.

Very enjoyable was that first day's journey, and when night came on we lay down on a mossy bank, with the gem-strewed heavens above us, and were lulled to sleep by the music of the murmuring river.

We were up betimes the next morning. Reversing the general order of things, we undressed on leaving our bed, and plunging into the river had a glorious swim; after which we made a hearty breakfast, with more regard to our appetites than to the quantity of food that remained in our wallets. The clear air intoxicated us, and the cold bath made us as hungry as wolves; we felt, somehow, as though we had come into a fortune and were on our way to enjoy it. Those fits of wild pleasure are as curious and unreasoning in their way as the more frequent "fits of the blues" with which most people are acquainted; in our case it was perhaps given to us to make the contrast of after-events but the stronger, with which rather grim remark I will " git," as the Yankees say.

On the evening of the third day we reached the mines; but, it being late, we contented ourselves with finishing the remains of our provisions, and, seeking the shelter of a friendly tree, slept the sleep of the just.

The next morning we went up to the mining offices to make inquiries about work. These buildings, of a fair size, though shabby in appearance, were some distance from the mine itself—a very necessary precaution with any work connected with that valuable but deadly fluid-metal, quicksilver. We stated to the first clerk we came across, our object in coming to Knoxville, and asked to whom we were to apply. With a grin that foreboded no good he referred us to the next office, who sent us to a third, where we were told calmly and coolly that no road was to be made yet.

The management of the place we soon discovered was one huge swindle, got up by a company as dishonest as it was discreditable. Started at a time when all the world seemed infatuated with the spirit of gambling, for it was nothing else, the heads of this concern followed the example of hundreds of others, with, however, more truth than many, for quicksilver was found here, and in not inconsiderable quantities, and advertised themselves widely. Trusting to the blind ardour and spirit of speculation in the public they announced, in magniloquent language, the glorious find they had made, and talked of their millions of capital (flourishing for the most part only on paper), inviting inspection, and guaranteeing large profits.

But to return to ourselves. The story of a road being needed was a mere invention made up to induce workmen to come to the place. Once on the spot they are sometimes persuaded to stay as miners, rather than have their journey for nothing. Indeed in most cases they are obliged to remain, having expended all their ready money in coming so great a distance. A fiendish piece of policy on the part of the Company to placard their pretended want of men for road-making at such an immense distance, which virtually prevented any immediate return of the workmen.

Other tricks they had also that spoke well of their ingenuity. For instance, if you tramp there (as we did) and do not take a seat in the Company's coach at $500 a head, they are down on you with contempt. Then they require $300 for poll tax, besides a couple of dollars for school tax; like the horse-leech's daughter their cry is ever, "Give, give!"

Gladly would we have turned our backs on Knoxville quicksilver mines, had it been possible; but having spent most of our money in getting here we must make some more before we could hope to get away.

The slenderness of our purses being so painfully apparent to the lynx-eyed Company (for, needless to say, we were unable to pour out dollars for poll tax, or school tax, or any other tax), the only work offered to us was the most dangerous and in which department they had the fewest men.

Until I came to the mine I knew very little about quicksilver, but although I stayed but a short time I knew more than enough to please me. A few words about it, however, may not be uninteresting. This mercury, or quicksilver, is always found in the strata of secondary formations, and is distinguished from all other metals by its extreme fusibility, for it does not become solid until cooled to the 39th degree below 0, Fahrenheit. It is not only found in cinnabar, a red sulphuret of mercury, but in other ores, and sometimes in a quite fluid and pure state in an accidental cavity of hard stone. Its power is very great, for it penetrates parts of all other metals, making them brittle and even dissolving some. The ore found here was amber in colour, a pretty crystalline matter mixed frequently with stone and other extraneous substances, all which impurities are chipped off, facetiously called "cherry picking." Very strong and long-continued heat is necessary, for which purpose immense kilns are kept heated up to a certain temperature, which heat, combined with the fumes of the mercury, makes working in these parts of the mines so dangerous.

Dangerous or not we could not refuse, the money offered to us being in fair proportion to the risk, so we determined to try it, for anything was better than to return penniless to the scene of our late troubles.

Gilbert's work, bad as it was, was not so deadly in its effect as mine. He was set to fix and clear out one of the reverberatory furnaces that were employed in the process of refining or cupellation. Curious furnaces these were, the lower part being covered with wood ashes and clay in order to form a cupel, a shallow chemical vessel in which the assay-masters try the metal. On one side of the furnace there is a hole for the exit of the litharge, on the opposite side another hole for the admission of air to the surface of the metal, which is introduced through an aperture above, to which a cover is fitted. This particular one required some cleansing, and that my friend was requested to do; I was told I should have a room to clean out, and followed my guide, feeling sorry Gilbert had not my good luck.

My sorrow, however, was soon changed into thankfulness, for as we neared the place, gaunt, grey spectres of men were moving about, looking scarcely human. My guide stopping to give some directions to a group of them, one of the party came up to me and in a hollow voice warned me not to attempt to work here.

I looked at the man; he appeared about sixty and was bent nearly double; but what struck me most was his face—it was livid in hue, and so lean that the skin seemed stretched over the bones until I wondered it did not crack, his eyes sunk into their sockets gave him a still more ghastly look, in fact a corpse buried and dug up again is the only simile

I can choose to express the effect this man gave one.

"Do not go there," he said, earnestly, pointing with a skinny, trembling finger to a block of buildings a little distance off; "no money is worth it."

"I am only going to clean out a room," I assured him; "but you, can you find nothing else to do, old and ill as you are?"

"Old," he answered, with a bitter laugh; "I am a younger man in years than you, I bet, for all I carry my forty-three years so badly. But this is not the first time I have worked at those furnaces there, and I tell you no money is worth it."

"Then why do you do it?"

"If you care to know come to my hut, that one that lies down yonder apart from the rest, and I will show you. But for you, don't do it—no money is worth it," he repeated for the third time.

"Go to h——ll," said my guide brutally, who had come up and heard his last sentence.

"I have been there, and come out again—all that is left of me," was the mournful reply, as the man moved slowly away in an opposite direction.

"He needn't complain, I'm sure," grumbled my cicerone, "he's got his pockets full of dollars, and after all has only been here five days this time."

Five days, and looked like that! a man of forty-three! A cold shiver passed over me.

"They call him 'Mercury Jack,'" volunteered my companion, "and he's a queer fish, always coming back here and always abusing the place; now I don't call that acting quite on the square, do you?"

"That depends greatly on how he is treated," I replied, "for sometimes it happens that big mining companies don't act quite on the square with their workmen."

My friend made no reply—perhaps because we had reached the place over whose portals might surely be written Dante's words:

"Abandon hope, all ye who enter here."

My guide quickly told me what I was to do, pushed open the door, and—bolted. I was in a large condensing chamber completely saturated with mercury. It needed cleaning, certainly, and I doggedly cleaned it, and, what is more, came out alive, neither crippled nor disabled, but feeling weak, sick, weary, worn-out, and hopeless.

In these condensing chambers no man ever stays more than a few days; they are always coming and always going; coming, fairly strong and healthy; going, decrepit, broken down, and ill.

After I had emerged alive from the mercury chamber I was set to tend the kilns, *i.e.*, keep the fires at full blaze, technically called "feeding the mouths." This is done by stoving in huge logs of oak into the kilns, each log taking three men to raise and push in.

Gilbert and I took lodgings in a little hut built up of wood, of which there were a good many dotted about, and a woman, wife of one of the miners, "did" for us, as they call it. She certainly did do for us in more ways than one, but we were at her mercy, and could say nothing. One thing she did well, I must allow—she made a rabbit stew better than any one I have ever known; still, good as that was in its way, it did not make up for all the discomfort she put us to; she was dirt personified, talked like—no, I can find no simile, and being of a lachrymose turn, favoured us with long and watery accounts of all her troubles. She was a huge woman, with unkempt hair and a decided moustache, of which, far from being distressed at, she gloried in, smoothing it down and caressing it with all the pride of a young man who, after long watching and careful shaving, welcomes at last the few soft hairs that he twists and torments until he thinks that he has proved to all the world that he has that much-longed-for adornment on his upper lip. But I am forgetting the fair Ophelia Cox, who " did for " several other men besides ourselves, going from hut to hut, cooking the meals that she left ready on the fire, and "smoothing over" the beds, as she described it. Gilbert and I always made ours ourselves; the mere thought that they had been touched by that creature would have driven away the gentle god from our pillows. Her attire was as remarkable as all the rest. To begin at the end, she wore a pair of Wellington boots that had long since seen their best days, and that formerly encased the feet and legs of "as fine a gent as ever put foot to ground." Stockings she dispensed with altogether, she volunteering this interesting piece of information herself. Certainly, I should never have dreamed of asking, but she did not sin by too much reticence at any time, or on any subject. A short petticoat that had once been scarlet, but was now, by time and stains, turned into patches of all colours, was surmounted by a man's rough pilot jacket, a blue checked neckcloth, tied in a knot around her throat, and a billycock hat completed a costume that did not err on the side of elegance.

I forgot two long, deep bags or pockets that she wore, one on each side of her. These pockets, empty when she left her own hut in the morning, had a way of getting filled as the day advanced, and she returned in the evening bulging out right and left, like a donkey with panniers.

She had a husband who worked in the mines, "a poor mess," as she graphically described him. No need for me to enlarge on Jabez Cox after that terse and comprehensive delineation of him by his better half; and also six children of doubtful parentage, to fill whose ever hungry mouths she "did for" the various men around.

Among her victims was "Mercury Jack," and one day, very shortly after we were there, my work for the day being over before Gilbert's, I thought I would go down to his hut and see him, for somehow he had interested me.

A short walk past the straggling houses and

huts that formed the village, if it could be so called, brought me to the outskirts of a small wood, where, quite alone, stood a tiny hut. The little plot of ground in front had at one time been laid out as a sort of flower garden, and there were still some rose-bushes, and a few plants. No one was in sight, but the door being open I went up to it and entered. A horrible yet pathetic sight met my eyes. Seated on a low stool, swaying himself to and fro, and piping out in a thin, quavering voice the hymn, "Abide with me," was "Mercury Jack." On his knees lay what at first sight I took to be the corpse of a child, but disturbed by my footsteps, both turned towards me, and then I saw it was a living creature.

The child, a girl of some thirteen years, was a victim of the most virulent form of scrofula; many of the bones were eroded, and ophthalmia had done its work with hideous malignity. "Mercury Jack" ceased his singing as I entered, and, inviting me to sit down on the only chair the place possessed, said, without further preamble: "You have come to know why I work in the mercury chambers. I want money for Molly; it will take a lot to cure her, but we are on the road, ain't we, Moll?" and he bent over the emaciated, revolting object in his arms, and passionately kissed the top of her head.

Bit by bit he told me his story. He was a Cornishman, who had worked in the mines there, but the one on which he was engaged was closed up for want of money, and he started, like many another, for California, with his wife and two children. At first all went well, but several of the mines he worked at went smash, his wife's health failed, and every year he had another child, sickly or deformed, that dragged on a miserable existence for a year or two and then died.

"I have lost seven," said "Mercury Jack" (whose real name was Mitchell). "A sad thing for a man to see them die off one by one; it breaks the heart."

"And your wife?" I asked.

"Dead too, she was always sickly. Molly got her illness from her; she is our first child, and is now thirteen past; none lived to be so old, so I think she'll do. The doctors have given her a power of iron and hemlock."

"Is there a doctor here?"

"Yes, but I won't have him again, he don't know. He said the little maid couldn't be cured; I say she can."

During our talk the child had lain quietly in her father's arms, moaning now and again, but not speaking. The room was almost destitute of furniture, but there was a good bed in a corner, and on the table some white bread, a chicken, and a bottle of wine. There went the money which Mitchell procured by that deadly work which sapped up his life's blood, and made him at forty a decrepit old man. There and into the capacious pockets of "Ophelia Cox," who traded on such a good opportunity of filling the six ever open mouths of her own olive branches.

Whenever I had time I went down to the little hut, and always came away with a feeling of wonder at the man's devotion to the child and faith in her recovery. Mitchell was a Methodist, like, I believe, many Cornishmen, and was deeply religious, so I hoped that when the trouble fell upon him he would find comfort in his belief that the poor child was safe, and I did all I could to prepare him for what was inevitable—with, I fear, but poor success.

During this time I had gone on with my work of "feeding the mouths," just like Ophelia Cox, but my companions dropped off, finding the work too hard and the pay too small, others that replaced them refusing to stay, until I was left alone.

I went to the office to know what was to be done.

"Why, feed the mouths yourself," was the cool reply.

I explained—what they knew perfectly well—that such a thing was a simple impossibility, as no one man could raise the end of a log by himself; whereupon I was ordered "to git," as they laconically put it, meaning that my services were no longer required, and I might go elsewhere, to live or die as I chose.

Gilbert would not stay on without me, though

he had got into better work and was doing well; so we decided to leave when his next week was up. For the few days intervening I was at liberty, and spent many hours with Mitchell and his child, whose end was near at hand. How I strove to make the poor father see it! But all in vain—he only got angry. Molly had begun to recognize me by this time, and would [receive me with what would have been a smile on any other face, but on hers was only a frightful contortion of the muscles of the mouth.

One morning when I went down I saw a great change in her, and by Mitchell's sharp inquiry as to what I was looking at, knew that he had perceived it also.

"Please God, she may die quietly," I murmured, as I looked at the poor child lying a mass of ulcers and corroding sores, swollen joints, and wasted body.

But that mercy was denied the wretched father. Almost as I spoke the death agony began, and was fierce and terrible. How so much strength could exist in so frail a body was a marvel, but the poor child writhed and tossed with convulsive movements that shook her from head to foot, and opening some of the ulcers on her face and throat, deluged her with blood and matter.

"Jesus, have mercy!" cried Mitchell, almost mad with terror and grief.

I wiped the child's face and laid her back on the pillow, when there came a struggle; she beat the air frantically with her hands, uttering hoarse cries of agony, while she glared at us wildly from her lidless eyes. A final struggle, a final cry, and, thank God, the little one was dead.

Shaking from head to foot, without a dry thread on me, I turned away for a moment and went to the open door. I was stifling.

"Don't leave me," said Mitchell, in a hollow voice, and I went back to him. He was kneeling by the bed, and was gazing at his dead child, who now presented a most awful spectacle. Hastily I drew the sheet over her face, then pouring out some wine into a tumbler, forced Mitchell to drink it. It revived him, and I drew him out into the open air.

"She must be buried!" said Mitchell, suddenly, in the voice of a man talking in his sleep.

I started; we were miles away from any cemetery, and neither clergyman, priest, nor minister lived here. To get one would involve a heavy expense and loss of time. From the nature of the disease, and the great heat, the funeral must be held the next morning at the latest.

I think I have said that, years before, I had been ordained, and for over twenty years was a curate in Ireland. Religious scruples had induced me to leave the Church, and I had never since performed any ceremony whatever in connection with the Church. Now I felt myself in a difficulty; the child must be buried, and, unless I took the service, must be buried without any.

Mitchell seemed almost more broken down by that thought than any other, so after a struggle with myself I said to him, " I will read the service over Molly, if you like; I am a clergyman."

The poor fellow's joy was so great that I felt I had done the right thing. That evening he and I, with Gilbert's help, dug the grave, not far from the hut. He would have no coffin made, though we offered to help him.

The next morning at five we went down to him. He had lain her on the mattress of her bed and covered her with flowers. Cox helped us to carry her and lay her in the grave, where once more I gave out that message of love:

" I am the resurrection and the life: he that believeth in Me, though he were dead, yet shall he live."

Gilbert and Cox then went back to their work, and Mitchell and I spent the day in fencing the grave around to protect it from the wild beasts. He seemed like a man in a dream, and showed no feeling whatever until, our work over, we re-entered the hut.

I had told the woman Cox to put out of sight everything belonging to the child—she did, into her pockets, as it turned out afterwards—and to thoroughly wash and clean the room. This she had done, and when poor Mitchell saw it in its unfamiliar state, and empty, he gave a heart-broken cry—" My little maid! I want my little maid!" and fled back to the grave.

I was afraid to leave him that night, and, indeed, spent the remaining few days of our time at Knoxville with him. His patient submission was most touching to witness. All his spare time—for I persuaded him to go to work, though not in the mercury chambers again—he spent in carving a tombstone, and making the grave a very garden of flowers. That would henceforth be his one object in life.

So one morning Gilbert and I said goodbye to him, and turned our backs on the quicksilver mines and Ophelia Cox, who stood a colossal mass of damp sorrow—" Never had she done for any one with greater pleasure than for us," which was quite easy to believe. The "poor mess" stood meekly by her side, and the six children of doubtful parentage rolled in the dirt and squabbled around her.

We had decided to tramp it back again as far as we could, for although we had money, we would not give those skunks a cent, added to which our open-air life on the Tarwin had made this gipsy mode of travelling a pleasant and healthy one, far more to our taste than being boxed up in a coach with very indifferent companions.

On the evening of our first day's journey, as we prepared to bivouac under a large tree, I saw a curious figure coming along in a sneaking sort of way, and reaching us, stood right in front of me, gazing not at us, but at the food that we had spread out before us.

It was a boy of some thirteen or fifteen years, with the face of a beautiful girl. His clothes were a mass of rags and tatters, it being really a marvel how he kept them on his limbs. A man's coat, of course miles too big for him, reached to his heels, and gave him at a distance the appearance of a dwarf.

"How did you come here, and what do you want?" I asked, for we were some twenty miles and more from any habitation.

"Want something to eat," he answered, replying only to my last question.

"But how did you come here? Where's your father?"

"Dunno!"

"Or your mother?"

"Never had none."

Though I somehow doubted that last statement, still I did not insist, but, giving him a great piece of bread and meat, told him to sit down.

He did so, and ate away calmly, his lovely eyes searching first Gilbert's face and then mine with a wistful, pleading look in them that quite won my heart. Not so Gilbert; he seemed to take a violent and, as I thought, unjust dislike to the boy, and spoke so harshly that I was not astonished when the little fellow's eyes filled with tears, and he turned away as if to leave us.

"How can you be so cross!" I cried, indignantly; "you have driven him away."

"No fear," said Gilbert, with a sort of suppressed

irritation that I could not understand, and made me fear another attack of illness, though since Dr. Fernnoh's care he had seemed quite cured.

I called the boy back and tried to get from him where he came from and what he was doing out here alone, but he appeared unable to give any account of himself.

"The poor child is an idiot," I said; "what on earth are we to do with him?"

"You had better adopt him, as you seem so fond of him," answered Gilbert, savagely; "but you'll choose between him and me."

I stared at him in astonishment; the boy, having finished eating, stood watching us with pleading eyes.

"We had better sleep on it," I said; "to-morrow, if you are in the same mind, we might take him back to Knoxville, for I suppose he must have come from there, or take him on to Napa; there's sure to be some Home or other in a big town."

So having replenished the fire, and returned the remainder of our supper to the wallets which we placed by our side, we lay down and were soon fast asleep.

At daybreak the next morning I woke and looked round for the boy. He was gone, and on further investigation my wallet containing some food, a change of linen, and some money—luckily not all—was gone too! I woke Gilbert and told him what had happened.

He burst out laughing. "So much for your

adopted son. Far from being an idiot, he has shown himself sharper than either of us."

"But how could he get here, such a distance from any town, quite alone?"

"Who says he's quite alone? Most likely he's one of a party of thieves who followed us. We may think ourselves lucky that we were not murdered."

That surmise of Gilbert's must have been the correct one, for as we journeyed on we came across my little volume of Tacitus that had evidently been thrown away as useless, and the trodden-down grass near it showed that several people had encamped there. Somewhat crestfallen, and exceedingly disgusted at having been so thoroughly done by a mere child who had feigned idiotcy to avoid the difficulties of talking, I pocketed my Tacitus, and we went on our way in silence.

"You might have warned me," I grumbled at last, "for from your manner you evidently had some suspicion."

"I thought he was shamming certainly, but it wasn't that that made me so cross. The little wretch had a face that reminded me of Curly, and I could not bear it."

I knew the story of poor Curly, and could quite understand the effect the resemblance had upon him.

In due time, without further incident or adventure, we again entered the "Golden City." A road was being made at the Lime Point Government Works: we applied, and got taken on at once. I forget how many hundred men were working on it, but was told that nine-tenths of them were gentlemen. Certain it is that all we came across were unmistakably of gentle birth.

It was curious to notice the different effects adverse circumstances had upon the different characters. Some were reckless and devil-me-care; others morose and sullen; some again viewing their fate with philosophical indifference; others with poor Curly's bright, hopeful belief in the good time coming.

The work here was horribly hard, pick and shovel business, and very soon I was obliged to give it up, having lost so much strength at the quicksilver mines. Gilbert had secured easy work on the same road as surveyor's auxiliary, so he remained there, while I sought other employment.

Behold me next as groom and coachman to a Yankee gentleman at San Rafeel; wages $10 a month. He was a kind-hearted, good man, with whom I was very comfortable. We used to have long talks about the Old Country, which he had only visited once, but for which he had a strong affection and passionate admiration.

"You are such aristocrats," he said one day, adding with a sigh, "You have such a long line of ancestors."

"A very nice thing, I allow, if the descendants have money enough to keep up the old prestige," I answered, "otherwise it is but another suffering added to many."

"I don't see how," replied Mr. Horner, twisting a button of his coat round and round, which was a trick of his when talking on anything that interested him. I have known him go home with not a button left on either coat or waistcoat, as was the case on the day this conversation took place.

"Simply because, although a gentleman can bear misfortune and starvation with more or less patience and fortitude, he cannot bear without pain and disgust the forced companionship with the low, uneducated, and degraded class of men that his poverty throws him among."

"Yes, I can quite understand that, though perhaps you will say that I can know nothing about it. I began life as a newspaper boy, and my father kept a small tripe-shop."

"The nobly born are not the only noble," I quoted. "I have myself known men whose pedigree was lost in the mist of past ages, guilty of low and dishonourable actions that would put an honest coalheaver to the blush." It did not strike me at the time how comical it was master and man talking so together.

Many weeks passed by; Gilbert and I had the same lodgings, and met every evening. We began to put a little money by, and felt getting on in the world, when one evening on returning I found Gilbert feverish and ill. His old enemy had overtaken him again. The day had been very hot, and he had passed it measuring the road under a blazing sun.

I left my "situation" to nurse him, bidding goodbye to Mr. Horner with a regret that was mutual; he left San Francisco just at that time to go and live with a married daughter.

Thanks probably to old Dr. Fernnoh, Gilbert was neither ill so long nor so seriously as the last time, but on his recovery we did not think it advisable for him to continue the same work, as it exposed him to the heat of the sun.

A fellow-lodger mentioned that there was a berth vacant on board a man-of-war then in the docks for repairs; he had a brother on board, and advised Gilbert to try for it.

Rather reluctantly he went, hoping he would not be accepted—so secretly did I, but he was. The doctor who examined him passed him at once, and he had his credentials proving him to be a lieutenant in seamanship.

Very gloomily we took this piece of good luck, Gilbert at first absolutely refusing to accept the offer; but I persuaded him to do so, though my heart was very sad at the thought of the separation after so many years' close friendship; but it seemed to me wrong to refuse such a chance. I tried to get employment on board, I didn't care in what capacity, but the ship's crew was complete.

Gilbert had money enough to buy his outfit, and I left him one morning to do it while I went to work (gardening this time), feeling thoroughly depressed and disheartened, overshadowed with the thought of parting from my only friend. When

I returned in the evening to the room where we lodged I found him quietly smoking a pipe.

"Got your kit?" I asked, in rather a choking voice—something seemed to have got into my throat.

"No, old man, and what's more, I don't mean to get it; another fellow has got the berth."

"What do you mean? Why it was promised to you."

"I gave it up myself. I couldn't bear the thought of leaving you, Haln; we have been everything to each other for years; please God, we will live and die together."

And so it was settled—an immense relief to both, nor have either of us ever regretted it. Instead of buying a "kit" Gilbert added his money to what I had saved when "coachman" (I had often been a coach-man in the old days in Ireland, and if I must speak the truth, much prefer the four-legged animals to the two-legged ones), and we purchased the interest in a boot-blacking saloon in Market Street. No great art was required in this line of business, nor was it a difficult one to acquire. Nevertheless, although brain-work pays not, shoe-blacking pays well, and rather to our astonishment we made a lot of money. True, we worked hard for it, were busy from "dawn to twilight grey" shining away with might and main.

Some months after we were settled in, the block of houses in which our saloon was situated changed owners, and our place would have to come down in a couple of months; we were greatly put out about it, and were wondering what it was best to do, when a man told us he was willing to take the place on chance, giving us in exchange another similar saloon in Sacramanto Street. This offer we gladly accepted, for although it was a much smaller business, still it was sure, and we had no expenses connected with settling in.

So we went on our "polishing" way, and by strenuous exertions built up a good trade. Soon we undertook other work, such as cleaning out offices, errands, &c., keeping a small staff of boys for the purpose.

Next door to us was a drinking saloon where the proprietor gave a free lunch every day. That meal was well attended, and others too, for the sprat so sent out caught many a whale, and it became the best lounging saloon in that part of the town. We reaped the benefit of being so near, as many of the loungers turned in to us to be "polished!" David Levy, the proprietor, was very friendly, and —unheard-of thing—trusted to our honesty, not hesitating to leave us in charge whenever he wanted to go elsewhere.

At first we slept in a tiny room that was cut off from our business apartment—hard work to place two beds, narrow as they were. Now and then it had to accommodate three. I remember on one occasion Gilbert had taken Levy's place for him, and I had spent a long day of hard work alone, so was very glad when, evening coming on,

I could shut up for the night, and dismissing the boys, had my supper, and, without waiting for Gilbert, went to bed.

I was awakened in the midst of my beauty sleep by hearing voices in the other room. Then Gilbert poked his head in. "I say, Haln, get up; I've met a fellow from Truro; you know, where my people live."

I grunted.

"He's in there; we are going to have a pipe and a talk. Come along, he's from Truro."

"Well, black his boots, give him my blessing, and send him back to—Truro," I said, letting my head sink down contentedly on my pillow.

"Surly old bear," laughed Gilbert, "I'll leave the door open, so you can hear if you won't come in."

I groaned. I didn't want to hear. I wanted to recover the fleeting moments of that beauty sleep from which I had been so rudely aroused. In vain my efforts, those two voices sounded through the thin partition, though I had made a long arm and shut the door.

Before long I knew the whole of that blessed town situated somewhere down in the west of Cornwall by heart. Every house did they enter, and various exclamations broke from my friend suitable to the pieces of news, that this one had married, this one had died, or this one had done worse; for that little town down in the west of Cornwall did not appear to be behind her more important sisters in the matter of morals, or want of morals. I dozed off, and was awakened by a loud "By Jove! you don't say so!" from Gilbert, then chatter, chatter. Talk about magpies or women! In desperation I sprang out of bed, pulled open the door, and appeared before them.

"That's right, old fellow, come along in," cried my friend, adding insult to injury. "Here, take a pipe. This is Mr. T—— from Truro."

I acknowledged the brief introduction as gracefully as I could under the circumstances, but was not astonished as I dived back into the bedroom to put on some clothes to catch Mr. T—— from Truro in the act of putting his finger to his forehead inquiringly, and nod his head in my direction.

Again, as I appeared, "By Jove! you don't say so!" burst from Gilbert. "Just fancy, Haln——"

"I've heard it all," I interrupted quickly. "I can tell you everything about your confounded town, from the one monument it possesses, that stands like an exclamation point on the top of a street, which street bears the acid cognomen of Lemon, to the river that deposits gallons of liquid mud twice a day into the very midst of the town. I could take you up Pydar Street and on the Cross, over to the Parade and across Strangeways Terrace, to St. Mary's, St. Paul's, St. John's, St. George's, not forgetting various chapels and meeting-houses."

"Then you know it well," said Mr. T—— of Truro. "Were you born there?"

"That were an honour unto which I was *not* born," I answered. " All my knowledge of your town is from my friend there, and a few photographs lately sent him; nor can I with truth say that I burn with a desire to visit it. One thing strikes me in favour of the town—it seems a splendid place to get away from, every facility being afforded for that laudable act."

Mr. T—— of Truro looked puzzled, and no wonder. Should any Truronians ever read these pages I can only make the same excuse to them that I made to him. I was tired, I wanted to sleep, and being disturbed by a duet that went on into the small hours of night, conceived a violent dislike to Truro, a small town in the west of Cornwall, noted, as I read in a certain dictionary, for the pride and poverty of its inhabitants. You can only pity my ignorance and despise me, which will make us quits.

Mr. T—— of Truro left us the next morning, nor have we ever seen or heard of him again. In due course I left off saying to Gilbert every time I came across him, "By Jove! you don't say so!"

Shortly after this our business flourished so much that we took lodgings near at hand, and had our meals always at a restaurant. In 'Frisco the shoe-blacking trade is as much a business as a draper's or any other storekeeper's, and no one is looked down upon or despised for making a living how best he can. Any one showing that sort of feeling is at once recognized as a snob, and soon has the starch taken out of him. Here one man is as good as another as long as he acts on the square and makes money; there is no rotten pride of caste, it is too well known that it is, alas! generally gentlemen who, being uneducated in the lower walks of life, find themselves out of their own country, obliged to do many queer things in order to live.

So behold us now with our saloon handsomely carpeted, large mirrors (for we soon found out how fond men were of looking at themselves in the glass—those mirrors brought us many a customer!), grand black walnut armchairs comfortably cushioned with velvet, some nice pictures, and a lounge or two. Added to this, we took in the morning papers and the illustrated periodicals, kept perfumes and flowers, which last sold amazingly well. This year we cleared $1,500 net profit over and above our expenses of living, board, and rent, yet we lived well, going to the theatres whenever anything was worth seeing, and haunting the concerts.

Finding we were doing so well, we ventured after a time to give up the "shining line" and took a book and stationery store in Stockton Street. Here we sold all sorts of things, possible and impossible—inks, from the common black to the beautiful carmine of Guyot; drawing necessaries of every description; school books and school requisites, such as desks, slates, pens, and pencils; the chief daily papers; forty different illustrated periodicals; curious toys, cards, and many other things too numerous to mention.

I began to think I had missed my vocation, surely I had been intended all along for a shopman in the Golden City, only hadn't the "nous" to find it out until towards the end of my life.

We have taken in one day $127 for school books alone when the schools opened after recess. Our average was about $12 a day. Then our rent was $40 a month. Most of the money we made we put into the business, buying whatever we thought would entice customers. We sold great quantities of photographs of the great actors and actresses, eminent men and beautiful women; these we always procured from the best artists in 'Frisco, Bradley, and Rulofhor, and although we paid very high for them we found they were a good investment. We slept in a room at the back of our stores—the best way of protecting them at night—but we took our meals at a restaurant. About this time I made a great find. I had been without a violin for years, but now that we were flourishing I thought I would like to get up my music again, so looked about in the various music shops for one that would be to my taste. Whether I was fidgety, or the instruments I saw were not good, at any rate I let the weeks go by without being suited.

One evening I went back to our old lodgings that we occupied when in the "polishing line," as I missed an old book that was a favourite, and thought perhaps I may have left it there. And there I found it, the landlord and his wife, old people, having taken the rooms to live in themselves.

"I put it up in that cupboard with a lot more rubbish," remarked Mrs. Spence, with unconscious contempt. "Many a lodger leaves something, some of 'em naught but a heap of trash, which is all I've got sometimes in the place of money due."

"I daresay you have had a very varied experience in your time," I remarked, "and might write an interesting book on your lodgers."

"Lor, sir, that I couldn't, for I can't write a word, and it always have seemed to me to be one of they silly, useless things as never did no good to nobody."

"Well, I don't quite agree with you," I answered, watching the old woman somewhat anxiously, for she was perched up on the top of a step-ladder, which, although I held it and was able to steady it, yet the wood was so old and rotten, that I feared it would collapse altogether.

"There it is," she cried at last, triumphantly, handing me down my precious little volume, which she first politely dusted with her apron. "It was hid a bit under an old fiddle."

I pricked up my ears at the word, having fiddles on the brain just then, and laughingly asked her if she played.

"No, no," she replied, quite seriously. "It was left by a lodger in part payment; not that it would pay a quarter of what he owed me. But there, you can't get money out of dead men; it's hard enough to get it out of living ones sometimes."

"Would you mind my seeing it?" I asked, though I could not have explained what motive or feeling induced me to do so.

"There it is; but it can't be no good now, for the strings is all broke. I didn't like to burn it, for I was fond of the man, though he was a bit daft, poor soul, but harmless as a child, and full of trouble. I've taken the worst of the dust off," and she handed it to me.

Somehow, even before I took it to the window to examine it, I felt a tremor of excitement run through me as one on the very verge of a great discovery. My presentiment had not played me false; there, under the dust, were the magic words, "Antonius Stradiuarius Cremonensis faciebat, 1720." With a beating heart I carefully wiped it, and passed my fingers over the loosened strings. A plaintive sound, like the wail of a broken heart, was the result.

Mrs. Spence seemed uneasy, for she said, "It ain't no good; it only crys like a creetur in pain. I'm sure I don't know why ever I kept it. I'll sell it to get rid of it; the wood will fetch a few cents, perhaps."

A genuine violin of the eighteenth century to be sold for a few cents! Oh, Stradiuarius of Cremona, my heart burnt with shame at this appalling ignorance of thy great art!

"If you are thinking of selling it," I answered, "I will buy it, for I play the violin, and was on the look-out for one. Have you the bow?"

"Do you mean the thing you scrape it with?" asked worthy Mrs. Spence, and on my answering in the affirmative, mounted once more the rickety steps, and, after some searching and fumbling among the heterogeneous mass of dust-covered articles, produced the bow.

I tightened the strings as well as I could, and passed the bow over them. Oh, the mellow, plaintive sound, how sweet it was! Like a miser gloating over his gold, I examined my prize inch by inch, held it sideways to admire that beautiful curve in the back that is one of the characteristics of all violins that come from the hands of Stradiuarius, at the quaint cutting of the F holes, at the time-blackened wood, with a feeling of reverence, with a joy that was almost painful. More than a hundred years had passed since the cunning hands of the great artist had ceased their work for ever; he was gone, but the fruits of his labour remained to stir the hearts and raise the souls of those to whom the blessed gift of music is given, a foretaste, as it were, of that other world to which we look for the completion and fulfilment of our greatest hopes and desires.

I had let my thoughts wander far away while my fingers unconsciously tapped the sounding-board of the instrument, every slight touch producing soft, sweet murmurs, for the very fibre of the wood was impregnated with music. Many may smile at me for this extravagant praise even of a Stradiuarius; enthusiastic lovers of music, however, will understand and pardon me.

Mrs. Spence recalled me to mundane things by saying anxiously, "You don't find it worth the buying, though to hear poor old Mr. Tom talk, you'd think it was as good as a gold mine; but then he was off his head with trouble and that. You shall have it for a dollar, if you like, sir."

I smiled at the shrewd old woman. Before I had spoken of buying it she had thought to get but a few cents for the wood, now she immediately asks a dollar. I, knowing the value of the instrument, feel that I should offer more, so I said:

"Mrs. Spence, this violin is by a very old maker, and there are many people who would give a good deal of money for it. I can't afford to do that, but I offer you two dollars and a half (10s.) if you care to let me have it for that sum."

"That I will, sir, and thank you, too, for I shouldn't know how to go about getting it sold. Sometimes you gentlemen think a sight of things as ain't of no valley."

From which remark I understood that Mrs. Spence considered me in the same state as her late lodger, *i.e.*, off my head, and thought herself a very clever and lucky woman to get the two dollars and a half that I paid her on the spot.

"I wish you would tell me something about

your lodger; I mean the one who owned this violin. I think you said he was dead."

"Well, he killed hisself, which is the same thing," answered Mrs. Spence, settling herself down for a chat, while I took a chair opposite her and hugged my violin in my arms.

I will tell you Mr. Tom's history in my own words, for good Mrs. Spence not only took one hour and three-quarters over it, but she added so many remarks of her own, that, although I was a victim, I don't wish my readers to share the same fate.

Mr. Tom, evidently a fictitious name, was an Englishman by birth, a peculiar, sensitive man, one of those that Dame Fortune seems to choose now and then as the sport of her every whim, and the victim of her every cruel joke. The thirteenth son of a rather poor rector in the north of Yorkshire, he had always been the butt of his brothers and sisters, for his prolific father was the happy possessor of twenty children, of whom seven were girls. This one, Amos, appears from the beginning of his life to carry out the sad meaning of the name bestowed upon him—a burden. Truly he was, a burden to all around him, worst of all a burden to himself. Misfortune seemed to dog his footsteps. Did he go to school, he was sure to meet with an accident; was he going up for an exam., an attack of illness would seize him and prevent his attending.

Finally it seemed as though Fate was tired of

dealing him bitter blows. He was employed as engineer in the mines that were situated in his father's parish, and lodged with the curate, a man of low birth, which he tried to hide by haughty and supercilious airs—a miserable failure, for being very poor, and having seven children, he found it as much as he could do to get on.

Of course, before his rector's twenty encumbrances his seven looked small, still it was no easy matter to get them all clothed and educated. His wife, a good, honest, hard-working woman, daughter of a former landlady, firmly believed that her husband was a grand gentleman and a fine fellow, simply because he said so. The eldest child, a girl, just grown up when Amos went there to live, appeared to be a modest, charming young creature, with whom he fell in love at once.

It was just at this time in his life that he was sent by the head of the mines over to Liguria, in Italy, to the iron mines there. He left England, not daring to speak of his love to the curate's daughter, seeing how unsettled were his prospects, still he doubtless said enough to her to make her understand what were his feelings towards her.

I had forgotten to say that he had early shown a great love for music, but that being considered a useless profession, as far as bringing in money was concerned, he was commanded to give it up and turn his thoughts to engineering. With the patient submission which seemed to be his most striking characteristic he did so, but once in Italy his fate threw him among musical people. A young girl, daughter of the first violinist in the Opera House at Liguria, herself a violinist, fell in love with the Englishman.

Amos either did not or would not see it, and with unconscious cruelty took Florence C—— into his confidence, and was wont to pour out his love for the curate's daughter at every possible opportunity. He remained there five years, and on leaving to return to Yorkshire threw away his one chance of happiness in life.

It is said that there comes to every one in our sojourn here on earth one opportunity of happiness. How many of us miss that chance, and, failing it, get shipwrecked on life's stormy sea!

Poor Amos was one of the unlucky ones, and drew but blanks in the lottery of life. He left Italy and the girl who loved him with singleness of heart to give all his affection to a worthless woman.

The curate's eldest daughter, modest and simple in appearance, was a true child of her father, and her haughty, overbearing temper kept from her several suitors who would otherwise have offered. So at twenty-four she found herself still unsought, although three of her younger sisters had already flitted from the parent nest.

When Amos returned in a fairly good position, and showed unmistakable signs that he had not changed, she thought it worth her while to play the amiable, and when he asked her, which he did as soon as possible, to accept him, giving him to understand, however, that she only did it because she really loved him, as two other wealthy aspirants to her hand were sighing in vain.

The marriage turned out a very unhappy one, and when money difficulties came, Mrs. Amos showed herself in her true character, and made life intolerable to him. The Yorkshire mines failing, they went to California, but things only went from bad to worse.

I forgot to mention that soon after his marriage he received a letter and a violin, a Stradiuarius, from Florence C——. The poor girl in dying had sent her greatest treasure to the only man she had ever loved, and he, already finding out his wife's real character, must often have wished his eyes had been open and he could have distinguished the true from the false.

After years of struggling and misery and sorrow, during which his wife would leave him sometimes for months together, saying she was in some situation or other, poor Amos, broken down in health, and overcome with sorrow, took to drinking to drown his troubles. Several children had been born to them, but all died in infancy, with the exception of one girl, a handsome creature and her father's joy and pride. For her sake he worked like a black, hardly eating enough to keep him from starvation, that she might have luxuries to eat and dainty clothes to wear. He gave violin lessons for sixpence an hour, and sometimes got hired to play dance music at some low music-halls.

It was one evening in one of these places that he saw his wife enter, grandly dressed, in company with a well-known gentleman, notorious for his bad life. Wild with rage and shame, he accosted her, when the gentleman ordered him to be turned out as a madman. Amos replied by striking him on the face, whereupon a fight ensued, and Amos was ejected wounded and bleeding, some one flinging his violin after him.

For months he and his daughter had been lodging with Mrs. Spence, sometimes paying, sometimes not. When he managed to crawl back to his room and say what had happened, the girl, furious with him, told him brutally that she knew the life her mother led, and meant to do the same herself, as she was sick of the misery and poverty, and left the house there and then. Amos was laid down with brain fever, during which Mrs. Spence nursed him, from sheer pity. He pulled through, but was an aged, broken-down man, weakened alike in mind and body. All day long he paced the street searching for his daughter, playing airs on his violin that she was accustomed to hear. Many passers-by threw him pence, which he always faithfully brought to his landlady.

So time went on; she had not the heart to turn him out, for what with the effects of the fever, and drink and exposure in all weathers in the endless search for his daughter, he became more and more imbecile.

One morning he came in unexpectedly, looking wild. "I've seen her," he said; "but she denied being my child, she ordered her servants to drive me away." Mrs. Spence could get nothing else from him; he sat down, took his violin on his knees, wiped it, and handed it to her, saying, in quite a natural tone of voice, "I can't pay you what I owe you, but I leave you this, it will more than repay you."

Then he went out, walked quietly to a deserted part of the wharf, and drowned himself. Finding he did not return, Mrs. Spence made inquiries, saw a description of a body found that made her think it was his; finding that to be the case, old Spence and she identified him, and followed him, the only mourners to his pauper's grave.

Such is the outline of the story Mrs. Spence told me, and I looked at the violin with even greater interest. With that in my hands and my recovered book in my pocket, I returned home. Gilbert was almost as much interested as I was, and we sat up late that night talking over the sad story I had heard. There were some people, then, more unlucky and with harder fates than ours—indeed, we now seemed to be at the end of our troubles.

At this time every one in 'Frisco went mad on stock gambling. The papers were full of nothing else, and no two men could get together for five minutes without entering into a warm discussion on the topic.

I ought not to say much, for, bitten by the prevailing epidemic, we ventured some money, like every one else. More cautious than most, however, we did not risk a heavy sum, nor did we even lose all that we did put in. Frightened by the endless stories of ruin, we sold out at a great loss before things came to the worst, and were by far not so unfortunate as many of our acquaintances.

A terrible time followed for San Francisco—indeed, for the whole of California, and extended even to other countries. Thousands of families were completely ruined, for every one seemed infected with the fever of gambling that raged alike among rich and poor.

The great stockbrokers gobbled up all the small fry. It was one giant swindle, followed by all sorts of evils—ruin, despair, and endless suicides.

For many weeks the whole country was panic-struck, and painful tragedies were of daily occurrence. Here the head of a family, having lost every cent he possessed, would blow his brains out; there the head of a bank, gone smash, would do the same, or would be murdered by some infuriated creditor who had been ruined.

Nearly every morning, and at intervals through the day, we were startled by pistol-shots quite near our office, the great B. and S. E. (or for fear you may not understand these mysterious letters—Book and Stationer's Emporium), and would as frequently see the bodies of the shot ones carried past, some to the Morgue, some to their private dwellings. So common were these occurrences that no one was much disturbed or troubled by them, and the police took as little notice as any one else; the man was dead, nothing could bring him back to life, even if any one desired his resuscitation, which was doubtful, and any looking into the matter involved loss of time and money, so what was the good, particularly as these little events followed each other with considerable rapidity?

The truth is that, as far as I could learn, no one was ever shot in the streets of 'Frisco who did not richly deserve his fate. Every bullet has its billet, and although nervous people might think it dangerous to walk the streets at that time for fear of meeting a stray bullet, they need not have disturbed themselves, for all well-disposed persons were, on the whole, as safe as they would be in London or any other great city.

The panic over, things settled down more or less in the usual way, and life went on with its daily routine. The gaps made by death or departure were quickly filled up, and the city resumed its normal aspect.

Our business had become a really prosperous affair, and the time came when, as once before, we found ourselves the possessors of sufficient funds to enable us to have our heart's desire, *i.e.*, to leave city life, with its uncongenial work, its temptations to gamble, and its ups and downs, and live once more the free, healthy life in the country.

We longed to have if only a two-roomed hut in the forest, where among the trees and flowers and the animals we could be independent of men, and quietly and peacefully pass our days—Lust in Rust. Gilbert heard of a small ranche on Mark West Creek, some eight miles from Santa Rosa. It consisted of about thirty acres of land, with vineyard and orchard, the latter well stocked with fruit-trees; while from the creek which ran past the house we could procure fish in plenty.

So one day we left the "Emporium" in the hands of an assistant and went off to Mark West Creek to see for ourselves. It was a lovely day, and we were both in high spirits, and felt more like a couple of schoolboys out on a spree than two staid, serious men.

The proprietor of the ranche in question was to meet us at the place, and as we drove up, having hired a sort of dog-cart at Santa Rosa, we beheld him sitting like another Job under a fig-tree.

Though he saw us entering the opening of the fence he did not condescend to move towards us, or even to get up, but contented himself with sitting a little more upright, and, extending a couple of fingers of his right hand, which mark of politeness neither Gilbert nor I pretended to see.

"Almighty proud, you bet," observed Mr. Ruthven; but to whom the remark was addressed it would be difficult to say, unless to a small sandy-coloured terrier that bolt upright between his feet presented a striking personal resemblance to his master.

"This ranche belongs to you, I believe?" began Gilbert.

Mr. Ruthven, chary of his words, nodded.

"Well," cried Gilbert, getting impatient, "my friend and I have come out by appointment to see the place, which we understand is to be sold. Are you Mr. Ruthven?"

"You bet," was the reply, accompanied with a look as much as to say, "I wouldn't advise any one to play with my name."

"Then, Mr. Ruthven, will you take the trouble to show us over the ranche, as we have come here for that purpose by your own desire?"

"Have a drink first," said our strange host, rising to his feet, and pitching a soft-felt hat on his head, that had been lying on the ground by his side, shook it into its place. He was the tallest man I think I have ever seen, thin too, and with the true Yankee type of features. His small, grey eyes twinkled with a mixture of fun and cunning. He walked as though he were throwing his feet before him, and had a trick of suddenly jerking his head on one side, in which he was always immediately imitated by his dog, Dollar by name.

Mr. Ruthven and his dog led the way into the house; a rather poor affair it looked, although there were four rooms in it, all more or less out of order and nearly destitute of furniture; that, of course, did not matter, as we should bring our own.

In one of the downstair rooms was a large table on which was laid out a sort of lunch, more for the purpose of satisfying hunger than to pander to the taste of an epicure. There was no cloth, which after all is not a necessity in the bush, but the huge lump of cold beef might have been placed on a dish instead of right down on the bare and not over clean table; four plates more or less broken and cracked, and a knife or two, thrown pell-mell among spoons and forks, which latter were of pewter and very dirty, completed the chattels on the table. I forgot a large loaf of bread and two quarts of ale.

Our host motioned us to the only two seats the room possessed, seating himself on a block of wood that he rolled in for the purpose. Dollar sat on the table by his master's elbow, and when that worthy put too large a piece of meat in his mouth, sagaciously bit off the end that protruded from between his teeth.

"Help yourselves," said Mr. Ruthven, pushing the meat across the table with his bare hand, and pouring out some ale in large glass pots, with handles and covers—the German beer glass—raised his to his lips, wished us good luck, and drained it in one gulp. That ale was certainly good, the best I have ever tasted; for the rest I will say nothing, except that we made a good supper when we got back to 'Frisco that night!

This feast over, Mr. Ruthven's tongue being a

little untied, he proceeded to take us over the ranche, which really seemed to be all that was promised in the way of vineyard, orchard, and fishing. Of course it was small, and very much out of order, having only been lived on now and then for a few months at a time, and our host, having invested in a larger concern on the other side of Santa Rosa, was anxious to part with this one. Not that he let his anxiety be seen—on the contrary, it was his very indifference of manner that made us suspect that he would be glad to get rid of it.

We thoroughly examined everything, Mr. Ruthven honestly pointing out various defects, such as bad fencing, rotten vines, some dead fruit-trees, and so on, flinging his feet before him and jerking his head, which latter movement Dollar repeated with unfailing fidelity.

"'Cute little brute that seems to be," I remarked, hoping to hide an irrepressible smile that the abovementioned movement on the part of man and dog had forced from me.

" You bet he's the 'cutest terrier in Sonoma by a long shot," said Dollar's master, becoming eloquent; " I wouldn't take fifty dollars for him— no, nor a hundred."

"What made you give him that queer name?" asked Gilbert, puffing some tobacco smoke into the dog's face, who seemed to like it, opening his mouth and breathing in the fumes of the fragrant weed with evident relish.

" Wall, he gave it to himself—leastways he took

it," replied Mr. Ruthven. "It's seven years ago now I was walking down one of the back streets in 'Frisco, and came along a lot of lads who were tormenting the poor little brute, and meant to kill it, because he had bitten one of them. I said I'd take him; they asked a dollar for him. I told them to git, for no dollar should they have; so what with cuffing and banging at them I drove them off and picked up the dog and brought him home. I thought of calling him Snap, but he wouldn't take no notice, though whenever the word dollar was mentioned he'd prick up his ears—perhaps because he heard it so often," concluded Mr. Ruthven, naïvely. "He is a 'cute cuss; look at him now, he knows we are talking about him," and he jerked his head in the direction of Dollar, who immediately reproduced the movement with ludicrous fidelity.

On the whole we were charmed with the place, agreed to buy it, got through all the formalities as quickly as possible, and I went down to Mark West Creek to take charge of the ranche until our store in Stockton Street could be disposed of.

The ranche was very prettily situated, surrounded by hills both high and steep, and which were called about here mountains. They ought to be ashamed to claim any such dignity, but "some have honour thrust upon them."

Mountains or hills, they are exceedingly beautiful, whether enveloped in the grey, pink mists of early dawn, or flooded with the full force of the golden light of a mid-day sun, or tinted with the amber, crimson, and purple glow of late evening; abundantly wooded, too, with grand, mighty trees. The fertile soil of the valleys is most favourable to agriculture, for it produces grains and fruits both of the temperate and semi-tropical zones, so we felt we could not have chosen a better spot or one more likely to answer our purpose than this lovely valley on the Mark West Creek.

I found the house a very poor affair, even worse than it had appeared on the day we visited it. Mr. Ruthven had of course cleared away his own things, and the place looked bare and dirty and desolate. But I soon altered that with the aid of a man I hired for the first day. We thoroughly cleaned out the four rooms, and arranged the plain but solid furniture we had chosen for the purpose. The bedrooms were of Spartan-like simplicity. Small iron beds, iron washstands, a couple of chairs, and a table was all the furniture. Gilbert had a looking-glass—I think it right to mention this fact, for I had not.

In the kitchen was a wide fireplace (we burnt wood chiefly, of course), a table, and four chairs. I adorned the walls artistically by arranging our rifles, pistols, and the heads and tails of various animals that we had preserved. The fourth room was our reception room! In it we had really good furniture, a carpet, curtains, and rugs. Pictures hung on the wall, and our pet books in a case, while my beloved violin lay in a bran-new violin case I had had made for it.

All these arrangements I made gradually while

living in solitary grandeur, waiting for Gilbert to join me. There was no house, hut, or shanty of any sort for miles near us, though during the day traffic was not unfrequent, as the road was not far from us, and led into Santa Rosa.

The first night or two when I was alone I was frequently disturbed by strange, unearthly noises. Now I do not believe in ghosts, and have no faith in any spiritualistic humbug whatever, so after looking into each room and finding nothing, not even a stray rat, I concluded that some one else was also struck with the charm and beauty of the little ranche, and finding that only one man lived there, thought it a good opportunity to become possessor of it gratis by knocking the said one man on the head, and taking possession of the house, which would of course be useless to the dead owner. But two can play that little game, so, loaded rifle in hand, I waited on the third night to make a corpse, rather than be made one.

Judge of my disgust when, after waiting hours, during which I dozed off several times, only to be awakened by the same mysterious sounds, I discovered the true cause. The old timbers of the house, a wooden one, scorched by the intense heat of the autumn day, stretched, and creaked, and groaned, while the loose and broken shingles on the roof clattered in the damp night air. Only that and nothing more. Another fit of the heroics for nothing, *ex nihilo nihil fit.*

But the sound of the wind among the trees gave

me an idea: I prepared an Æolian harp, which I placed in our "drawing-room" window, taking care that the strings were very powerful. The effect delighted me; each blast of wind passing by produced the sound of a distant choir of music, sweetly mingling all the harmonic notes, swelling or diminishing according to the strength or weakness of the wind. So we could always have a beautiful voluntary, or involuntary, if you like it better, by simply opening the window and letting the winds tell their secrets in sweet sounds through the medium of the Æolian harp. Soon Gilbert joined me; he had had a good deal of worrying work arranging for the sale of the stock, and finally had settled with two young men in 'Frisco, who went as partners together. They took our store, agreeing to pay us $20 a month until the whole purchase money was paid up.

We knew both men well, and they had always been strictly honest, so we began our new life on Mark West Creek with the future smiling upon us, and every prospect of doing well.

Having spent a day or two in lazy enjoyment of our free life, we set to work in good earnest putting things in order. And no sinecure we found it, for the vineyard, in particular, had been much neglected and yielded badly. So we pruned it, uprooted the decayed or dying plants, and fenced it all around, all of which took some time, but repaid us well later on for our trouble.

We next turned our attention to the orchard, in

which were almond, plum, pear, apricot, apple, and peach trees in plenty. We grafted a good many young ones, and planted some new. Then we enclosed a tolerably large piece of ground for vegetables, where, the ground being so fertile, we had little trouble beyond the planting and eating of them.

In front of the house is a flower garden of our making, which by giving half an hour every day is in beautiful order. In the centre bed stands a maguary, or centaury plant; around it various species of verbenas, mignonette, and roses of every sort and kind, perfuming the whole place with their sweet odours.

We had been here but a few months, when Fortune, not yet content with having battered us about with so many and grievous blows, dealt another that well-nigh crushed me, for it threatened me with the loss of my friend.

The two young men who had taken our store paid very regularly, and we never had the smallest hint that things were not flourishing. But whether they neglected their business, or did not understand it, or gave way to the spirit of gambling, I know not; one thing only was sure—we heard suddenly that they had gone smash, sold the business, and vanished with the money, leaving us without means to carry on the work of the ranche.

We had been too short a time to have been able to reap any profit from our work, and the farm was still in a bad state, requiring both labour and money to put it into anything like order and make it repay us. Also there was a $1,000 debt on it, which we now saw no chance of paying off. One trouble follows another. The anxiety and worry occasioned by this loss brought on one of Gilbert's attacks of fever—the worst he had ever had. I sent into Santa Rosa for the most skilful physician, who, directly he saw him, told me there was no hope.

This happily was a false diagnosis. After a struggle, which it is painful for me to remember, I brought Gilbert round. And here I will bring my narrative to an end, my life not being sufficiently diversified to interest my readers. Gilbert and I are still in California, and, I may add, we are doing well.

The Gresham Press,
UNWIN BROTHERS,
CHILWORTH AND LONDON.

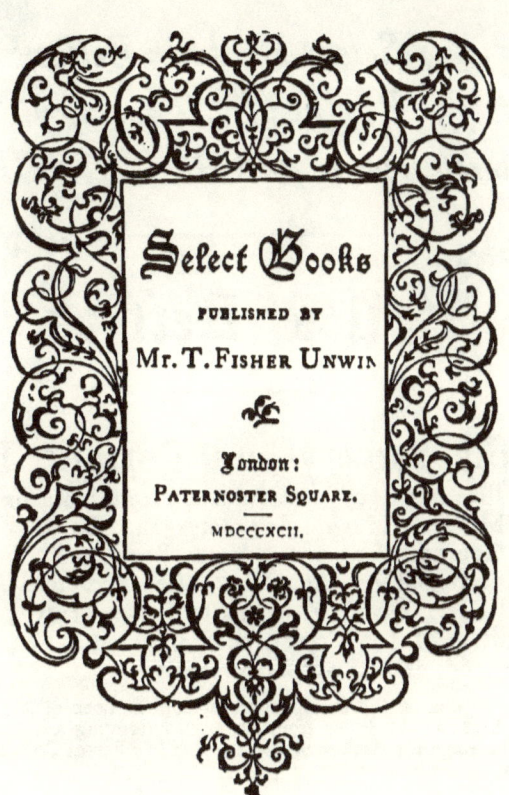

Catalogue of Select Books in Belles Lettres, History, Biography, Theology, Travel, Miscellaneous, and Books for Children.

Belles Lettres.

Gypsy Sorcery and Fortune Telling. Illustrated by numerous Incantations, Specimens of Medical Magic, Anecdotes and Tales, by CHARLES GODFREY LELAND ("Hans Breitman"), President of the Gypsy Lore Society, &c., &c. With numerous Illustrations and Initial Letters drawn by the Author. Small 4to., cloth, 16s. Limited Edition of 150 Copies, numbered and signed, demy 4to., price £1 11s. 6d. nett, to subscribers only.

This volume is one of the most important contributions of late years to the study of Folk Lore, and is drawn from the most interesting and curious sources, setting forth the magical practices of the Romany in different Countries, and their strange beliefs.

Dreams. By OLIVE SCHREINER, Author of "The Story of an African Farm." With Portrait. Fcap. 8vo. buckram, gilt, 6s.

CONTENTS :—1. The Lost Joy.—2. The Hunter.—3. The Gardens of Pleasure.—4. In a Far-off World.—5. Three Dreams in a Desert.—6. A Dream of Wild Bees.—7. In a Ruined Chapel.—8. Life's Gifts.—9. The Artist's Secret.—10. I Thought I Stood——.—11. The Moonlight Fell across my Bed.

Gottfried Keller : A Selection of his Tales. Translated, with a Memoir, by KATE FREILIGRATH KROEKER, Translator of "Brentano's Fairy Tales." With Portrait. Crown 8vo., cloth, 6s.

Keller is the greatest Swiss romancer of modern days.

The English Novel in the Time of

Shakespeare. By J. J. JUSSERAND, Author of "English Wayfaring Life." Translated by ELIZABETH LEE, Revised and Enlarged by the Author. Illustrated by Six Heliogravures by DUJARDIN, of Paris, and 21 full-page and many smaller Illustrations in facsimile. Demy 8vo., handsome cloth, gilt tops, 21s.

"Here we have learned, yet not at all wearisome, descriptions of the works which led up to the novel as we now understand it. . . . Dr. Jusserand's agreeable style in recounting the origin of the modern literary 'three decker' makes his book, though historically valuable, very pleasant reading."
Daily Telegraph.

English Wayfaring Life in the Middle

Ages (XIVth Century). By J. J. JUSSERAND. Translated from the French by LUCY A. TOULMIN SMITH. Illustrated. Third Edition. Demy 8vo., cloth, 12s.

"This is an extremely fascinating book, and it is surprising that several years should have elapsed before it was brought out in an English dress. However, we have lost nothing by waiting."—*Times.*

The Letters of Horace Walpole.

Selected and Edited, with Introduction and Notes, by CHARLES DUKE YONGE, M.A. Portraits and Illustrations. Limited Edition of 750 copies in Two Vols., medium 8vo., cloth, 32s.

"Have been carefully edited, and, moreover, contain admirable illustrations."
Guardian.

The Trials of a Country Parson: Some Fugitive

Papers by Rev. A. JESSOPP, D.D., Author of "Arcady," "The Coming of the Friars," &c. Crown 8vo., cloth, 7s. 6d.

"Sparkles with fresh and unforced humour, and abounds in genial commonsense."—*Scotsman.*

The Coming of the Friars, And other Mediæval Sketches. By the Rev.

AUGUSTUS JESSOPP, D.D., Author of "Arcady: For Better, For Worse," &c. Third Edition. Crown 8vo., cloth, 7s. 6d.

"Always interesting and frequently fascinating."—*St. James's Gazette.*

Arcady : For Better, For Worse. By AUGUSTUS JESSOPP, D.D., Author of "One Generation of a Norfolk House."

Portrait. Popular Edition. Crown 8vo., cloth, 3s. 6d.

"A volume which is, to our minds, one of the most delightful ever published in English."—*Spectator.*

The Twilight of the Gods. By RICHARD GARNETT, LL.D.
Crown 8vo., cloth, 6s.

"If imagination and style constitute the true elixir of literary life, Dr. Garnett's 'Twilight of the Gods' should live."—*British Weekly.*

Light and Shadow: A Novel. By EDWARD GARNETT,
Author of "The Paradox Club." Crown 8vo., cloth, 6s.

"An exceedingly clever book."—*Daily News.*

The Paradox Club. By EDWARD GARNETT. With Portrait of Nina Lindon. Second Edition. Crown 8vo., limp cloth, 3s. 6d.

"Mr. Garnett's dialogue is often quite as good as his description, and in description he is singularly happy. The mystery of London streets by night is powerfully suggested, and the realistic force of his night-pieces is enhanced by the vague and Schumann-like sentiment that pervades them."—*Saturday Review.*

Soul-Shapes. Crown 4to., with four coloured plates of Souls on hand-made paper, with Japanese vellum cover, 3s. 6d.

Robert Browning: Personal Notes.
Frontispiece. Small crown 8vo., parchment, 4s. 6d.

"Every lover of Browning will wish to possess this exquisitely-printed and as exquisitely-bound little volume."—*Yorkshire Daily Post.*

Old Chelsea. A Summer-Day's Stroll. By Dr. BENJAMIN ELLIS MARTIN. Illustrated by JOSEPH PENNELL. Second Edition. Crown 8vo., cloth, 7s. 6d.

"Dr. Martin has produced an interesting account of old Chelsea, and he has been well seconded by his coadjutor."—*Athenæum.*

Euphorion: Studies of the Antique and the Mediæval in the Renaissance. By VERNON LEE. Cheap Edition, in one volume. Demy 8vo., cloth, 7s. 6d.

"It is the fruit, as every page testifies, of singularly wide reading and independent thought, and the style combines with much picturesqueness a certain largeness of volume, that reminds us more of our earlier writers than those of our own time."
Contemporary Review.

Studies of the Eighteenth Century in Italy. By VERNON LEE. Demy 8vo., cloth, 7s. 6d.

"These studies show a wide range of knowledge of the subject, precise investigation, abundant power of illustration, and hearty enthusiasm. . . . The style of writing is cultivated, neatly adjusted, and markedly clever."—*Saturday Review.*

Belcaro: Being Essays on Sundry Æsthetical Questions. By VERNON LEE. Crown 8vo., cloth, 5s.

Juvenilia: A Second Series of Essays on Sundry Æsthetical Questions. By VERNON LEE. Two vols. Small crown 8vo., cloth, 12s.

"To discuss it properly would require more space than a single number of 'The Academy' could afford."—*Academy.*

Baldwin: Dialogues on Views and Aspirations. By VERNON LEE. Demy 8vo., cloth, 12s.

"The dialogues are written with . . . an intellectual courage which shrinks from no logical conclusion."—*Scotsman.*

Ottilie: An Eighteenth Century Idyl. By VERNON LEE. Square 8vo., cloth extra, 3s. 6d.

"A graceful little sketch. . . . Drawn with full insight into the period described."—*Spectator.*

Introductory Studies in Greek Art.

Delivered in the British Museum by JANE E. HARRISON. With Illustrations. Square imperial 16mo., 7s. 6d.

"The best work of its kind in English."—*Oxford Magazine.*

The Fleet: Its River, Prison, and Marriages. By JOHN ASHTON, Author of "Social Life in the Reign of Queen Anne," &c. With 70 Drawings by the Author from Original Pictures. Second and Cheaper Edition, cloth, 7s. 6d.

Romances of Chivalry: Told and Illustrated in Fac-simile by JOHN ASHTON. Forty-six Illustrations. New and Cheaper Edition. Crown 8vo., cloth, 7s. 6d.

"The result (of the reproduction of the wood blocks) is as creditable to his artistic, as the text is to his literary, ability."—*Guardian.*

The Dawn of the Nineteenth Century in

England: A Social Sketch of the Times. By JOHN ASHTON. Cheaper Edition, in one vol. Illustrated. Large crown 8vo., 10s. 6d.

"The book is one continued source of pleasure and interest, and opens up a wide field for speculation and comment, and many of us will look upon it as an important contribution to contemporary history, not easily available to others than close students."—*Antiquary.*

Chopin, and Other Musical Essays.

By HENRY T. FINCK, Author of "Romantic Love and Personal Beauty." Crown 8vo., cloth, 6s.

"The six essays are all written with great thoroughness, and the interest of each one is admirably sustained throughout."—*Freeman's Journal.*

The Temple: Sacred Poems and Private Ejaculations. By Mr. GEORGE HERBERT. New and fourth edition, with Introductory Essay by J. HENRY SHORTHOUSE. Small crown, sheep, 5s.

A fac-simile reprint of the Original Edition of 1633.

"This charming reprint has a fresh value added to it by the Introductory Essay of the Author of 'John Inglesant.'"—*Academy.*

Songs, Ballads, and A Garden Play.

By A. MARY F. ROBINSON, Author of "An Italian Garden." With Frontispiece of Dürer's "Melancholia." Small crown 8vo., half bound, vellum, 5s.

"The romantic ballads have grace, movement, passion and strength."—*Spectator.*
"Marked by sweetness of melody and truth of colour."—*Academy.*

Essays towards a Critical Method.

Studies in English Literature. By JOHN M. ROBERTSON. Cr. 8vo., cloth, 7s. 6d.

"His essays are always shrewd and readable. His criticisms on the critics are enjoyable for the irony (conscious or unconscious) that is in them; and the book will not fail to please lovers of literature and literary history, and to prove suggestive to the critical."—*Scotsman.*

The Lazy Minstrel.

By J. ASHBY-STERRY, Author of "Boudoir Ballads." Fourth and Popular Edition. Frontispiece by E. A. ABBEY. Fcap. 8vo., cloth, 2s. 6d.

"One of the lightest and brightest writers of vers de société."
— *St. James's Gazette.*

Caroline Schlegel,

and Her Friends. By Mrs. ALFRED SIDGWICK. With Steel Portrait. Crown 8vo., cloth, 7s. 6d.

"This is a singularly brilliant, delicate and fascinating sketch—one of the most skilful pieces of literary workmanship we have seen for a long time. . . . Mrs. Sidgwick is a writer of very unusual equipment, power and promise."
British Weekly.

Amos Kilbright:

His Adscititious Adventures. With other Stories. By FRANK R. STOCKTON. 8vo., cloth, 3s. 6d.

"Mr. Stockton is the quaintest of living humorists."—*Academy.*

www.ingramcontent.com/pod-product-compliance
Lightning Source LLC
Chambersburg PA
CBHW030424300426
44112CB00009B/840